**A SAMPLING OF THE 300+ DELICIOUS RECIPES
FOR ALLERGICS YOU'LL FIND
IN THESE PAGES:**

- Honey–Oatmeal Bread (no corn, egg, or milk)
- Wheat-free Noodles (no corn, milk, or wheat)
- Stuffed Flank Steak (no corn, egg, or wheat)
- Eggplant "Cannelloni" (no corn, egg, wheat, or gluten)
- Chilled Zucchini Bisque (no corn, egg, milk, wheat, or gluten)
- Sweet Basil Pasta (no corn, or egg)
- Bagels (no corn, egg, or milk)
- Fluffy Lemon Cheese Cake (no corn, wheat, or gluten)
- Quick Gingerbread (no corn or milk)
- No-Bake Peanut Butter–Carob Cookies (no corn, egg, wheat, or gluten)

*"While my credentials include a B.S. degree in Nutrition
and Dietetics from the University of Washington
and years of experience in practical dietetics, my best
recommendation to write a book of this kind is simply
the fact that 'I've been there.' My husband has
been allergic to milk and eggs for years, and our son
is allergic to wheat and corn. Every one of the recipes
in this book was created out of my personal needs
as a wife and mother to prepare tasty,
nutritious meals for my family."*
                                                        —*Ruth R. Shattuck*

THE ALLERGY COOKBOOK

TASTY, NUTRITIOUS COOKING WITHOUT WHEAT, CORN, MILK, OR EGGS

Ruth R. Shattuck

WITH A FOREWORD BY
George K. Hurwitz, M.D.

A PLUME BOOK

NEW AMERICAN LIBRARY

NEW YORK AND SCARBOROUGH, ONTARIO

NAL BOOKS ARE AVAILABLE AT QUANTITY DISCOUNTS
WHEN USED TO PROMOTE PRODUCTS OR SERVICES.
FOR INFORMATION PLEASE WRITE TO PREMIUM MARKETING DIVISION,
NEW AMERICAN LIBRARY, 1633 BROADWAY, NEW YORK, NEW YORK 10019.

PLUME TRADEMARK REG. U.S. PAT. OFF. AND FOREIGN COUNTRIES
REGISTERED TRADEMARK—MARCA REGISTRADA
HECHO EN WESTFORD, MASS., U.S.A.

SIGNET, SIGNET CLASSIC, MENTOR, PLUME, MERIDIAN
and NAL BOOKS are published *in the United States* by New
American Library, 1633 Broadway, New York, New York 10019,
in Canada by The New American Library of Canada Limited,
81 Mack Avenue, Scarborough, Ontario M1L 1M8

Library of Congress Cataloging in Publication Data

Shattuck, Ruth R.
   The allergy cookbook.

   Includes index.
   1. Food allergy—Diet therapy—Recipes.   I. Title.
RC588.053S53   1984   641.5′63   83-19400
ISBN 0-452-25718-2

First Printing, April, 1984

3 4 5 6 7 8 .9

PRINTED IN THE UNITED STATES OF AMERICA

CONTENTS

FOREWORD

The field of allergy and immunology has undergone immense changes in the last few years, and there is increasing evidence that proper diet is important for all of us but especially the allergic patient.

Some patients are overly allergic to foods, dyes, and drugs; but there are many others allergic to pollens and environmental factors who would benefit by the principles outlined by Mrs. Shattuck—proper diet and nutrition. When combined with rest, exercise, and avoidance of nonspecific irritants, avoidance of food allergens is of immense help to the allergic patient.

This book will be of value to those who must restrict or eliminate common food allergens. The recipes are clearly outlined, time tested, and nutritious. It is a real service to have this book available.

—GEORGE K. HURWITZ, M.D.
Fellow, American Academy of Allergy,
and Associate Clinical Professor
of Medicine, University of California
School of Medicine, San Francisco

INTRODUCTION

Countless thousands of persons know that they are allergic to specific foods or "families" of foods. And every day hundreds more learn of their intolerance to various foods. The situation is widespread and serious. The most common allergens are wheat, milk, corn, and eggs. Unfortunately, in today's society, these are also the most difficult ones with which to cope.

A completely unknowledgeable person might say, for example, "If you're allergic to milk, just don't drink any!" But only a little critical investigation will show that avoiding milk is easier said than done. Not only do many canned products we eat contain milk or fractions of milk, as do almost all baked goods, but even fresh meat products purchased at the butcher's counter can contain added dry milk solids.

The same is true of corn. Not eat corn? Easy, if it were only on the cob. But the fact is that many, many products we eat—without ever reading the labels—contain corn syrup, cornstarch, or corn in other forms. It is not too great an overstatement to say that individuals allergic to all four—wheat, milk, eggs, and corn—could figuratively starve to death in the middle of their favorite supermarket.

And yet, some are allergic to all four. It is the nature of allergies to multiply themselves—particularly when individuals have been unaware of their problems for a long time, or have not given careful attention to their eating habits after learning of their allergies. Avoidance of one food tends to increase the usage of another. And the overuse can create a new sensitivity.

The inconvenience of not being able to eat what one likes—or, in many instances, not being able to eat at all—is inevitably disruptive. In some cases it can create havoc with one's life-style. Worst of all, it makes getting proper nutrition much more difficult. This can have serious consequences. It is essential to maintain the best possible health at all times, and adequate, enjoyable nutrition is a key factor.

This was what motivated me to publish my first allergy cookbook in 1974 and to create this second, new one now. While my credentials include a B.S. degree in nutrition and dietetics from the University of Wisconsin and two years of experience in practical dietetics, my best recommendation to write a book of this kind is simply the fact that "I've been there." My husband has been allergic to milk and eggs for years, and our son is allergic to wheat and corn. Every one of the recipes in this book was created out of my personal needs as a wife and mother to prepare tasty, nutritious meals for my family.

Every one of these recipes has been tested again and again—scoured clean of "unpermissibles" and revised until it could pass a taste test by myself and at least one other very critical person. (Many of these recipes have also been enjoyed by my friends and neighbors.)

In creating these recipes, four factors were always in my mind:

1. Each recipe must meet the needs of the allergic person, based on my latest information on the causes and nature of food allergies. Substitution of foods must be such as not to encourage a new allergy.
2. All the products used must be obtainable by the average cook. Those that are not standard shelf products in your markets will be found in health food stores and nutrition sections of the supermarket. Each recipe must be easy to prepare by anyone with only moderate kitchen skills, and must offer good value for its cost.
3. Each recipe must look good, smell good, taste good, and must be suitable in every way for even the nonrestricted members of the family to enjoy.
4. Each recipe must follow the best guidelines I know for healthful nutrition. This means fresh ingredients and as few processed foods as possible. Whenever possible, whole grains and whole flours are used; honey instead of sugar; unsaturated cooking oil instead of margarine; carob instead of chocolate; a minimum of salt, and lots of unroasted nuts and seeds, legumes and vegetables.

Living on a restricted diet is certainly not a great pleasure. But it need not be a hardship either. I hope that with my book in hand, an allergic individual will find exciting new adventures in eating for every item of food no longer allowed.

I have tried to present in these 300 recipes the widest possible choice of fine eating from many different cuisines. Moreover, recipes are included for every possible need, from snacks to desserts.

It is my hope that with my book you will no longer be "locked out" of the world you enjoyed, but will instead be "locked in" to a whole new world of pleasurable dining.

Bon appétit!

—RUTH R. SHATTUCK

THE ALLERGY COOKBOOK

A NUTRITIONAL BRIEFING

If you are undergoing an allergy elimination diet, it is important to know how to compensate for foods omitted. Some basic knowledge of food and nutrition is more than helpful—it is essential. We are what we eat. Health is not merely the absence of an allergic reaction.

My recipes provide good nutrition in foods that also taste and look good. They call for ingredients that provide maximum food value, and they solve the problem that the allergy diet poses for both the restricted person and the homemaker responsible for meal planning and preparation—how to ensure attractive, palatable dining and adequate nutrition, too.

The food that fuels our bodies is composed of various elements, each of which plays a vital role. The chemical structure of all these elements is highly complex, but the fundamental way in which they work is easy to understand.

- Proteins build and restore body tissue, including muscle.
- Carbohydrates provide energy and are an important factor in vital metabolic processes.
- Fats are also essential to metabolism and are another source of energy.
- Minerals and vitamins function as catalysts enabling the body to utilize proteins, carbohydrates, and fats, as well as playing important roles of their own.

An allergy diet should be a wholesome diet, with adequate amounts of all the food elements that fuel the human body and as little as possible of the ones that can do it harm. The following information will help you recognize what those food elements are and explain why it is so important to use only the most wholesome ingredients possible.

1

PROTEINS

Proteins are composed of combinations of any of twenty-two "subparticles" called amino acids. The body can manufacture most of them, but there are eight that are "essential" to include in our diets daily because the body does not manufacture them itself.

Some proteins may be described as "complete" because they contain all eight of the essential amino acids. Complete proteins are found in meat, fish, fowl, eggs, wheat germ, and milk (including secondary milk sources such as cheese and yogurt). Another protein group is "partially complete." In these, most of the necessary amino acids are present, one or two missing. Foods that provide proteins of this type are legumes (beans and peas), nuts, tofu, seeds, brown rice, whole grains, and brewer's yeast. Still a third group of proteins is "incomplete"—few of the essential amino acids are present. Fruit, corn, and other vegetables contain proteins in this group.

The body can properly utilize those incomplete and partially complete proteins only if all eight essential amino acids are ingested at, or at about, the same time. This means that our menus must be planned so that foods that are sources of some but not all of the essential amino acids are *combined* to produce a complete protein. Cereal or toast or beans or rice are not adequate proteins if eaten separately. Beans *and* rice are, because in combination they provide a complete protein. So do beans and whole wheat toast. So do milk and cereal or milk and whole wheat toast.

Other useful combinations are: legumes with wheat, corn, oats, barley, or sesame or sunflower seeds; rice with legumes, grains, or seeds; grains with legumes.

Foods that contain complete proteins can of course be combined with foods that are only partially complete. The above example of milk and cereal or toast shows this combination.

Particular mention must be made of two much overlooked, useful foods which, although not able to provide a complete protein, have other nutritional virtues—sunflower seeds and legumes.

Sunflower seeds, whether used as a snack or incorporated in recipes, are a great booster to good nutrition. They contain 24 percent protein of a quality almost equal to meat. They are a good source of polyunsaturated oils, including one believed to be important to our hearts. They contain six vitamins and six minerals, including zinc and B-6, which are both difficult to get in sufficient quantity in our normal diets.

Legumes are a useful, low-cost alternative to meat. They are low in saturated fats and much lower in calories. They easily combine with other foods to make complete proteins. They are rich in fiber. Legumes include soybeans and tofu, black-eyed peas, peanuts, garbanzo beans or chick peas, navy beans, kidney beans, pinto beans, lima beans, cranberry beans, and lentils.

CARBOHYDRATES

Carbohydrates include sugars and starches. Sources of sugars are brown and white sugar; the many canned and prepared foods that contain them; and honey, molasses, and fruits. Sources of starches are flours made from grains, grains themselves, prepared foods made from grain flours, and vegetables.

Refined sugars are of minimal utility in nutrition. They provide energy (calories) and nothing else of value. Indeed, they are detrimental not only to diabetics and hypoglycemics but to good nutrition. There is increasing evidence that refined sugars disrupt calcium levels, increase the need for vitamin B complex (which is often in short supply in our diets), decrease the body's ability to combat infection and recover from disease and surgery, and lower immune responses to infection. They certainly reduce the appetite for nutritionally sound foods. And they are often combined commercially with synthetic flavors and colors that contain allergens and are particularly harmful to children.

Natural sugars are those found in honey, molasses, and fruits. The sugars in fruits are valuable because they are digested more slowly than refined sugar, and the fruits themselves contain important bulk, which slows down digestion. Honey is another useful source of the sweetness to which our palates are attuned. Only half as much honey as sugar is needed to produce the same degree of sweetness, and according to *The Composition of Foods, Agriculture Handbook No. 8*,* strained or extracted honey contains trace amounts of protein, phosphorus, sodium, and potassium. Selenium and B vitamins have also been mentioned as present. Raw honey contains even more of these elements.

Starches are also a source of energy, and complex starches (unrefined) are excellent foods. They are absorbed much more slowly and efficiently than sugars, thus helping to maintain level blood sugars. Their bulk aids in digestion and elimination and decreases the risk of colon cancer.

The Composition of Foods, Agriculture Handbook #8, United States Department of Agriculture.

Whole grains and flours made from them are rich in vitamins, minerals, and unsaturated oils. Particularly valuable is raw wheat germ. It is a prime source of essential food elements and also is readily combined with many other foods. Raw wheat germ is 26 percent complete protein—more complete protein than is in meat. It is high in fiber, B vitamins, zinc, and vitamin E. Brown rice is even richer than wheat in several minerals and vitamins. Both raw wheat germ and brown rice are especially rich in B vitamins.

Refined flours and the products made from them are not good foods. They provide little but starch—"empty" calories. Vitamins and minerals are found mainly in the husks and oils of the grains, which have been removed in the processing. Only about half a dozen needed nutrients are replaced in the much advertised "enriching" process of refined flours out of the more than twenty that are removed. Unfortunately, some of the trace minerals hardest to get in our diets are among the ones not replaced, and the iron used is in a form the body cannot absorb. White flour combined with refined sugar and fat in numerous popular pastries, desserts, and snack foods become empty calories. In contrast, using whole grain flours, unsaturated oil, and honey or molasses produces a nutritious, still tasty product.

FATS

Fats are of three types: saturated, monounsaturated, and polyunsaturated. Of these, the last is to be preferred in nutrition. Polyunsaturated oils are essential in the formation of cell membranes and assist in the metabolism of some vitamins. Good sources—in descending order of saturation—are safflower, sunflower, soybean, corn, and cottonseed oils. The common salad or vegetable oils in supermarkets are only partially polyunsaturated and not as beneficial as the types listed above, which are slightly more expensive but worth the difference in price. Most diets are woefully deficient in unsaturated fats so vital to our hearts and arteries. Polyunsaturated oils should be kept refrigerated. They will not thicken in the refrigerator, but can become rancid if left at room temperature.

Monounsaturated fats appear to be neutral factors in the body, doing neither good nor harm except as calories. Olive oil is a monounsaturated fat.

Saturated fats are the least desirable. They tend to clog arteries and foster obesity. Sources are meats (most of which contain as much or more fat than they do protein), dairy products, hydrogenated (solid) shortenings, and products made from coconut and palm oils (these oils are used in many processed foods because they are less expensive).

Most of us eat too much fat. The average diet in this country is said to contain 40 to 45 percent fat, far more than is desirable. Thirty percent or less would be enough for our body requirements. The problems that result from excess fat intake are compounded by the presence in many diets of the less desirable types of fat.

VITAMINS and MINERALS

These are essential components of a sound diet and are vital to many functions of our bodies. They are too often lost in the processing and refining that much of our food now undergoes. Use of unprocessed foods such as whole grains (including brown rice), raw wheat germ, sunflower seeds, sesame seeds, sprouts, fresh vegetables, and fresh fruits is a sound safeguard. Vitamin and mineral supplements may also be necessary as a precaution. They should certainly be considered.

THE ALLERGY DIET

Living with food allergies requires much cooking from scratch. It is no easy task, but it can be done, even though allergy diets pose plenty of problems for both the allergic person and anyone who cooks for him or her. These problems can usually be resolved with only a little extra effort if you keep a few key principles in mind:

- Take great care to study labels
- Be especially nutrition-conscious
- Try new ingredients and cooking techniques

TAKE GREAT CARE TO STUDY LABELS

For someone with a food allergy, forbidden substances can appear in unexpected places. Corn, for example, is present not only in corn syrup and cornstarch. It can also be found in canned fruits, catsup, baking powder, cocoa, chocolate syrup, dry cereals, soft drinks, and sauces. Milk, milk products, and eggs appear in a wide range of unsuspected products. Wheat lurks in many processed foods as well as in baked goods.

Specific information about ingredients should be obtained by writing food manufacturers if information on labels is not specific enough. Hydrolyzed protein, for instance, a common ingredient in commercial chicken and beef stock bases and instant bouillon cubes, may be derived from corn, milk, egg, or wheat. When its source is unidentified, it should be avoided by anyone who is allergic to any of these foods. By making a practice of reading ingredient lists, you soon learn which products to use. Swanson's broths, for example, contain no hydrolyzed proteins and can be used in my recipes. Campbell's broths, however, do contain hydrolyzed protein and should be avoided. Spice Island chicken and beef broth stock base contain corn and hydrolyzed vegetable protein. Herb Ox beef or chicken bouillon contains hydrolyzed vegetable protein—unidentified, and Steero instant beef bouillon and beef cubes both contain hydrolyzed vegetable protein and probable corn.

If you make your own stock, of course, you don't have to worry because then you know what's in it.

BE ESPECIALLY
NUTRITION-CONSCIOUS

If your diet must be milk-free, for example, you must contend with the fact that milk is a prime source of calcium, which is necessary for healthy cell tissue, for proper blood structure and heartbeat, and for strong bones and teeth throughout our lives. If calcium intake and assimilation are deficient, the tissues and blood will withdraw calcium from bones and teeth. The result may be lost teeth and/or osteoporosis—the bone softening that afflicts many older people. If milk is eliminated from a diet, other sources of calcium must be substituted or augmented. There is some calcium in legumes, blackstrap molasses, sesame seed meal, and tofu. Still smaller amounts are found in some green vegetables. However, none of these supply the amount needed. How can the allergic person get enough?

Calcium supplements are easier taken as tablets than incorporated in recipes. Calcium ascorbate, the only powdered calcium supplement I know of without a milk base, has a strong flavor which would not be good in recipes.

In some instances, modifying the milk by cooking it or using it evaporated makes it acceptable to the body. The albumin and globulin in milk are both proteins that trigger allergies. Cooking modifies them.

There are milk substitutes available (such as Coffee Rich, Cereal Blend, and Mocha Mix), but they have little food value and contain casein, a milk ingredient that must be approached with caution. Some other substitutes such as Cool Whip and imitation margarine contain too much saturated fat to be healthy. I do not recommend any of these products. For cereals or fruits, try adding nut milks (see page 16), homemade soybean milk, fruit sauces such as apple or pear sauce thinned with a little juice instead of milk. If you do use commercial milk substitutes, remember they are empty calories.

Butter and margarine are other milk-based products to be eliminated in milk-free diets. For table use, as on toast, nut spreads are nutritious alternatives.

TRY NEW INGREDIENTS AND COOKING TECHNIQUES

Eggs are found in commercial pies, cakes, cookies, pastries, sauces, many breads, noodles, and some meat dishes, so if you are allergic to eggs you must cook these foods from scratch. Yet cooking without eggs can be frustrating, for they impart a tenderness and texture that are difficult to replace. There really is no substitute for an egg in baking.

Special care and precautions are necessary with eggless cooking. Because eggless cakes are fragile, it helps to line the pans with greased and floured waxed paper, and keep the shape and size of the pan simple. Underbaked, an eggless cake may fall when removed from the oven. Opening the oven door to test for doneness prematurely will also make an eggless cake fall.

Eggless dips and binders for fish and meat recipes can be made from canned milk, half and half, or undiluted canned soup, if allowed. Adding a little gelatin or minute tapioca gives a firmer texture. Moist bread, bread soaked in milk, or broth in which a little minute tapioca has softened for 10 to 15 minutes and then wrung dry is good for stuffing and filling (you add whatever seasoning you desire).

Milk, oil with lemon juice, or melted butter can replace an egg as an adhesive for crumbs for broiling or pan-frying lean fish or meat. Tomato juice is another possibility where flavors are compatible. Whipped tofu is also an excellent egg substitute in some recipes.

Diets that must be both wheat-free and gluten-free are also especially difficult for cooks to accommodate. The conditions called celiac disease and sprue necessitate elimination of the gluten found in many grains. Gluten is well named, for it is the "glue" that gives the texture to leavened breads and pastries. Without it, baking breadstuffs is difficult. When gluten must be eliminated, not only wheat but also oats, rye, barley, and buckwheat cannot be used, as well as any foods with gluten-bearing ingredients such as malt and brewer's yeast made from barley mash, any cold cereal coated with malt, alcoholic beverages made from the offending grains, all commercial sauces, soups, puddings, and baked products, and all store-bought products that do not include a full list of ingredients. This leaves rice, cornmeal, millet, soybeans (soya), and potato flours with which to cook. Nuts and other legumes and seeds can be ground into a meal and combined with them. In wheat-free diets without gluten restrictions, the use of oat and rye flour makes possible more variety and a closer resemblance to wheat breads.

It is necessary to recognize, though, that a cake without egg will have a different texture, and bread without gluten will not be the same. Some of my recipes include egg but can be made without it. The texture is just slightly different.

Breads and baked goods are definitely the most difficult aspect of allergy cooking. Few people are willing to or should completely give up breads and baked goods. They should be part of your daily diet. Whole grains are important sources of minerals, vitamins, and bulk, as well as complex starches and some good-quality protein. They are also low in fat. The recipes I have given you not only for bread but also for cakes, cookies, and desserts are all nutritious.

HOW TO
USE THIS BOOK

It is a challenge to prepare nutritious, interesting meals to save jaded appetites from boredom while maintaining allergy-diet restrictions, but it can be done. My recipes should make your task simpler and enable you to serve the same interesting menu to the entire family—and guests—in spite of restrictions.

The sections called "Basic Ingredients for Cooking" and "Some Hints About Cooking Techniques" will add to your skill and expand the number of dishes you can healthfully prepare and enjoy.

There are charts at the beginning of each chapter so you can find the recipes eliminating your particular allergen. There are also variations, so that if a recipe excludes milk, for example, but milk is not an offender for you, you can use it in place of the liquid called for in the recipe. The appendix lists the food values of many different foods. Compare brown rice flour and whole wheat flour as an example to show what your substitutions are adding to or detracting from your diet. Check legumes with meat; sunflower seeds and raw wheat germ together and with meat. (Though sunflower seeds are 24 percent protein, more than in meat, they do lack one essential amino acid so are not quite a complete protein.)

Although this book is primarily for allergy diets, because minimum amounts of honey replace sugar, because unsaturated oil is used in nearly all the recipes, and because salt is used in small amounts that can be replaced with a salt substitute (or reduced even more), the recipes are also excellent for those with heart and circulation problems.

BASIC INGREDIENTS FOR COOKING

Baking Powder

Double-acting baking powder is used whenever "regular baking powder" is called for. *For corn-free recipes*, substitute arrowroot baking powder for regular baking powder. To make arrowroot baking powder, combine ⅓ cup of baking soda or potassium bicarbonate, ⅔ cup of cream of tartar, and ⅔ cup of arrowroot. Mix well and store in an airtight container. 1 teaspoon of regular baking powder = 1½ teaspoons of arrowroot baking powder.

Bread Crumbs

For wheat- or gluten-free recipes, bread crumbs can be made from wheat- or gluten-free breads or crackers (the recipes are given in this book) as you would any bread crumbs—dried and blended. (Note: Avoid rice crackers.) Nut or seed meal can be combined with the crumbs.

Butter and Oil

Butter is essential in very few recipes other than for flavor. Shortbread, for example, is not the same at all if butter is not used. But in most recipes, oil or vegetable shortening plus butter flavoring, if desired, is most satisfactory. Nearly all of my recipes use safflower oil. For flavor, olive oil or sesame oil, or even bacon fat, can replace butter in meat, fish, and vegetable cookery. For baking, safflower oil works very well in most recipes. A nonallergenic hydrolyzed shortening such as Crisco is best for greasing baking pans.

Both butter and margarine are to be eliminated in a milk-free diet. When they are not allergens, they are in most instances interchangeable. They both contain 100 calories per tablespoon. Butter has more cholesterol than margarine, but margarine has a detrimental hydrolyzed fat. When cholesterol is not a problem, butter is a preferable choice.

Carob, Cocoa, and Chocolate

Carob powder and cocoa powder are interchangeable in recipes, but carob contains milk and cocoa contains cornstarch. *For milk-free recipes*, use cocoa; *for corn-free recipes*, use carob. *For milk-free, corn-free recipes*, use chocolate. For each 3 tablespoons of carob or cocoa powder, use 1 square of chocolate and decrease the milk, water, or other liquid in the recipe by 1 tablespoon.

Cornstarch

For corn-free recipes, substitute arrowroot for cornstarch: 1 tablespoon of cornstarch = 2½ teaspoons of arrowroot. Do not use arrowroot in a recipe that has to be rewarmed. It loses its thickening capacity. Instead, use tapioca flour, potato flour, or brown rice or wheat flour as a substitute for cornstarch.

Flour

Whole Wheat Flour: Whole wheat flour is heavier in texture than refined flour and may produce breads and cakes heavier than you are used to or prefer. If so, use part whole wheat flour and part unbleached flour until you get used to the difference. Or substitute a small amount (1 to 2 tablespoons per cup of flour) of cornstarch or arrowroot to lighten the texture of cakes and pastries. The nutritional benefits of whole wheat flour are worth the effort of getting used to it. Compare the food value of white and whole wheat flour in the Appendix.

Homemade breads tend to be crumbly, especially breads made with whole wheat flour, because the increased amount of roughage lessens the proportion of gluten. To compensate, add gluten (1 tablespoon per cup of flour) to the flour. If the recipe calls for 4 to 5 cups of flour, substitute ¼ cup of gluten and reduce the flour by that amount. For 7 to 8 cups of flour, substitute ½ cup of gluten. It is obtainable at health food stores. (If gluten is not permitted, neither is the wheat.) Whole wheat flour should be stored in the refrigerator to prevent loss of vitamin E and prevent rancidity, but should not be frozen, as freezing destroys vitamin E.

Brown Rice Flour: *For wheat-free recipes*, brown rice flour is as nutritious as whole wheat flour, and in case of gluten sensitivity, it is the most acceptable substitute. Cornmeal can be used but is not nearly as nutritious. Where gluten sensitivity is not the problem, brown rice flour is best replaced or combined with oat, rye, or barley flour. They, in turn, can be combined with nuts and other legumes and seeds ground into a meal. If corn is not an allergen for you, substituting 1 tablespoon of cornstarch for 1 tablespoon of brown rice flour in each cup of flour gives a better texture. Brown rice flour has a slightly gritty texture and produces bread of a texture that is not as fine as that of breads made with other grains.

Rice polish and bran can also replace up to one fourth the rice flour and have more calcium, iron, thiamin, riboflavin, and niacin (B vitamins) than whole wheat flour. Everyone is familiar with wheat bran, the outer husk of the wheat. Brown rice has the same type of husk which, when removed, is sold as rice bran. In polishing rice to make white rice (empty calories), all the important nutrients, the minerals and vitamins in the rice, are removed but are fortunately then available as rice polish. Rice bran and rice polish are as valuable as wheat germ for their nutrients and are available in health food stores.

In many of the recipes in this book, cornstarch is given as an alternative to brown rice flour. It should be pointed out that if another kind of flour is allowed, it should be used instead of cornstarch, which gives a different-textured sauce. It is best for desserts or when a clear sauce is desired, but is not as good for meats and vegetables.

Other Flours and Meals: Soya and potato flour are very heavy, and soya has a rather strong flavor. These flours should be used sparingly. Breads made from brown rice, soya, and potato flour must be kept in the refrigerator, as they mold very easily. Freezing for very long will dry them, causing them to become crumbly. It is best to bake often and not too much at a time.

Rye flour and cornmeal are available at supermarkets; brown rice flour at some markets or at health food stores. Soya, rice polish or rice bran, barley flour, millet flour, tapioca flour, chick pea flour, and potato flour are all health-food store items.

You can also make your own flour *for wheat-free recipes*. To make oat flour, put about 2 cups of oats in a blender or food processor and blend at high speed. This makes about 1½ cups of flour. It is easiest to process 6 or 8 cups of oats, in batches, and store in an airtight container ready for immediate use. It does not need refrigeration.

To make nut or seed flour or meal, follow directions for making oat flour, using almonds, walnuts, filberts, or peanuts instead of oats. Flours blended from nuts and seeds have a different consistency from wheat or rice flours. They are coarser and more like a meal. The moisture and the oil content of seeds and nuts tend to be higher, giving them a silky feeling.

Use only raw, unsalted seeds. We do not need extra salt, and toasting destroys the vitamin E. Refrigerate seed meals.

½ cup raw unblanched almonds yields
    ½ cup + 3 tablespoons meal
3 cups filberts yields 2 cups meal
½ cup chopped walnuts or peanuts yields
    ½ cup + 2 tablespoons meal
½ cup sunflower seeds yields ½ cup + 3 tablespoons meal

To make safflower seed meal, follow directions for making nut flour or meal and use interchangeably.

To make millet flour, take 1 cup of millet and put in the blender; blend at high speed for several minutes. Then put through either a very fine strainer or a sifter until you have removed the grit. This should make about ½ to ⅔ cup of flour. Commercial millet flour is best.

For thickening for sauces, gravies, puddings and such *in wheat-free recipes*, a number of substitutes are available. Cornstarch (not for corn-free diets), brown rice flour, tapioca flour (available in some nutrition and health food stores), and potato flour are all possibilities. Use about the same amount of tapioca as cornstarch, half as much cornstarch as wheat flour, and not quite as much brown rice as wheat flour.

Milk

Nut Milk: *For milk-free recipes* for desserts and beverages, nut milk may be substituted for cow's milk. To make 4 cups of nut milk, whirl 1 cup of cashews with 4 cups of water and 2 teaspoons of honey to taste for two minutes in a blender or food processor, and strain; or whirl ¾ cup of sesame seeds with 2 cups of water and 4 teaspoons of honey for two minutes in a blender or food processor, and strain.

Soybean Milk: Available in health food stores, soybean milk may be substituted for cow's milk *in milk-free recipes*. But commercially prepared soybean milk has a strong, rather bitter, unpleasant taste. Soybeans contain the enzyme lipoxidase, which is released when the beans are ground in water and triggers a chemical reaction that affects the flavor. If the enzyme is inactivated, however, the bitter taste does not develop. Cornell University has developed a process that inactivates the enzyme and produces a mild, bland soybean milk. The process is time-consuming, but the result is a nutritious alternative to cow's milk that can be fortified and is especially valuable for children who are allergic to milk. Here's how to make it:

Wash and pick over beans, discarding any broken ones. Soak 1 cup of beans overnight in 3 cups of cold water. They should double in size. Pour off the water and drain well. Preheat the blender by pouring very hot water into it and running it for one minute. Have 6 cups of boiling water ready. Don't remove it from the heat except to measure. Divide beans into three parts. Grind each third with 2 full cups of *boiling* water for 2 to 3 minutes. If the water is not boiling, the process will not work. Wrap towels around the blender to keep in the heat. Strain through several layers of cheesecloth in a colander or use a jelly bag to remove the residue. Squeeze the cheesecloth or jelly bag to get as much milk as possible. Measure the amount. You should have approximately 6 to 7 cups. Heat the milk in an uncovered double boiler for 30 minutes, stirring occasionally. Remeasure and replace with cold water the amount lost to evaporation. Refrigerate immediately.

Soybean milk has the same amount of protein as cow's milk and a third as much fat—most of it unsaturated—but it has no carbohydrates, no vitamin B-12, and very little calcium. To remedy this, to each cup of soybean milk add ½ teaspoon of calcium carbonate (300 milligrams), available at health food stores, and for each 6 to 7 cups of soybean milk add one crushed vitamin B-12 tablet (25 to 50 micrograms). Add 1 teaspoon of soybean or safflower oil if the fat equivalent of whole milk is desired. Sweeten with up to 2 teaspoons of honey depending on how you plan to use it.

The lack of carbohydrates is easily compensated for with other foods. Calcium carbonate is available in drugstores. *Please note*: Calcium carbonate does not dissolve, so it is important to *shake or stir the milk before each use*.

If the strong taste of commercial soybean milk is not objectionable, it can be used in these recipes. I would recommend diluting it to a skim milk consistency. My recipes call for the homemade mix.

Potato Water: Peel and chop 2 medium-sized potatoes. Cover with 3 cups of water. Boil until potatoes are soft. Set potatoes aside. Use potato water as a milk substitute *for milk-free bread recipes*. Yields 1½ to 2 cups of potato water. It should be made as needed or at least used the same day. Refrigerate if not used quickly.

Milk Powder: 1 cup of nonfat, noninstant milk powder equals 2 cups of instant, nonfat milk powder.

Seasonings

To replace cheese flavor *in milk-free recipes*, use equal amounts of nutmeg, paprika, celery salt, plus pepper to taste if desired. Pepper is not included in any of my recipes. It is very simple to add it at the table but impossible to remove from prepared dishes.

There are commercially mixed spices, such as Spice Island "fines herbes," or you can make your own, using primarily 1 T. sweet basil, 1 T. oregano, 1 T. taragon, ½ T. marjoram, ½ t. thyme, 1 t. sage, and 1 t. minced fresh rosemary if available.

Salt is used sparingly in these recipes, and often left up to you. The body needs only ½ teaspoon of sodium as salt daily, but the average daily consumption is 4 to 5 teaspoons. It is hidden in practically all prepared or processed foods. Everything from soup to catsup, from canned foods to cheese has too much salt. Most tastebuds are trained to the taste of salt rather than the food it is in. The excess salt upsets the mineral and chemical balance of the body, contributing to circulatory and heart problems.

Tofu

Many supermarkets as well as health food stores and Oriental and specialty markets carry tofu—the nutritious soybean cakes used in so many Oriental dishes. Tofu comes in soft, medium, or firm cakes. The soft is best for recipes requiring creaming, the firmer or medium is best where the tofu is to be cut into pieces and where the tofu needs to keep its own identity. The recipes for desserts and sauces use the soft. The firmer cake is used for meat substitutes and extenders.

For milk-free, egg-free recipes, tofu can be a welcome ingredient. Interesting pies and puddings are possible. Tofu does have a soybean flavor, but it also absorbs quite readily the flavors of the food it is used with. If there is still a distinguishable tofu flavor, add additional flavorings to taste. For example, use 2 teaspoons of vanilla instead of 1 or more of cinnamon, nutmeg, etc., or orange juice instead of water to make the difference.

To prepare the tofu, drain and rinse the cake in cold water. Split into two horizontal sections and place cakes side by side on three or four thicknesses of paper towels. Cover with more paper towels and place a heavy skillet on top to press out the moisture. Repeat if necessary. If all excess moisture is not removed, your dish will be runny. Pat dry.

Yeast

1 packet of dry yeast = 2 teaspoons of dry yeast. It is more economical to buy yeast in bulk, or 8-ounce packages, which are available at many health food stores. It is best stored in the refrigerator. Cake yeast can be substituted in these recipes though I have used dry yeast throughout. Dry yeast keeps better, especially if refrigerated, and for me it is easier to use.

SOME HINTS ABOUT COOKING TECHNIQUES

All oven temperatures in this book are for preheated ovens. All are Fahrenheit. All measurements and temperatures are for low altitude.

Kitchens differ. Even in your own kitchen, baking pans and cookie sheets may differ. Ovens have their own eccentricities. Oven temperatures given in the recipe may need some adjustment. Reduce temperature 25 degrees for glass containers. All recipe temperatures given here are for metal unless otherwise specified.

When measuring oil and honey, measure the oil first; then measure honey in the same spoon or container. The oil remaining in the measurer will wash out all the honey—quick and easy, and no waste.

When transferring from beater to spoon mixing, be sure to clean all batter off beaters or proportions will be changed.

To simplify legume cookery, soak beans 3 to 4 hours or overnight. Throw away the soak water. Cook beans in boiling water for ½ hour. Drain, discarding water. Finish cooking with fresh water until tender, as long as 2 to 3 hours. This process greatly reduces the flatulence associated with beans and the nutrition loss is minimal. You may compensate for it, if you wish, by adding 1 teaspoon of brewer's yeast for each ½ cup of beans to the fresh water during the final cooking process.

Beans can be frozen in the soaking water for future use. They will cook faster after freezing. Cooked beans can also be frozen.

Flour consistency varies with temperature and humidity. Moisture from the air is absorbed in humid or rainy weather. Hot, dry weather makes for a dry, light flour, which produces a better bread texture. In dry weather, fewer cups of flour are needed than in moist temperatures. Thus, 5 cups may be sufficient on a dry day but 6 cups will be needed on a moist one.

A quick, easy, and clean method of sifting is to stir or whip the flour with a fork in its sack or container and then spoon it gently into a measuring cup. Whole wheat and unbleached flours especially need sifting for cakes or pastries, as they are not as light as bleached flour. Sifting incorporates air into flour and helps produce a more tender product.

To lower cholesterol and calories without jeopardizing quality, whipped, evaporated milk replaces whipped cream in many recipes. Canned milk is inexpensive and can be stored for instant availability. Proper flavoring masks the caramelized canned-milk flavor.

Whipped, nonfat milk makes a good topping. It must be whipped just before using, as it breaks down if allowed to stand. Bowls and beaters must be very cold. Follow the directions on a nonfat milk package, and be sure all ingredients are chilled before you begin.

To enhance orange and lemon flavor, use grated peel. Frozen juice does not supply peel flavor. To make peel, use a vegetable peeler on an orange or lemon to remove a very thin skin. Store it in your freezer in an airtight bottle.

A pastry cloth and rolling pin stocking can be very helpful. Because less flour is used to prevent dough from sticking, a lighter-textured pastry or dough results. It is easier to handle and the cleanup is quicker and easier.

YEAST BREADS

	NO CORN	NO EGG	NO MILK	NO WHEAT	NO GLUTEN
Oat and Wheat Bread	X	X	⊗		
Refrigerator Wheat Germ Bread	X	X	⊗		
Cracked Wheat Bread	X	X	X		
Potato Whole Wheat Bread	X	X	X		
Rye Bread	X	X	X		
Rye Batter Bread	X	X		X	
Bagels	X	X	X		
Honey-Oatmeal Bread	X	X	⊗		
Zucchini Yeast Bread	X	X	⊗		
Applesauce Loaf	X	X	X		
Date Loaf	X		X		
Jule Kaga—Christmas Bread	X	X	⊗		
Pumpkin Rolls	X	X	⊗		
Buttermilk Rolls	X	X			
Cracked Wheat Rolls	X	X			
Whole Wheat Sally Lunn	X	X			
Whole Wheat Buns	X	X	X		

⊗ means that the recipe includes instructions for adding that ingredient if allowed.

21

Oat and Wheat Bread

NO CORN, EGG, OR MILK*
Yield: 2 loaves (16–18 slices per loaf)

2 T. dry yeast
½ c. warm water
2 T. honey
2 T. safflower oil
2½ c. warm potato water (see
    page 17)

2 t. salt
2 c. whole wheat flour, unsifted
½ c. gluten
2¼ c. unbleached flour,
    unsifted
1¼ c. oat flour (see page 15)

In a mixing bowl, dissolve yeast in warm water. Add honey, oil, potato water, salt, and whole wheat flour. Add gluten. Thoroughly blend. Beat at medium speed in electric mixer for 3 minutes. By hand, beat in most of the unbleached flour and the oat flour.

Turn out onto a floured board and knead 10–15 minutes, adding remaining flour. The dough should be quite stiff. Put into a greased bowl, turning once to grease the top. Let rise covered with a cloth in a warm place until almost doubled in bulk, about 1 hour.

Punch down dough and knead again about 5 minutes. Shape into two loaves and let rise, covered, in two 8 × 4-inch greased bread pans until almost doubled in bulk, about 25 minutes. Bake at 375° 35–40 minutes, or until lightly browned and loaves sound hollow when tapped on the bottom. Turn out onto wire racks to cool.

Variations: *If you can use milk,* use scalded and cooled milk instead of potato water.

The oat flour can be replaced with all whole wheat flour.

Refrigerator Wheat Germ Bread

NO CORN, EGG, OR MILK*
Yield: 3 loaves (16–18 slices per loaf)

This dough can be mixed ahead and refrigerated for up to 24 hours to meet the demands of a busy schedule, and the bread is just plain super good. The lemon peel in this bread adds an interesting, tantalizing flavor.

2 T. dry yeast
¾ c. warm water
2 c. potato water (see page 17)
⅔ c. honey
1½ T. salt
½ c. safflower oil

4 c. whole wheat flour, divided
½ c. gluten
2 c. raw wheat germ
2 T. grated lemon peel
4 c. unbleached flour (approx.)

Dissolve the yeast in warm water until bubbly. Add potato water, honey, salt, oil, 2 cups of the whole wheat flour, and the gluten. Beat until smooth at low speed in an electric mixer or with a rotary beater. Add remaining whole wheat flour. Beat 2–3 minutes at medium speed or 150 strokes by hand. The dough should be thick and elastic. Stir in wheat germ and lemon peel. Add enough unbleached flour to make a soft dough that will leave the sides of the bowl. Turn out onto a floured board. Knead, working in more flour if needed to make a smooth and elastic dough, about 10 minutes. Cover with plastic wrap, then a tea towel. Let rest 20 minutes on the board.

Punch down, divide into three equal portions, shape into loaves, and place in lightly greased 8 × 4-inch bread pans. Brush surface of loaves with safflower oil. Cover loaves loosely with oiled waxed paper, then plastic wrap (*do not make them airtight*). Refrigerate 2–24 hours.

Remove from refrigerator. Uncover. Let stand 10 minutes. Puncture any surface bubbles. Bake at 400° 35–40 minutes on low rack of oven until lightly brown and loaves sound hollow when tapped on the bottom. Turn out onto wire racks to cool.

Note: If preferred, divide dough into two portions and use 9 × 5-inch pans.

*Variation: *If you can use milk*, use 2⅔ c. scalded and cooled milk instead of potato water.

Cracked Wheat Bread

NO CORN, EGG, OR MILK
Yield: 2 loaves (18–20 slices per loaf)

3½ c. warm water, divided
½ c. bulgur
1 T. dry yeast
3 T. honey, divided
2 c. whole wheat flour
2 T. safflower oil
2 t. salt

3–4 c. unbleached and whole wheat flour, combined half and half or to taste
1 c. raw wheat germ
1 c. rolled oats
2 T. sesame seeds

Pour 1½ cups of the warm water over the bulgur. Let sit about 1 hour, or until most of water is absorbed and bulgur is soft. In large bowl of mixer, add the remaining 2 cups water to dissolve yeast. Stir in 1 tablespoon of the honey, the whole wheat flour, and the bulgur. Beat at low speed until well mixed, about 3 minutes. Let rest about 20 minutes or until bubbly. Add remaining ingredients. Beat to mix. When dough leaves sides of bowl and can be handled, roll out onto floured pastry cloth. Knead 15–20 minutes, adding flour as necessary to make a nonsticky, springy dough. Place in a greased bowl, turning once to grease top. Cover with a cloth and let rise in warm place until doubled in bulk, about 1½ hours.

Turn out onto lightly floured board and knead lightly. Divide into two equal parts. Pat and stretch dough and roll into loaves. Put into well-greased 9 × 5-inch bread pans. Let rise, covered with a cloth, until almost doubled in bulk, about 45 minutes.

Bake at 375° 45 minutes, or until browned and loaves sound hollow when tapped on the bottom. If top gets too brown, cover with foil during the last part of baking. Turn out onto wire racks to cool.

Potato Whole Wheat Bread

NO CORN, EGG, OR MILK
Yield: 2 loaves (18–20 slices per loaf)

2 t. dry yeast
1 c. water, divided
1 t. sugar
½ c. honey
1½ t. salt

3 T. safflower oil
1½ c. potato water (see page 17)
8–9 c. whole wheat flour (part unbleached if desired), divided

Dissolve yeast in ¼ cup warm water. Add sugar. Let sit until bubbly. Combine in large bowl of electric mixer ¾ cup water and the honey, salt, and oil. Add the yeast, potato water, and 3 cups of the flour. At medium speed of mixer, beat until well blended, 2–3 minutes. Cover the sponge with a cloth and let rise in a warm place until doubled in bulk, 1–1½ hours. Stir down the sponge and add 3 cups more flour. Turn out onto a floured pastry cloth and knead in enough more flour to make a firm dough, 2–3 cups. Knead until smooth and elastic, about 10 minutes. Put into a greased bowl, turn once to grease top, cover with a cloth, and let rise until doubled in bulk, about 1–1½ hours.

Punch down the dough. Knead lightly a few times. Divide in half, shape into two loaves, and put into greased 9 × 5-inch loaf pans. Let rise, covered, until almost doubled. Bake at 400° 10 minutes. Reduce heat to 325° and continue baking about 50 minutes, or until well browned and loaves sound hollow when tapped on the bottom. Turn out onto wire racks to cool.

Rye Bread

NO CORN, EGG, OR MILK
Yield: 1 loaf (16–18 slices)

2 t. dry yeast
¼ c. warm water
1 T. molasses
¾ t. salt
1 T. grated orange rind
½ t. crushed fennel seeds
  (optional)

1 c. beer or water
1½ c. rye flour
1 T. safflower oil
2¼ c. unbleached flour

In a large bowl, dissolve yeast in warm water. Add molasses, salt, orange rind, fennel, and beer or water. Stir in rye flour. Beat by hand or in electric mixer until smooth. Blend in safflower oil. Stir in most of the unbleached flour to make a soft dough. Use remaining flour on pastry cloth and knead until smooth and elastic, about 10 minutes. Place in a greased bowl, turning once to oil top. Cover with a cloth. Let rise in a warm place until doubled in bulk, 1–1½ hours. Punch down dough, shape into a loaf, and put into a greased 8 × 4-inch or 9 × 5-inch loaf pan. Let rise until almost doubled, about 45 minutes. Bake at 375° 50 minutes, or until well browned and loaf sounds hollow when tapped on the bottom. Turn out onto a wire rack to cool.

Rye Batter Bread

NO CORN, EGG, OR WHEAT
Yield: 20–24 slices

This bread is excellent for sandwiches. It slices well and is not crumbly. The lemon peel cuts any strong rye flavor and adds a nice flavor of its own.

2 t. gelatin	1 T. safflower oil
¼ c. cold water	4 t. dry yeast
1 c. buttermilk	¾ c. warm water
1 T. honey	4½ c. rye flour
1 t. salt	1 T. grated lemon rind

Stir gelatin into cold water. Warm to dissolve. Warm buttermilk, honey, salt, and oil to lukewarm. (Overheating will cause buttermilk to separate.) In mixing bowl dissolve yeast in warm water; add milk mixture and gelatin to yeast. Add 2 cups rye flour. Beat about 2 minutes at medium speed in electric mixer, or beat vigorously by hand until batter is satiny. Remove and clean beaters. Add lemon rind and about 2½ cups more rye flour to make a medium-stiff dough. Blend well.

Cover and let rise about 45 minutes. (Do not allow to over-rise.) Stir down the batter. Scrape into well-greased 1½-quart casserole. Smooth top. Let rise again 15–20 minutes. (Again, do not allow to over-rise.) Bake at 375° 45–50 minutes. Remove from oven. Cool in casserole a few minutes, then turn out onto wire rack to finish cooling.

Bagels

NO CORN, EGG, OR MILK
Yield: 12 bagels

2 t. dry yeast
1½ c. warm water
1 T. salt
4 T. sugar, divided

5–6 c. sifted whole wheat and
    unbleached flour, combined
    half and half or to taste
1 gal. water for simmering

In a large bowl, dissolve yeast in the warm water. Mix in salt and 3 tablespoons of the sugar. Add flour and blend well to make medium-stiff dough. Knead dough on a lightly floured board or cloth, about 10 minutes. Place in a greased bowl, cover with a cloth, and let rise 15 minutes. Return dough to board, roll out and flatten with hands to a 1-inch-thick square. Cut into twelve strips. Shape bagels with hands, rolling each strip on board until long enough to shape as a doughnut. Press ends together to seal. Let rise 20 minutes, covered. (They do not rise much, but if left too long, they will not sink in the water bath.)

Put water in a large pot, add the remaining 1 tablespoon sugar, and heat to simmering. Add bagels one at a time until four or five are in the pot. They should sink, then come to the top. Simmer each bagel 7 minutes. Remove from water with a slotted spoon. Place on a tea towel to dry and cool. Then remove to an ungreased baking sheet, leaving space between them. Bake at 375° 25–30 minutes, or until brown. Serve warm or cold, cut crosswise, buttered and broiled or as sandwiches.

Honey-Oatmeal Bread

NO CORN, EGG, OR MILK*
Yield: 1 loaf (16–18 slices)

1 c. boiling water
1 c. rolled oats
2 T. safflower oil
1 t. salt
2 T. honey

½ c. warm water
1 T. dry yeast
1½ c. whole wheat flour
1 c. unbleached flour
¼ c. raw wheat germ

Pour the boiling water over the rolled oats in a large mixing bowl. Add oil, salt, and honey. Let stand until cooled to lukewarm. Dissolve yeast in warm water. Let stand until bubbly. Combine flours and wheat germ. Stir yeast mixture into oatmeal in mixing bowl. Add half of the flour mixture and blend 3–4 minutes in electric mixer at medium speed or 100 strokes by hand. Clean beaters. Stir in enough more flour to make a medium-stiff dough. Use any remaining flour on pastry cloth or pastry board and knead 8–10 minutes, or until smooth and elastic.

Put in an oiled bowl, turn once to grease top, cover with a cloth, and let rise in a warm place until doubled in bulk. Return dough to bread board, punch down, and shape into a loaf. Place into a greased 8 × 4-inch bread pan. Cover and let double in bulk. Bake at 350° 50–60 minutes. Turn out onto a wire rack to cool.

*Variation: *If you can use milk*, add ¼ c. dry skim milk powder with the flour and wheat germ.

Zucchini Yeast Bread

NO CORN, EGG, OR MILK*
Yield: 1 loaf (16–18 slices)

⅓ c. warm water, orange
   juice, or soybean milk (see
   page 16)
1 T. safflower oil
1½ T. honey
2 t. dry yeast
2 T. warm water
¾ c. whole wheat flour

1 c. unbleached flour
2 T. raw wheat germ
1 t. grated orange rind
1 t. ground cardamom
½ t. salt
¾ c. shredded zucchini
½ c. raisins (optional)

Over medium heat, warm the water, orange juice, or soybean milk. Add oil and honey. Dissolve yeast in the 2 tablespoons warm water. Let sit 5 minutes. In a large bowl, combine the oil mixture and the yeast. Blend together flours, wheat germ, orange rind, cardamom, and salt. Stir about half into the yeast mixture. Stir in zucchini and raisins. Gradually add the remaining flour to make a stiff dough. On a well-floured pastry cloth, knead about 10 minutes, or until dough is smooth and elastic. Add more flour if needed. Put dough in a greased bowl, turning once to grease top. Cover with a cloth and let rise in a warm place until doubled in bulk, about 1–1½ hours.

Punch down the dough, shape into a loaf, and put into a greased 8 × 4-inch loaf pan. Cover and let rise until doubled in bulk, about 45 minutes. Bake at 350° 40–45 minutes, or until loaf sounds hollow when tapped on the bottom. Turn out onto a wire rack to cool.

Variation: If you can use milk, use ⅓ c. scalded milk instead of the water, orange juice, or soybean milk, and let cool to lukewarm after adding oil and honey.

Applesauce Loaf

NO CORN, EGG, OR MILK
Yield: 1 loaf (16–18 slices)

This makes a very tender loaf, good for special occasions as well as every day.

*1 c. thick, unsweetened
  applesauce*
2 t. dry yeast
½ T. safflower oil
½ t. salt

3 T. honey, divided
1⅔–2 c. whole wheat flour
½ c. seedless raisins
¼ c. water
¼ t. cinnamon

Warm the applesauce. Place in a mixing bowl and stir in yeast, oil, salt, and 2 tablespoons of the honey. Gradually add flour to make a soft dough. Knead until smooth. Place in a greased bowl, cover with a cloth, and let rise in a warm place. In small saucepan, combine raisins, water, cinnamon, and the remaining 1 tablespoon honey. Cook over low heat until moisture is absorbed and raisins are plump. Stir often to keep from scorching. Cool.

When dough is doubled in bulk, punch down; remove to a floured pastry cloth. Roll out to an 8 × 10-inch rectangle. Spread raisin mixture evenly on dough. Roll up like a jelly roll. Place seam-side-down into an 8 × 4-inch greased loaf pan, cover, and let rise until light. Bake at 425° 10 minutes. Reduce heat to 350° and bake 45 minutes. Turn out onto a wire rack to cool.

Variation: If desired, ¼–½ c. chopped nuts or sunflower seeds can be combined with the cooled raisins.

Date Loaf

NO CORN OR MILK
Yield: 1 loaf (18–20 slices)

3 t. dry yeast
1 c. warm water
2¼–2½ c. whole wheat
   flour, divided
½ c. honey
1 c. chopped dates

2 eggs, beaten
¾ c. raw sunflower seeds,
   chopped
½ t. salt
½ t. allspice
1 t. cinnamon

Dissolve yeast in warm water. Add 1 cup of the flour. Mix until spongy. Let rise until light and frothy. Add the remaining flour and the honey, dates, beaten eggs, sunflower seeds, salt, and spices. Blend well. It should be a fairly firm mixture.

Spoon into a greased 9 × 5-inch bread pan, cover with a cloth, and let rise until nearly doubled in bulk (about 40 minutes). Bake at 375° 45 minutes, or until a toothpick inserted in center of loaf comes out clean. Turn out onto a wire rack to cool.

Jule Kaga—Christmas Bread

NO CORN, EGG, OR MILK*
Yield: One round loaf (18–20 slices)

1 c. soybean milk (see page 16)
⅓ c. honey
⅓ c. safflower oil
1 t. salt
2 T. dry yeast
¼ c. warm water

2 c. sifted whole wheat flour
2–2½ c. sifted unbleached
   flour
1½ t. ground cardamom
1¼ c. combined chopped
   dates, raisins, nuts, and seeds

Warm the soybean milk. Stir in honey, oil, and salt. Transfer to a large mixing bowl and cool to lukewarm. Dissolve yeast in warm water. Stir into lukewarm milk mixture. Add whole wheat flour and beat vigorously. Cover with a cloth and let rise in a warm place until doubled in bulk, about 30 minutes. Stir down. Add remaining ingredients. The dough should be just stiff enough to handle. Turn out onto a lightly floured board or pastry cloth and knead until smooth and elastic, about 10–15 minutes. Place in a greased bowl, brush with oil, cover, and let rise until doubled in bulk, about 1 hour. Punch down. Knead lightly 1–2 minutes.

Form into a round loaf. Place on a large greased baking sheet, cover, and let rise about 1 hour, or until doubled in bulk. Bake at 400° 10 minutes. Reduce heat to 350° and continue baking about 40 minutes until lightly browned and loaf sounds hollow when tapped on bottom. Cool on a wire rack. Frost with confectioners icing (see page 91) and decorate with more nuts and fruit.

Variation: *If you can use milk*, use 1 c. milk instead of the soybean milk.

Pumpkin Rolls

NO CORN, EGG, OR MILK*
Yield: 16–18 rolls

2 t. dry yeast
½ c. warm water
½ c. pumpkin
1 T. safflower oil
2 T. honey
¼ t. ginger
¼ t. ground cloves

½ t. nutmeg
¾ t. cinnamon
½ t. salt
2½–3 c. whole wheat and
    unbleached flour, combined
    half and half or to taste

Dissolve yeast in the warm water. Let sit 5 minutes. Combine remaining ingredients except flour in bowl of electric mixer. Stir in the yeast. Spoon about half of the flour into the yeast mixture. Beat at low speed of mixer for 2 minutes. Stir in most of the remaining flour, or enough to make a medium-stiff dough. Turn out onto a pastry cloth using remaining flour for kneading. Knead until smooth and elastic, about 10–15 minutes, adding more flour if necessary. Place into a greased bowl, cover with a cloth, turn once to grease top, and let rise in a warm place until doubled in bulk, about 1–1½ hours.

Turn out onto a pastry cloth. Punch down. Divide dough into sixteen–eighteen balls. Place in a greased 9-inch round cake pan, cover, and let rise until doubled in bulk, about 45 minutes to 1 hour. Bake at 375° about 25 minutes, or until browned.

Variation: *If you can use milk*, add ¼ c. nonfat, noninstant dry milk with the pumpkin.

Buttermilk Rolls

NO CORN OR EGG
Yield: 12 rolls

Tender and good.

1 c. buttermilk	*¼ t. baking soda*
1 T. safflower oil	*½ t. salt*
1 t. dry yeast	*1 c. whole wheat flour*
2 t. honey	*1 c. unbleached flour*

Warm buttermilk over low heat (if overheated, it separates). In bowl of electric mixer, combine buttermilk, oil, yeast, honey, baking soda, salt, and whole wheat flour. Beat at medium speed for 3 minutes. Stir the unbleached flour into the mixture. Turn out onto a lightly floured pastry cloth. Knead until smooth and elastic. Roll out to ½-inch thickness. Cut into desired shapes. Place on a greased baking sheet. Brush tops with melted butter or safflower oil.

Cover loosely with a tea towel.

Let double. Bake at 375° 15–20 minutes or until golden brown. Serve hot.

Cracked Wheat Rolls

NO CORN OR EGG
Yield: 16–18 rolls

¼ c. bulgur	*1 t. salt*
½ c. cold water	*¾ c. plus 2 T. milk, scalded*
1 t. dry yeast	* and cooled*
2 T. warm water	*1 c. whole wheat flour*
2 T. honey	*2 c. unbleached flour (approx.)*
2 T. safflower oil	

Soak bulgur in cold water until moisture is absorbed, an hour or more. Dissolve yeast in warm water. Stir in honey, oil, salt, cooled milk, and bulgur. Mix in the flour to make a stiff dough. On a floured pastry cloth, knead until dough is smooth and elastic. Place into a greased bowl, turning once to grease top. Cover with a cloth and let rise in a warm place until almost doubled in bulk.

Punch down. Roll out on a lightly floured pastry cloth or bread board. Cut into desired shapes. Arrange on a greased baking pan and let rise in a warm place, covered, until almost doubled. Brush tops of rolls lightly with melted butter or safflower oil. Bake at 375° 15–20 minutes until golden brown. Serve hot.

Whole Wheat Sally Lunn

NO CORN OR EGG
Yield: 10–12 rolls

Light and tender without kneading or rolling. Allow to rise for 3 hours.

1 T. honey
1 heaping T. corn-free vegetable
*   shortening (see page 13)*
1 t. salt
1 scant c. milk, scalded

2 t. dry yeast
¼ c. warm water
⅔ c. whole wheat flour
1⅓ c. unbleached flour

Combine honey, shortening, and salt in a large mixing bowl. Pour scalded milk over mixture. Cool. Dissolve yeast in warm water. Add to milk mixture. Add flours. Beat well by hand as you add the flour. (This is not a mixture you can handle except with a spoon.) Cover with a cloth and let rise until doubled; then beat it down with a spoon. Repeat. Spoon into well-greased muffin tins, filling two-thirds full. Cover and let rise again. Bake at 450° about 15 minutes.

Whole Wheat Buns

NO CORN, EGG, OR MILK
Yield: 4 buns

2 t. dry yeast
3 T. warm water
½ t. sugar
3 T. olive oil
1¼ c. unbleached flour

¾ c. plus 1 T. whole wheat
    flour
1 t. salt
⅔ c. warm water
sesame seeds

Dissolve yeast in the 3 T. warm water. Add sugar and set aside. Combine the remaining ingredients. Add yeast mixture. Stir with a fork until it forms a ball. Knead on a floured pastry cloth about 10 minutes, or until smooth and elastic. Divide into four equal-sized balls. Flatten with rolling pin or by hand to ¼-inch thickness. Let rise in a warm place, covered, for 45 minutes. Transfer to a lightly greased baking sheet. Brush the tops lightly with olive oil (or melted butter if milk is allowed). Sprinkle with sesame seeds. Bake at 475° 12–15 minutes, or until puffed and golden. Serve warm.

QUICK BREADS

	NO CORN	NO EGG	NO MILK	NO WHEAT	NO GLUTEN
Avocado Bread	⊗		X		
Wheat-Free Avocado Bread	⊗		X	X	X
Quick Pumpkin Bread	X	X	X		
Quick Brown Bread	⊗		X		
Fresh Apple-Fruit Loaf	X	X	X		
Super Zucchini Bread	⊗	⊗			
Millet Muffins	⊗		X	X	⊗
Orange Muffins	X		⊗	X	
Cranberry-Orange Muffins	⊗	X	X		
Applesauce Muffins	⊗		X		
Bran Muffins	⊗	X			
Buttermilk Scones	X	X			
Chapati		X	X		
Tofu Muffins and Pancakes	⊗		X	X	
Whole Wheat Pancakes	⊗	X			
Yogurt Pancakes #1	⊗	X			
Yogurt Pancakes #2	⊗			X	X
Wheat-Free Pancakes	⊗	⊗		X	
Sunflower Seed Pancakes	X	X	X	X	X

⊗ means that the recipe includes instructions for adding that ingredient if allowed.

	NO CORN	NO EGG	NO MILK	NO WHEAT	NO GLUTEN
Brown Rice Flour Bread	⊗		X	X	X
Carrot Bread	⊗		X	X	
Corn Bread				X	
Multi-Grain Bread # 1 with Buttermilk	⊗	X		X	
Multi-Grain Bread # 2 with Eggs	⊗		X	X	
Multi-Grain Bread # 3, with Eggs and Milk	⊗			X	
Pumpkin-Peanut Butter Bread	⊗		X	X	⊗
Gluten-Free Banana Bread	⊗		X	X	⊗
Gluten-Free Carrot-Corn Bread				X	X
Millet-Barley Bread	⊗		X	X	
Rice-Soy Crepes	X		X	X	X
Oat Flour Crepes	X			X	
Chick Pea Crepes	X		X	X	X
Brown Rice Crackers	X	X	⊗	X	X
Rye Crackers	X	X	⊗	X	
Corn Crackers		X	⊗	X	X

Avocado Bread

NO CORN* OR MILK
Yield: 1 loaf (16–18 slices)

1 egg
2 T. safflower oil
½ c. honey
½ c. mashed avocado
¼ c. water
1 c. whole wheat flour
⅔ c. unbleached flour
1 c. raw wheat germ

2½ t. arrowroot baking
powder (see page 13)
½ t. salt
2 t. grated orange peel
¼ t. cinnamon
½ c. chopped nuts, sunflower
seeds, or raisins

Beat the egg until thick and lemon colored. Dribble in oil and honey. Still beating, add the mashed avocado and water. Combine remaining ingredients and stir into avocado mixture all at once—stirring until moistened. Spread batter into a greased 8½ × 4½ × 2½-inch loaf pan. Bake at 350° 55–60 minutes, or until a toothpick inserted in the center of the loaf comes out clean. Cool in pan 10 minutes. Turn loaf out onto a wire rack to finish cooling.

*Variation: If you can use corn, you can substitute 2 t. regular baking powder for the arrowroot baking powder.

Wheat-Free Avocado Bread

NO CORN,* MILK, WHEAT, OR GLUTEN
Yield: 1 loaf (16–18 slices)

This is an adaptation of the Avocado Bread recipe, above.

Use 2 eggs instead of 1
Replace whole wheat and
unbleached flours with 1⅔
c. brown rice flour or ⅔ c.
brown rice flour and 1 c.
millet flour

Replace wheat germ with ½ c.
peanut flour (see page 15) and
¼ c. rice bran
Increase baking powder to 1 T.
regular or 4 t. arrowroot

Proceed as directed in Avocado Bread recipe.

Quick Pumpkin Bread

NO CORN, EGG, OR MILK
Yield: 1 loaf (16 slices)

1 c. pumpkin
1/3 c. safflower oil
1/2 c. honey
1/2 c. raisins
1 2/3 c. whole wheat pastry
  flour

1/4 t. salt
1/2 t. cinnamon
1/8 t. nutmeg
1 1/2 t. baking soda

Combine pumpkin, oil, and honey. In a medium-sized bowl, combine remaining ingredients. Stir pumpkin mixture into flour mixture and blend well. Pour into a well-greased 8 × 4-inch loaf pan. Bake at 350° 50–60 minutes, or until a toothpick inserted in center of loaf comes out clean. Turn out onto a wire rack to cool.

Quick Brown Bread

NO CORN* OR MILK
Yield: 1 loaf (16–18 slices)

1 c. raisins
1 c. warm water less 3 T.
1 egg
1/4 c. safflower oil
1/4 c. honey
1 c. whole wheat flour
3/4 c. unbleached flour

1/2 t. salt
1/2 t. baking soda
3/4 t. arrowroot baking powder
  (see page 13)
1/4 c. molasses
1 c. unprocessed bran flakes

Soften the raisins in warm water and set aside. Beat the egg. Continue beating, adding oil and honey slowly. Set egg mixture aside. Measure and sift together the dry ingredients except the bran flakes. Set aside. Drain water from raisins, retaining water. Water should measure 1 cup less 3 tablespoons; add more water if necessary. Combine water with molasses. Add dry ingredients and molasses water alternately to the egg mixture, beginning and ending with flour mixture. Stir in bran flakes and raisins, combine thoroughly, and pour into a greased 8 × 4-inch loaf pan. Bake at 350° 1 hour, or until a toothpick inserted into the center of the loaf comes out clean. (*Do not undercook.*) Remove pan to a wire rack. Let sit 5 minutes, then remove loaf from pan to finish cooling on wire rack.

Variations: *If you can use corn*, you can substitute ½ t. regular baking powder for the arrowroot baking powder.

If desired, 2–3 T. raw wheat germ may be substituted for the same amount of the bran flakes.

Fresh Apple-Fruit Loaf

NO CORN, EGG, OR MILK
Yield: 1 loaf (18–20 slices)

½ c. firmly packed brown sugar
¼ c. safflower oil
¼ c. honey
2 T. sherry or orange juice
1 t. vanilla
1½ c. coarsely shredded, peeled raw apple
2 t. baking soda
1 c. raisins
1 c. pitted fresh dates, cut into pieces
½ c. chopped dried fruit
1 c. chopped nuts
½ c. sunflower seeds
2 c. sifted unbleached flour
½ t. salt
¼ t. cinnamon
¼ t. nutmeg

Combine brown sugar, oil, honey, sherry or orange juice, and vanilla in a large bowl. Set aside. Mix the shredded apple with the baking soda and stir it and the remaining fruits and nuts into the brown sugar mixture. Sift together the remaining dry ingredients and blend into fruit mixture. Turn into a greased and floured 9 × 5-inch loaf pan. Bake at 350° for 1 hour and 25 minutes, or until a toothpick inserted in the center of the loaf comes out clean. Allow to cool in pan about 3 minutes. Turn loaf out onto a wire rack to finish cooling.

Super Zucchini Bread

NO CORN* OR EGG*
Yield: 1 loaf (18–20 slices)

2 c. whole wheat flour
½ c. wheat germ
½ c. bran
4 t. arrowroot baking powder
  (see page 13)
½ t. baking soda
1 t. cinnamon
½ t. allspice

¼ t. ginger
½ c. sunflower seeds
½ c. raisins or chopped dates
½ c. honey
3 T. safflower oil
1⅓ c. buttermilk or yogurt or
  a combination
1 c. grated zucchini

Combine dry ingredients in a large bowl with seeds and raisins or dates. Combine honey, oil, and buttermilk and stir into dry ingredients. Mix well. Stir in zucchini. Pour into a greased and floured 9 × 5-inch loaf pan. Bake at 325° about 1 hour and 25 minutes, or until a toothpick inserted in center of loaf comes out clean.

   Variations: *If you can use egg*, decrease buttermilk to 1 c. and add 1 beaten egg to buttermilk.

   If you can use corn, you can substitute 3 t. regular baking powder for the arrowroot baking powder.

Millet Muffins

NO CORN,* MILK, WHEAT, OR GLUTEN
Yield: 12 muffins

1 c. millet flour
1 c. boiling water
1¼ c. brown rice flour
2 t. arrowroot baking powder
  (see page 13)

¾ t. salt
1 T. safflower oil
1 T. honey
2 eggs, separated

Pour boiling water over millet. Set aside. Combine dry ingredients. Set aside. Stir oil and honey into millet. Beat egg whites until very stiff. Set aside. Without cleaning beaters, beat yolks. Add to millet. Stir in dry ingredients. Stir in about 2 tablespoons of the whites into the mixture. Then, carefully fold in remaining whites. Spoon into well-greased muffin tins. Bake at 400° about 20 minutes, or until done.

Variation: *If you can use corn*, you can substitute 1½ t. regular baking powder for the arrowroot baking powder.

Orange Muffins

NO CORN, MILK,* OR WHEAT
Yield: 12 muffins

Although this recipe contains yeast, it is included here with the other muffin recipes.

1 c. oat flour (see page 15)
½ c. brown rice flour
½ t. salt
3 T. finely chopped raw
  sunflower seeds
2 t. dry yeast
¼ t. mace or coriander

2 eggs, separated
3 T. honey
2 T. safflower oil
1 c. soybean milk (see page 16)
⅓ c. seedless raisins or
  chopped dates
1 T. grated orange rind

Combine dry ingredients. Beat egg yolks until thick and lemon colored. Add honey, oil, and soybean milk. Stir in dry ingredients and raisins or dates. Beat egg whites until stiff peaks form. Fold gently but firmly into batter. Spoon into well-greased muffin pans, filling two-thirds full. Place in a warm place or in the oven with pan of warm water and let rise 30 minutes. Bake on middle rack of oven at 375° for 30 minutes, or until nicely browned. Serve immediately.

Variation: *If you can use milk*, substitute 1 c. nonfat milk for the soybean milk.

Cranberry-Orange Muffins

NO CORN,* EGG, OR MILK
Yield: 6 muffins

1 c. unbleached flour
1½ t. arrowroot baking
*   powder (see page 13)*
¼ t. salt
¼ t. baking soda

2 T. safflower oil
½ c. orange juice
½ t. grated orange rind
½ c. cranberries, cut in half
1 t. honey

TOPPING:
2 T. chopped sunflower seeds
¼ t. cinnamon

2 t. brown sugar

Combine flour, baking powder, salt, and baking soda. Set aside. Combine oil, orange juice, orange rind, cranberries, and honey. Pour all at once into the flour mixture. Stir just to moisten. Quickly spoon into well-greased muffin tins. Combine sunflower seeds, cinnamon, and brown sugar and sprinkle on top. Bake at 375° about 25 minutes, or until well browned. This recipe can be doubled.

Variation: *If you can use corn*, you can substitute 1¼ t. regular baking powder for the arrowroot baking powder.

Applesauce Muffins

NO CORN* OR MILK
Yield: 9 muffins

½ c. sifted, unbleached flour
¾ c. unsifted, whole wheat
  flour
2½ t. arrowroot baking
  powder (see page 13)
½ t. salt
¼ t. cinnamon (optional)

2 T. apple juice or water
½ c. less 2 T. unsweetened
  applesauce
1 egg, slightly beaten
¼ c. safflower oil
2 T. honey

Combine flours, baking powder, salt, and cinnamon. Set aside. Combine juice or water and applesauce. Set aside. Mix together egg, oil, and honey. Stir in applesauce mixture. Pour all at once into flour mixture. Stir just enough to moisten (*do not overmix*). It should be lumpy. Spoon batter into greased muffin tins. Bake at 375° about 25 minutes, or until browned.

Variation: *If you can use corn*, you can substitute 2 t. regular baking powder for the arrowroot baking powder.

Note: Applesauce thickness varies. Adjust juice or flour if necessary to make a typical muffin batter.

Bran Muffins

NO CORN* OR EGG
Yield: 10–12 muffins

1 c. whole wheat pastry flour
½ c. unprocessed bran
4 t. arrowroot baking powder (see
  page 13)

½ t. salt
1 c. plain low-fat yogurt
3 T. safflower oil
3 T. molasses

Combine flour, bran, baking powder, and salt. Set aside. Mix together yogurt, oil, and molasses and stir into flour until just moistened. Spoon into well-greased muffin tins. Bake at 425° for 15–20 minutes.

Variation: *If you can use corn*, you can substitute 1 T. regular baking powder for the arrowroot baking powder.

Buttermilk Scones

NO CORN OR EGG
Yield: 6 scones

1⅓ c. whole wheat flour, or a combination of whole wheat and unbleached flour
½ t. salt
½ t. baking soda
1 T. sugar

¼ c. butter, corn-free margarine, or corn-free vegetable shortening (see page 13)
2 t. grated orange peel
⅓ c. raisins (optional)
½ c. cultured buttermilk

Sift dry ingredients together. Cut in butter or shortening. Stir in orange peel and raisins. Add buttermilk. Stir until blended. Turn out onto a lightly floured board. Knead eight or ten times, until dough will form into a round ball. Pat or roll until ½-inch thick. Cut into six pie-shaped pieces. Put onto a lightly greased baking sheet. Brush with melted butter, if allowed. Bake at 400° for 15–20 minutes, or until lightly browned and cooked through. Serve hot (they can be reheated if made ahead).

Chapati

NO EGG OR MILK
Yield: 8 chapati

1 c. whole wheat flour
1 c. corn flour

¼ t. salt
¾–1 c. cold water

Sift together flours and salt. Gradually add water as for pie crust, to make a dough of pie crust consistency. Turn out onto a floured board. Divide into about eight equal portions. Roll very thin. Heat a dry cast-iron skillet to medium hot. Cook, one at a time, turning after about 30 seconds. They should be lightly toasted and cooked through. Serve warm, or reheat in medium-hot, oiled skillet. They become very hard when cold.

Tofu Muffins

NO CORN,* MILK, OR WHEAT
Yield: 9–10 muffins

8 oz. soft tofu (½ pkg.)
1 whole egg or 2 yolks
½ c. white grape or orange
juice, or water
1 c. barley flour
1 c. oat flour (see page 15)

2½ t. arrowroot baking
powder
½ t. baking soda
1 t. cinnamon
½–1 t. sugar (if water is used)

Rinse tofu in cold water. Wipe dry but do not press. Break it up into food processor with steel blade. Add egg and juice. Blend until very creamy. Transfer to a 2-cup measure. There should be 1¾ cups. The consistency should be that of buttermilk. If too thick, add more juice. Combine dry ingredients in bowl. Add tofu mixture all at once. Stir just until blended. It should be a typical muffin consistency. If too thick, add more juice. Spoon into well-greased muffin tins. Bake at 450° 15–20 minutes.

Note: If orange juice is used, about 2 teaspoons grated rind gives additional flavor. Any light-colored juice such as peach, pear, or apple can be used. Dark-colored juice gives an undesirable color to the muffins.

Tofu Pancakes

NO CORN,* MILK, OR WHEAT
Yield: 10–12 pancakes

Follow directions for muffins, but add enough juice to thin batter to pancake consistency. Cook on medium-hot griddle as usual.

*Variations: *If you can use corn*, you can substitute 2 t. regular baking powder for the arrowroot baking powder.

Chopped nuts, seeds, or raisins may be added to muffins.

Whole Wheat Pancakes

NO CORN* OR EGG
Yield: 7–8 pancakes

Tender and delicious! Serve with fruit such as crushed berries or applesauce and you have a nutritious meal as well.

¾ c. whole wheat flour
½ t. baking soda
½ t. salt
1½ t. arrowroot baking
   powder (see page 13)

1 T. safflower oil
1 T. honey
1 c. buttermilk

Combine dry ingredients. Stir oil and honey into buttermilk. Stir buttermilk mixture into flour mixture all at once. Mix just to moisten. (If a thinner batter is desired, add more buttermilk.) Cook on a lightly greased griddle.

   Variation: *If you can use corn*, you can substitute 1 t. regular baking powder for the arrowroot baking powder.

Yogurt Pancakes # 1

NO CORN* OR EGG
Yield: 6–8 pancakes

½ c. whole wheat flour
2 T. soya flour
2 T. bran
1½ t. arrowroot baking
   powder (see page 13)

½ t. baking soda
1 T. melted butter or safflower oil
¾ c. plain low-fat yogurt

Combine all ingredients in small bowl of electric mixer. Turn to high speed and mix until well blended. Pour about ¼ cup at a time onto a hot, lightly greased griddle and cook as usual.

   Variation: *If you can use corn*, you can substitute 1 t. regular baking powder for the arrowroot baking powder.

Yogurt Pancakes # 2

NO CORN,* WHEAT, OR GLUTEN
Yield: 6–8 pancakes

*½ c. brown rice flour or ¼
  c. each brown rice and millet
  flours
2 T. soya flour
1½ t. arrowroot baking
  powder (see page 13)*

*½ t. baking soda
1 t. sugar (optional)
¾ c. plain low-fat yogurt
2 eggs*

Combine all ingredients in small bowl of electric mixer. Turn to high speed and mix until well blended. Pour about ¼ cup at a time onto a hot, lightly greased griddle and cook as usual.

    Variation: *If you can use corn*, you can substitute 1 t. regular baking powder for the arrowroot baking powder.

Wheat-Free Pancakes

NO CORN,* EGG,* OR WHEAT
Yield: 6 pancakes

For larger amounts, double or triple the recipe.

*½ c. oat flour (see page 15)
½ c. barley flour
½ t. salt
1½ t. arrowroot baking
  powder (see page 13)*

*1 T. safflower oil
1 T. honey
1 c. buttermilk*

Combine dry ingredients in small bowl of electric mixer. Add oil and honey to buttermilk. Stir into dry ingredients. Add more buttermilk if mixture is too thick. Cook as regular pancakes.

    Variations: *If you can use corn*, you can substitute 1 t. regular baking powder for the arrowroot baking powder.

    If you can use egg, use 1 egg, beaten slightly, plus enough buttermilk to make 1 c., instead of 1 c. buttermilk.

Sunflower Seed Pancakes

NO CORN, EGG, MILK, WHEAT, OR GLUTEN
Yield: 6 pancakes

¼ c. raw sunflower seeds	½ T. dry yeast
¼ c. millet	½ c. water
½ c. water	½–1 T. molasses

Combine sunflower seeds, millet, and water. In a second dish, cover yeast with water. Let both containers stand overnight in a cool place. In the morning, whirl seed mixture in the blender at high speed. Add the yeast and molasses. If the batter is too thin, add enough barley, oat, rice, or wheat flour (depending on your restrictions) to thicken. Set pan in a bowl of warm water. When batter is doubled in bulk, about 20 minutes, stir and cook as other pancakes. This recipe can be doubled for larger amounts.

WHEAT-FREE and GLUTEN-FREE BREADS

Wheat-free and gluten-free (see Introduction, pages 14–16) breads have an entirely different flavor and texture from those containing gluten. The action of yeast on the moistened gluten gives the elastic quality we associate with breads. Without gluten, they tend to be either dense-textured, soggy, or crumbly. All rye and cornmeal breads are good examples. All rye bread has a little gluten and is dense-textured. Most recipes for gluten-free breads use baking powder and/or baking soda for leavening. The addition of eggs (if allowed), milk (if allowed), potato flour, cornstarch or arrowroot, gelatin, or tapioca improves the texture.

Grains containing gluten are wheat, rye, barley, buckwheat, and oats (see pages 14–16). Wheat has the highest percentage of gluten. For those individuals with the nonabsorption syndrome, celiac disease or sprue, no gluten is tolerated. This leaves flours made from rice, corn, soybeans, potatoes, and millet to cook with for gluten-free diets. For those with wheat allergies alone, oats, rye, and barley are usually acceptable.

Flavor is important. Nonwheat breads taste entirely different and must be accepted. The stronger flavors of rye, soy, and buckwheat can be unpleasant. Combining grains is one answer, and spices, peels, and juices can add interest and pleasing flavors.

Wheat-free and gluten-free breads do best baked as muffins or in small tins—preferably 5 × 3-inch, but 8 × 4-inch tins can be used.

Brown Rice Flour Bread

NO CORN,* MILK, WHEAT, OR GLUTEN
Yield: 2 small loaves (10 slices) or 1 large loaf (16 slices)

This bread has good texture and flavor and slices well. As it dries it will get crumbly, so it is best to use it quickly.

2 envelopes plain gelatin
½ c. cold water
1 t. liquid lecithin
1 c. brown rice flour with 1 c. millet flour, or 1 c. brown rice flour with 1 c. chick pea or garbanzo flour

3 t. arrowroot baking powder (see page 13)
1 t. salt
2 T. potato flour
2 eggs
2 T. safflower oil
2 T. honey

Stir gelatin into cold water. Add lecithin (it will not completely dissolve). Measure dry ingredients. Set aside. Beat eggs until thick. Add oil and honey. Heat gelatin just enough to dissolve it. Add to egg mixture. Stir in dry ingredients. (If you are using a mixture of brown rice flour and garbanzo flour, add 2 tablespoons of water. The batter should be medium-stiff but not dry.) Spoon into two well-greased 5 × 3-inch bread pans or one well-greased 8 × 4-inch bread pan. Bake at 375° 25–30 minutes for the small loaves or 35–40 minutes for the large loaf. A toothpick inserted into the center of the loaf should come out clean. Turn out onto a wire rack to cool.

Variation: *If you can use corn,* you can substitute 2 t. regular baking powder for the arrowroot baking powder and 2 T. cornstarch for the potato flour.

Carrot Bread

NO CORN,* MILK, OR WHEAT
Yield: 2 small loaves (10 slices) or 1 large loaf (16 slices)

1 c. oat flour (see page 15)
1½ c. plus 2 T. brown rice flour, or 1 c. millet flour and ½ c. plus 2 T. brown rice flour
6 T. arrowroot
3 t. arrowroot baking powder (see page 13)
½ t. salt
1 t. cinnamon
¼ t. allspice
2 envelopes plain gelatin
¼ c. cold water
2 eggs
2 T. molasses
¼ c. honey
½ c. safflower oil
1 c. grated carrots
½ c. chopped dates, raisins, or nuts

Combine oat flour, brown rice flour, arrowroot, baking powder, salt, cinnamon, and allspice. Set aside. Stir gelatin into cold water and dissolve over low heat. Lightly beat eggs. Slowly add molasses, honey, oil, and gelatin. Stir in carrots and fruit. Blend in dry ingredients. Mix well. Batter should be medium-stiff. Spoon into two well-greased 5 × 3-inch loaf pans or one 8 × 4-inch pan. Bake at 350° 30–35 minutes for the small loaves or 60 minutes for the large loaf. Bread should be lightly browned and a toothpick inserted into the center of loaf should come out clean. Turn out onto a wire rack to cool.

Variation: If you can use corn, you can substitute ½ c. cornstarch for the arrowroot and 2 t. regular baking powder for the arrowroot baking powder.

Corn Bread

NO WHEAT

Yield: One 7-inch square pan (about 9 squares)

2 t. plain gelatin
¼ c. cold water
½ c. cornmeal
½ c. oat flour (see page 15)
2 T. brown rice flour
¼ c. nonfat, noninstant milk
  powder

1½ t. regular baking powder
½ t. salt
1 egg
1½ t. safflower oil
1 T. honey

Stir gelatin into cold water and dissolve over low heat. Combine dry ingredients. Set aside. Beat egg. Slowly add oil and honey. Stir in half of cornmeal mixture. Add gelatin and remaining cornmeal. Stir just to mix. Pour batter into well-greased 7-inch-square pan. Bake at 350° 30–40 minutes. Serve warm.

Multi-Grain Wheat-Free Bread

Here are three different versions of multi-grain wheat-free bread. The dry ingredients are the same for all of them, but the liquid varies for different allergies. The best-textured loaf is produced by Number 3, Multi-Grain with Eggs and Milk. Number 1 uses buttermilk only and Number 2 has no milk, but adds eggs.

Multi-Grain Bread #1, with Buttermilk

NO CORN,* EGG, OR WHEAT
Yield: 3 small loaves (10 slices)
2 medium loaves (16 slices)
or 2½–3 dozen muffins

2 t. plain gelatin
1½ c. buttermilk, divided, plus
   ¼ c. if necessary
3 T. honey
1 t. liquid lecithin
3 T. safflower oil
2 c. oat flour (see page 15)
1 c. brown rice flour

1 c. millet or garbanzo flour
1 c. barley flour
1 c. rye flour
5½ t. arrowroot baking
   powder (see page 13)
4 t. baking soda
2 t. salt
1 T. grated lemon peel

Stir gelatin into ¼ cup of the buttermilk and heat gently to dissolve. Then combine with remaining buttermilk, honey, lecithin, and oil. Blend. Combine remaining ingredients in a bowl. Stir in the buttermilk mixture. Blend thoroughly. Batter should be medium-stiff; add more buttermilk if needed. If too dry, the bread will be crumbly. Spoon into three 5 × 3-inch or two 8 × 4-inch well-greased bread tins or muffin tins. Bake at 375° 25–30 minutes for the small loaves, 35–40 minutes for the medium loaves, or 15–20 minutes for muffins. Bread should be lightly browned and toothpick inserted in the center of the loaf should come out clean. (*Do not underbake.*)

   Variation: *If you can use corn*, you can substitute corn flour for the rye flour and 4½ t. regular baking powder for the arrowroot baking powder in this recipe and in #2 and #3.

Multi-Grain Bread #2, with Eggs

NO CORN,* MILK, OR WHEAT
Yield: 3 small loaves (10 slices),
2 medium loaves (16 slices),
or 2½–3 dozen muffins

This recipe and the one that follows are adaptations of Multi-Grain Bread #1, with Buttermilk, page 54.

Add 3 eggs   *Instead of buttermilk, use 1½*
c. water or orange juice

Stir gelatin into ¼ cup of the water and heat gently to dissolve. Add to remaining water. Add 3 eggs, beaten lightly, honey, lecithin, and oil. Combine remaining ingredients in a bowl. Stir in the egg mixture. Batter should be medium-stiff; add more water if needed.
    Proceed as directed in Multi-Grain Bread #1 recipe.

Multi-Grain Bread #3, with Eggs and Milk

NO CORN* OR WHEAT
Yield: 3 small loaves (10 slices),
2 medium loaves (16 slices),
or 2½–3 dozen muffins

Add 3 eggs   *Instead of buttermilk, use 1½–*
1¾ c. milk

Proceed as for Multi-Grain Bread #2, using milk instead of water.

Pumpkin-Peanut Butter Bread

NO CORN,* MILK, WHEAT, OR GLUTEN*
Yield: 1 loaf (16–18 slices)

This is a winner. Lovely for tea and good enough to replace cake.

1 egg
¼ c. plain or chunky peanut butter, preferably old-fashioned
⅓ c. honey
½ c. pumpkin
¼ c. sunflower seed meal (see page 15)
¼ c. almond or filbert meal (see page 15)
½ c. plus 2 T. brown rice flour, or part millet flour

2 T. arrowroot
½ t. baking soda
2 t. arrowroot baking powder (see page 13)
½ t. cinnamon
¼ t. nutmeg
⅛ t. allspice
¼ t. salt
¼ c. chopped nuts or seeds

Beat the egg well. Slowly beat in peanut butter and honey. Stir in the pumpkin. Set aside. Blend together remaining ingredients and stir into pumpkin mixture. Spoon into a greased 8 × 4-inch loaf pan. Bake at 375° 30–40 minutes, or until a toothpick inserted in the center of the loaf comes out clean. Remove from oven and let sit in pan on a wire rack a minute or two, then turn out onto rack to finish cooling.

Variations: *If you can use corn*, you can substitute 2 T. plus 1 t. cornstarch for the arrowroot and 1½ t. regular baking powder for the arrowroot baking powder.

If you can have gluten but not wheat, you can substitute oat or barley flour or a mixture of the two.

You can use either ½ c. sunflower seed meal or ½ c. filbert meal if you prefer, instead of the combination of the two different meals.

Gluten-Free Banana Bread

NO CORN,* MILK, WHEAT, OR GLUTEN*
Yield: 1 loaf (16 slices)

1 T. quick-cooking tapioca
¼ c. buttermilk, or 2 T.
orange juice
1 c. mashed banana (3–4
bananas)
2 large eggs
2 T. safflower oil
¼ c. honey
2 T. arrowroot

1¾–2 c. brown rice flour, or
1 c. brown rice flour and
¾–1 c. millet or garbanzo
flour
½ t. salt
½ t. baking soda
1 T. arrowroot baking powder
(see page 13)
1 t. grated orange rind
½ c. chopped nuts or seeds

Add tapioca and buttermilk or orange juice to banana. Set aside. In a large mixing bowl beat eggs until thick and lemon colored. Beat in oil and honey. Set aside. Put the arrowroot into a 1-cup measure and fill the cup level with brown rice flour. Empty into a bowl and add ¾ cup more flour, and the salt, baking soda, and baking powder. Add banana mixture and flour mixture alternately to the egg mixture beginning and ending with flour mixture. Add more flour if needed to make medium-stiff batter. Stir in grated rind and nuts or seeds. Spoon into a well-greased 8 × 4-inch loaf pan. Bake at 350° 50–60 minutes or until a toothpick inserted in the center of the loaf comes out clean. Cool on wire rack 10–15 minutes before removing from pan. When cold, wrap loosely and store overnight in refrigerator before cutting.

Variations: If you can use corn, you can substitute 2½ t. regular baking powder for the arrowroot baking powder.

If you can have gluten but not wheat, you can substitute a mixture of barley and oat flour.

Gluten-Free Carrot-Corn Bread

NO WHEAT OR GLUTEN

Yield: One 8-inch-square pan or one 9-inch pie tin (16 pieces)

Excellent!

2 T. butter
1 c. sliced, peeled carrots (2–3
carrots), tightly packed
1 c. buttermilk (¾ c. if
buttermilk is thin)

1 egg
1 c. yellow cornmeal
½ t. salt
½ t. baking soda
½ t. baking powder

In a 450° oven, heat butter in an 8-inch-square pan or a 9-inch pie tin until pan is hot and butter is melted. Set aside. Whirl carrots in blender or food processor with steel blade. Add buttermilk and egg and blend one minute more. In a large bowl, combine cornmeal, salt, baking soda, and baking powder. Pour carrot mixture all at once into cornmeal and mix well. Pour most of the butter into batter and blend well. (If necessary, increase cornmeal to make a medium batter.) Pour mixture into prepared pan. Bake at 450° for 20 minutes, or until browned on edges and beginning to pull away from pan. Serve immediately.

Millet-Barley Bread

NO CORN,* MILK, OR WHEAT
Yield: 1 loaf (16 slices)

2 t. plain gelatin
¾ c. cold water
⅔ c. millet flour (see page 15)
½ c. barley flour
1 c. grated carrots
1 T. honey

2 T. safflower oil
½ t. salt
1 t. arrowroot baking powder
  (see page 13)
2 eggs, separated
¼ t. liquid lecithin

Stir gelatin into water. Set aside. Combine in a large mixing bowl flours, carrots, honey, oil, salt, and baking powder. Beat egg whites to soft peaks. Set aside. Without cleaning beaters, beat egg yolks until thick and lemon colored. Heat gelatin water to boiling. Add lecithin and stir into flour mixture. Add the egg yolks. Gently fold in the egg whites. Spoon into 8 × 4-inch pan, well greased and then lined with greased brown paper. Bake at 350° 35–40 minutes, or until a toothpick inserted in the center of the loaf comes out clean (*do not undercook*). Cool in pan on a wire rack 10 minutes, turn out and remove paper. This bread is best served warm.

*Variation: If you can use corn, substitute ¾ t. regular baking powder for the arrowroot baking powder.

CREPES

None of the following crepes are made from empty-calorie white flour. For the best results, prepare batter in advance, strain into a bowl (unless made in a blender), and refrigerate, covered, from 2 hours to 2 days. The flour will settle as it sits, so be sure to stir before cooking. The batter should flow like heavy cream. If it is too thick or thin, adjust with either flour or water. If flour is used, let batter rest at least ¼ hour. Cook with an adequate amount of safflower oil in pan (the crepes must not stick) over a medium-high heat. Too low a temperature will produce tough crepes, too high will burn them before they are cooked. Add a little oil to the pan before cooking each crepe. Part butter, if allowed, gives a better flavor.

Pour the batter (about ¼ cup per crepe) into the hot skillet, tilting pan to distribute batter evenly and thinly. Pour out any excess. Cook until top appears dry, about 1 minute. Lift with edge of a metal spatula and if the bottom is golden, ease the whole crepe up with the spatula and turn. Cook about 1 minute more. Crepes can be stacked and kept warm in a low oven.

For dessert crepes, add 1 tablespoon honey to the batter.

Rice-Soy Crepes

NO CORN, MILK, WHEAT, OR GLUTEN
Yield: 8 crepes

A jewel for wheat- and gluten-free diets and a bonus for all except the egg-free.

⅔ c. plus 1 T. brown rice
  flour or ⅓ c. plus 1 T.
  brown rice flour and ⅓ c.
  millet flour
¼ c. soya flour

¼ t. salt
2 eggs
1 T. sesame oil
1 c. water

Combine all ingredients and thoroughly blend with an egg beater or electric mixer or in a blender. Proceed according to general directions, above.

Oat Flour Crepes

NO CORN OR WHEAT
Yield: 8 crepes

Substitute:
¾ c. oat flour for brown rice
  flour

1 c. milk for the water

Proceed as in recipe above.

Chick Pea Crepes

NO CORN, MILK, WHEAT, OR GLUTEN
Yield: 8 crepes

½ c. chick peas
1 c. water
1 T. olive oil

½ t. salt
2 eggs

Soak peas overnight in water. Drain and put in blender. Add the 1 cup water. Whirl at high speed, scraping down sides often until liquefied. Reduce speed. Add oil, salt, and eggs and blend. Proceed as in general directions, pages 59–60.

Brown Rice Crackers

NO CORN, EGG, MILK,* WHEAT, OR GLUTEN
Yield: 16–18 1½–2-inch crackers (depending on size)

The crackers in the following recipes should be used within 2 or 3 days.

½ c. brown rice flour
½ c. millet flour
2 T. potato flour
1 t. baking soda
1 t. baking powder

¼ t. salt
2 T. corn-free vegetable
   shortening (see page 13)
4–5 T. cold water

Combine flours, baking soda, and salt. Cut in shortening. Gradually add cold water, just enough to make a ball you can handle. Roll out between two sheets of flour-dusted waxed paper to ⅛-inch thickness. Carefully remove top sheet. Either flip the waxed paper onto a lightly greased cookie sheet before cutting into crackers or cut dough into desired cracker sizes and with a pancake turner, carefully transfer them to the cookie sheet. Bake at 400° 5–7 minutes, or until lightly browned and crisp. Remove from oven and place the cookie sheet on a wire rack to cool.

   *Variation: If you can use milk, you can substitute butter for the shortening.

Rye Crackers

NO CORN, EGG, MILK,* OR WHEAT
Yield: 18–20 2-inch crackers

1 c. rye flour
½ t. baking soda
½ t. salt

2 T. corn-free vegetable
*   shortening (see page 13)*
3–4 T. cold water

Proceed as in Brown Rice Crackers.
   *Variation: *If you can use milk*, you can substitute butter for the shortening.

Corn Crackers

NO EGG, MILK,* WHEAT, OR GLUTEN
Yield: 12–18 crackers (depending on size)

1 c. cornmeal
¼ t. salt
½ t. baking soda

2½ T. corn-free vegetable
*   shortening (see page 13)*
4–5 T. water

Proceed as in Brown Rice Crackers.
   *Variation: *If you can use milk*, you can substitute butter for the shortening.

CAKES

	NO CORN	NO EGG	NO MILK	NO WHEAT	NO GLUTEN
Banana Cake	⊗			⊗	⊗
Carob Cake	⊗				
Wheat-Free Carob or Chocolate Cake	⊗			X	⊗
Carrot Cake	⊗		X		
No-Egg Carrot Cake	X	X	X		
Wheat-Free Carrot Cake	⊗		X	X	⊗
Lackerlie #1	X	X			
Lackerlie #2	X			X	⊗
Hot Water Fruit Cake	X	X	X		
Honey Cake	⊗	X			
Quick Gingerbread	X		⊗		
Cherry Sauce	⊗	X	X	X	X
Raisin Fruit Cake	⊗		⊗		
Chocolate Pumpkin Cake	X	X	X		
Raisin Pudding Cake	X	X			
Molasses Pudding Cake	X	X	⊗		
Persimmon Pudding Cake	⊗	X	⊗		
Hawaiian Cake #1	X	X	X		
Honey-Milk Sauce	X	X		X	X
Pineapple Sauce	X	X	X	X	X

⊗ means that the recipe includes instructions for adding that ingredient if allowed.

63

	NO CORN	NO EGG	NO MILK	NO WHEAT	NO GLUTEN
Hawaiian Cake #2	⊗		X	X	⊗
Pumpkin Cake	⊗	X	X		
Filbert Cake	⊗		X	X	X
Almond Pear Torte	X		X		
Orange Glaze	X	X	X	X	X
Swedish Apple Cake	⊗		X		
Apple-Date Cake	X	X	⊗		
Wheat-Free Apple-Date Cake	⊗		X	X	⊗
Date-Nut Cake	X		X		
Date-Nut Torte	⊗		X	X	⊗
Almond Torte	⊗		X	X	X
Sponge Cake	X		X		
Fluffy Lemon Cheese Cake	X			X	X
Cherry Cheese Cake	X	X		X	X
Baked Cheese Cake	X			X	X
Apple Sponge Cake	X		X	X	⊗
Carob Frosting	X	X		X	X
Cream Cheese Filling	X	X		X	X
Creole Frosting	X	X		X	X
Cream Cheese Icing	X	X		X	X
Confectioners Icing	X	X		X	X
Creamy Icing	⊗	X		⊗	⊗
Orange Sauce	⊗	X	X	X	X
Cinnamon Sauce	X	X		X	X
Lemon Sauce	⊗	X	⊗	X	X
Mystery Sauce	X	X	X	X	X
Fruit Sauce	⊗	X	X	X	X
Raisin Sauce		X	X	X	X
Carob Sauce	X	X		X	X

The cake recipes presented here are nutritious as well as good eating, and are all good eaten just plain. Loading them with sugar-laden frostings is optional but is poor nutrition, as sugar provides empty calories and can actually be detrimental (see page 3). It is my hope that sprinkling a little powdered sugar or drizzling a little warm honey over the cake might satisfy the sweet tooth. Better yet, top with sliced fresh fruit or a fruit sauce such as applesauce.

I have stressed carob instead of chocolate. Carob is largely carbohydrate in the form of natural sugars. It has thirteen vitamins and minerals, especially calcium. In addition, it has half the calories of cocoa, one-hundredth of the fat, and no caffeine. All I can say about chocolate is that it is high in calories and fat, and contains caffeine. It is also a common allergen and should therefore be avoided by anyone who has a high degree of allergic reaction.

Banana Cake

NO CORN,* WHEAT,* OR GLUTEN*
Servings: 8

2 large eggs
¼ c. honey
¼ c. safflower oil
½ c. mashed banana
¾ c. brown rice flour, or ¼ c. each brown rice, millet, and garbanzo flours

¼ c. arrowroot
1 t. arrowroot baking powder (see page 13)
¾ t. baking soda
½ t. salt
1 t. plain gelatin
¼ c. buttermilk

In a large mixing bowl, beat the eggs until thick and lemon colored. Slowly beat in the honey and oil. Stir in banana. Set aside. Measure and sift together dry ingredients. Set aside. Add gelatin to buttermilk. Gently warm over hot water just to dissolve gelatin (if overheated, buttermilk will separate). Add flour and buttermilk alternately to banana mixture. Stir until well blended. Use 2 greased 8-inch pans, with removable bottoms if possible. If using regular 8-inch cake pans, cover bottoms with greased waxed paper. Pour batter into pans. Bake at 350° 35–40 minutes or until a toothpick inserted in center of cake comes out clean. Loosen edges. Invert onto a wire rack, remove paper, and cool. Use plain or frost as desired, or serve with sauce of choice (see sauces, pages 92–95).

Variations: If you can use corn, you can substitute 3⅓ T. cornstarch for the arrowroot and ¾ t. regular baking powder for the arrowroot baking powder.

If you can use wheat, you can substitute whole wheat pastry flour.

If you can use gluten but not wheat, you can substitute barley or oat flour.

Carob Cake

NO CORN*
Servings: 8–9

¼ c. safflower oil
2 T. brown sugar
¼ c. honey
½ c. carob chips, divided
1 egg
1 t. vanilla
¾ c. plus 1 T. whole wheat
   pastry flour

¾ t. arrowroot baking powder
   (see page 13)
½ t. baking soda
¼ t. salt
¼ c. chopped sunflower seeds
   or nuts

Combine oil, brown sugar, honey, and ¼ cup of the carob chips in a saucepan. Heat until chips are melted, stirring constantly. Remove from heat and cool. Beat egg. Stir into cooled mixture along with vanilla. Combine remaining ingredients. Stir into carob mixture. Pour into a greased 7-inch-square or 9 × 5-inch pan, greased and lined with greased waxed paper. Bake at 350° 25 minutes, or until a toothpick inserted in the center of the cake comes out clean. Remove from pan and cool on a wire rack. This recipe can be doubled to make a larger cake. Frost with frosting of your choice or see frostings (pages 90–91).

Variations: If you can use corn, you can substitute ½ t. regular baking powder for the arrowroot baking powder.

For a milk-free recipe, you can substitute chocolate chips for the carob.

Wheat-Free Carob or Chocolate Cake

NO CORN,* WHEAT, OR GLUTEN*
Servings: 8–9

¼ c. safflower oil
¼ c. honey
2 t. plain gelatin
1 t. liquid lecithin
½ c. carob chips, divided
1¼ c. brown rice flour, or
    ½ c. brown rice flour, ⅓
    c. millet flour, and ⅓ c.
    garbanzo flour

2½ T. arrowroot
¼ t. salt
1 t. baking soda
¼ c. chopped sunflower seeds
    or nuts
2 eggs, separated
1 t. vanilla

Combine oil, honey, gelatin, lecithin and ¼ cup of carob chips in a saucepan. Heat until chips are melted, stirring constantly. Remove from heat and cool. Combine flour, arrowroot, salt, baking soda, the remaining ¼ cup carob chips, and the seeds or nuts. Set aside. Beat egg whites. Without cleaning beaters, beat yolks slightly. Beat into cooled honey/carob mixture. Add vanilla. Stir into flour. Add about 2 tablespoons whipped whites and stir in. Gently fold in remaining whites. Pour into a greased 7-inch-square or 9 × 5-inch pan lined with greased waxed paper. Bake at 350° 25 minutes, or until a toothpick inserted into the center of the cake comes out clean. Remove from pan and cool on a wire rack. This recipe can be doubled to make a larger cake. Frost as desired or see pages 90–91.

*Variations: If you can use corn, you can substitute 3 T. cornstarch for the arrowroot.

If you can use gluten but not wheat, for a smoother-textured cake you can substitute ½ c. of barley or oat flour or a mixture of both for ½ c. of the brown rice flour.

For a milk-free cake, you can substitute ½ c. chocolate chips for the carob.

Carrot Cake

NO CORN* OR MILK
Servings: 16

2 large eggs
⅔ c. safflower oil
½ c. honey
1 t. vanilla
½ t. baking soda
½ t. salt
½ t. cinnamon

1 c. whole wheat pastry flour
½ c. unbleached pastry flour
*1¼ t. arrowroot baking
   powder (see page 13)*
1½ c. grated carrots
*½ c. chopped nuts or
   sunflower seeds*

Beat eggs until thick, fluffy, and lemon colored. Slowly add oil, honey, and vanilla. Combine dry ingredients and stir into egg mixture. Blend well. Stir in carrots and nuts or seeds. Pour into a well-greased 9-inch-square pan. Bake at 350° 30–35 minutes, or until a toothpick inserted in center of cake comes out clean. Remove from pan to cool on a wire rack. Spread with frosting of your choice or see frostings (pages 90–91).

Variation: *If you can use corn*, you can substitute 1 t. regular baking powder for the arrowroot baking powder.

No-Egg Carrot Cake

NO CORN, EGG, OR MILK
Servings: 16

*1½ c. whole wheat pastry
   flour*
½ c. wheat germ
1 t. baking soda
*½ c. chopped nuts or
   sunflower seeds*
1 c. grated carrots
1 c. dates, cut into small pieces
⅔ c. honey

2 T. safflower oil
½ t. salt
1¼ t. cinnamon
½ t. nutmeg
½ t. allspice
2 t. plain gelatin
½ t. liquid lecithin
¼ c. water

Combine first four ingredients. Set aside. Combine remaining ingredients in a saucepan. Bring to a boil. Turn down heat and gently simmer for 10 minutes. Stir occasionally. Cool. Stir flour mixture into cooled carrot mixture. Pour into a well-greased and floured 6 × 10-inch pan or 8-inch-square pan. Bake at 300° 45–50 minutes, or until a toothpick inserted in the center of the cake comes out clean. Remove from pan to cool on a wire rack.

Wheat-Free Carrot Cake

NO CORN,* MILK, WHEAT, OR GLUTEN*
Servings: 16

2 t. plain gelatin
⅔ c. safflower oil
½ c. honey
1 t. vanilla
1½ c. brown rice flour, or
  ½ c. brown rice flour, ½
  c. garbanzo flour, and ½ c.
  plus 2 T. millet flour
¼ c. arrowroot

1 t. baking soda
½ t. cinnamon
½ t. salt
2 t. arrowroot baking powder
  (see page 13)
4 large eggs
1½ c. grated carrots
½ c. chopped nuts or
  sunflower seeds

Stir gelatin into oil and heat just enough to dissolve. Add honey and vanilla to oil-gelatin mixture. Combine dry ingredients. Beat eggs. Proceed as in recipe for Carrot Cake.

   *Variations: *If you can use corn*, you can substitute 3⅓ T. corn-starch for the arrowroot and 1½ t. regular baking powder for the arrowroot baking powder.

   If you can use gluten but not wheat, you can substitute barley or oat flour.

Lackerlie #1

NO CORN OR EGG
Servings: 16

½ c. milk
2½ T. safflower oil
2½ T. molasses
3 T. honey, divided
1 c. whole wheat pastry flour
Scant ½ t. baking soda
1 T. carob powder

¼ t. salt
⅛ t. ground ginger
⅛ t. nutmeg
Dash of allspice
Dash of cloves
½ t. cinnamon
1 t. lemon juice

Scald milk. Add oil, molasses, and 2 tablespoons of the honey. Pour into a bowl to cool. Sift dry ingredients together. Stir into cooled mixture in two or three additions. Beat well each time. Pour into a well-greased 8-inch-square pan. The batter should not be more than ¼ inch thick. Bake at 375° 15 minutes. Cool in pan on a wire rack. While still warm, drizzle with a mixture of the remaining 1 tablespoon honey and the lemon juice. Serve topped with applesauce.

Lackerlie #2

NO CORN, WHEAT, OR GLUTEN*
Servings: 12–16

1 t. plain gelatin
½ c. milk
2½ T. safflower oil
2½ T. molasses
3 T. honey, divided
1 egg, lightly beaten
1¼ c. less 1 T. brown rice
  flour, or ¾ c. less 1 T.
  brown rice flour and ½ c.
  millet flour

½ t. baking soda
½ t. salt
½ t. cinnamon
1 T. carob powder
⅛ t. ground ginger
⅛ t. nutmeg
Dash of allspice
Dash of cloves
1 t. lemon juice

Add gelatin to milk. Scald milk mixture. Add oil, molasses, and 2 tablespoons of the honey. Pour into a bowl to cool. When cool, stir in lightly beaten egg. Sift dry ingredients together. Stir into cooled mixture in two or three additions. Beat well each time. Pour into a well-greased 8-inch-square pan. The batter should not be more than ¼ inch thick. Bake at 375° 15 minutes. Cool in pan on a wire rack. While still warm, drizzle with a mixture of the remaining 1 tablespoon honey and the lemon juice. Serve topped with applesauce.

Variation: *If you can have gluten but not wheat,* you can substitute barley or oat flour.

Hot Water Fruit Cake

NO CORN, EGG, OR MILK
Servings: 8

½ c. seedless raisins
1 c. honey
⅓ c. safflower oil
1 t. baking soda
1 c. boiling water or coffee
¾ c. chopped, mixed dried
    fruit (if dried fruit is not soft,
    soak it until it is, drain
    thoroughly, and pat dry)

½ c. chopped nuts
1¼ c. whole wheat pastry
    flour
1 c. plus 2 T. unbleached flour
½ t. salt
½ t. cinnamon
¼ t. cloves
¼ t. nutmeg

Combine raisins, honey, oil, and baking soda in large bowl. Pour water or coffee over mixture. Mix well and cool to room temperature. Prepare and set aside the dried fruit and nuts. Sift together dry ingredients and stir into cooled raisin mixture. Blend in dried fruit and nuts. Grease sides of a 9 × 5-inch loaf pan and line bottom with greased paper. Pour in batter. Bake at 350° 1 hour, or until a toothpick inserted in the center of the cake comes out clean. About 10 minutes before cake is done, brush top with honey. Remove from pan to a wire rack to cool.

Honey Cake

NO CORN* OR EGG
Servings: 12

2 c. whole wheat pastry flour
1½ t. arrowroot baking
   powder (see page 13)
½ t. salt
½ t. baking soda
¼ c. safflower oil
¼ c. corn-free vegetable
   shortening (see page 13)

½ c. honey
1 t. vanilla, or ½ t. almond
   extract
1 c. milk
Additional honey, warmed

Sift flour, baking powder, salt, and baking soda together. Set aside. Cream together oil and shortening. Slowly add honey and vanilla. By hand, alternately mix together with flour mixture and milk. Pour into a well-greased 8-inch-square pan lined with greased waxed paper. Bake at 350° 35–40 minutes. Remove cake from oven and drizzle warm honey over top. Let sit 2–3 minutes. Remove from pan, remove waxed paper, and cool on a wire rack.

*Variations: If you can use corn, you can substitute 1 t. regular baking powder for the arrowroot baking powder.

Instead of the honey topping, a confectioners icing or Carob Frosting (page 90) is excellent. Or use a topping of your choice.

Quick Gingerbread

NO CORN OR MILK*
Servings: 12

¾ c. whole wheat flour
¾ c. unbleached flour
⅓ c. sugar
1 t. ground ginger
1 t. baking soda

½ c. molasses
1 egg, unbeaten
½ c. corn-free vegetable
   shortening (see page 13)
1 c. boiling water (approx.)

In a large bowl, combine flours, sugar, ginger, and baking soda. Add molasses and egg. Measure shortening in a large measure and fill to the

1-cup level with boiling water. Add to flour mixture. Mix for 4 minutes at medium speed of electric mixer. Pour into a well-greased 8-inch-square pan. Bake at 350° 30 minutes, or until done. Serve with Cherry Sauce (below), applesauce, or any sauce of your choice.

Variation: *If you can use milk,* you can substitute butter for the shortening, or use a mixture of the two.

For egg-free, modify the recipe as follows:

Eliminate egg. Stir 2 t. gelatin into 2 T. cold water. Heat to dissolve. Add with molasses to the boiling water. Add ½ t. regular baking powder or ¾ t. arrowroot baking powder to the dry ingredients.

Cherry Sauce

NO CORN,* EGG, MILK, WHEAT, OR GLUTEN
Yield: 2½ cups

⅓ c. honey, or ½ c. sugar
1 c. water
2½ t. arrowroot
1 T. water

1½ c. fresh or thawed frozen
cherries
¼ t. almond extract (optional)

In a small saucepan, bring honey or sugar and the 1 cup water to a boil. Mix arrowroot with the 1 tablespoon water. Stir into honey water. Add cherries. Cook and stir until cherries begin to soften and mixture thickens slightly. Add the almond extract. Serve warm or cold.

Variation: *If you can use corn,* substitute 1 T. cornstarch for the arrowroot. If arrowroot is used, do not try to rewarm.

Raisin Fruit Cake

NO CORN* OR MILK*
Servings: 16–20

3 eggs
1/3 c. safflower oil
1/2 c. honey
1 c. whole wheat pastry flour
1 c. unbleached flour
3 t. arrowroot baking powder
    (see page 13)
1 t. cinnamon

1 t. grated orange peel
1/2 t. baking soda
1/2 t. salt
1/2 t. ground cloves
1 c. raisins
1 c. mixed chopped dates and
    other moist dried fruits
1/3 c. orange juice

SAUCE:
1/2 c. orange or pineapple juice
1/4 c. honey

2 T. corn-free vegetable shortening
    (see page 13)

Beat eggs until light and fluffy. Slowly add oil and honey. Set aside. Combine dry ingredients. Dust raisins and fruit with 1/4 cup of the flour mixture. Stir remainder of flour mixture into egg mixture alternately with orange juice. Add fruit. The batter should be medium-stiff. Spoon into a well-greased and floured bundt pan. Bake at 350° about 50 minutes, or until a toothpick inserted in the cake comes out clean. Cool for 10 minutes in the pan. Invert on a wire rack. While cake is cooling, combine juice, honey, and shortening to make sauce. Cook over low heat until sauce thickens. Spoon sauce over warm cake.

*Variations: If you can use corn, you can substitute 2 t. regular baking powder for the arrowroot baking powder.

If you can use milk, you can substitute butter for the shortening in the sauce.

Chocolate Pumpkin Cake

NO CORN, EGG, OR MILK
Servings: 15

½ c. safflower oil
1 oz. semisweet baking chocolate
1 c. pumpkin
½ c. honey
2 t. frozen orange juice
    concentrate, thawed
2 c. plus 2 T. whole wheat pastry
    flour
2 t. baking soda
1 t. cinnamon

½ t. nutmeg
¼ t. salt
¼ t. ground cloves
½ c. raisins (soak raisins in
    water until plump, drain off
    any excess water, then
    measure)
1 c. chopped nuts or sunflower
    seeds

Combine oil and chocolate in a small saucepan. Warm over low heat until chocolate is melted. Set aside. Combine pumpkin, honey, and juice. Set aside. Sift the dry ingredients into a bowl. Add raisins and nuts or seeds. Stir in the pumpkin and chocolate mixtures until well blended. Pour into a greased 7 × 11-inch baking dish. Bake at 325° 45 minutes, or until a toothpick inserted in the center of the cake comes out clean. Remove from pan. Cool on a wire rack.

Raisin Pudding Cake

NO CORN OR EGG
Servings: 9–12

4 T. butter or margarine, divided
⅔ c. honey, divided
½ c. whole wheat flour
½ c. unbleached flour
½ t. baking soda

¼ t. salt
½ c. buttermilk
½ c. raisins
¼ c. chopped nuts or seeds
1 c. boiling water

Cream together 2 tablespoons of the butter and ⅓ cup of the honey. Combine dry ingredients. Add dry ingredients and buttermilk alternately to honey-butter mixture. Stir in raisins and nuts. Spread in lightly greased 8-inch-square pan. Set aside. Combine the remaining butter and honey and the boiling water. Pour over batter already in pan. Bake at 350° 45–60 minutes. Serve warm.

Molasses Pudding Cake

NO CORN, EGG, OR MILK*
Servings: 12–14

1 c. whole wheat flour
1¼ c. unbleached flour
1½ t. cinnamon
¾ t. nutmeg
¼ c. sugar
¼ t. salt

⅓ c. corn-free margarine or
corn-free vegetable shortening
(see page 13)
¾ c. molasses
1½ c. warm water
1 t. baking soda

Combine dry ingredients. Cut in margarine or shortening until mixture resembles coarse meal. Distribute 1 cup of the mixture in a greased 9-inch-square pan. Set aside. Combine molasses, water, and baking soda. Spoon half of the molasses mixture into baking pan. Sprinkle half of the remaining flour mixture over liquid. Spoon on remaining molasses mixture, then remaining flour mixture. Use a fork to gently cut through the batter in a wide zigzag pattern to create a marbled effect (*be careful not to cut into bottom crumb layer)*. Bake at 350° 50 minutes, or until top is set. Serve with your choice of sauce.

*Variation: If you can use milk, you can substitute butter for the margarine or shortening.

Persimmon Pudding Cake

NO CORN,* EGG, OR MILK*
Servings: 8–9

*2 T. corn-free vegetable
  shortening (see page 13)*
½ c. honey
*2–3 medium-sized persimmons
  (approx.)*
1 T. arrowroot
*1 c. less 1 T. whole wheat pastry
  flour*

2 t. baking soda
1½ t. pumpkin pie spice
1 c. soybean milk (see page 16)
½ c. chopped raisins
½ c. chopped nuts

Cream together shortening and honey. Puree persimmons in blender or food processor with steel blade. Blend 1 cup puree into honey mixture. Sift together dry ingredients. Add to persimmon mixture alternately with the soybean milk. Stir in raisins and nuts. This makes a thin batter. Pour into greased 8-inch-square pan and set in a pan of hot water to bake. Bake at 350° 1¼–1½ hours, or until a toothpick inserted in the center of the cake comes out clean. Serve with Lemon Sauce (page 93) or Mystery Sauce (page 94).

*Variations: If you can use corn, you can substitute 1 T. plus 1 t. cornstarch for the arrowroot.

If you can use milk, substitute butter for the shortening and 1 c. milk for the soybean milk.

Hawaiian Cake #1

NO CORN, EGG, OR MILK
Servings: 12–14

2 c. whole wheat pastry flour
1 c. honey
1½ t. baking soda

2 8-oz. cans crushed,
  unsweetened pineapple, juice
  included
⅓ c. shredded coconut

Combine all ingredients in a large bowl. Stir until completely moistened. Pour batter into a greased and floured, 9-inch-square pan. Bake at 350° 35–40 minutes, or until a toothpick inserted in the center of the cake comes out clean. About 15 minutes before cake is done, prepare either Honey-Milk Sauce or Pineapple Sauce (see below). Remove cake from oven. Pierce top with a toothpick. Pour sauce over cake.

Honey-Milk Sauce

NO CORN, EGG, WHEAT, OR GLUTEN

¼ c. honey
⅔ c. evaporated milk

2 T. butter
1 t. vanilla

Combine honey, milk, and butter. Cook over low heat until sauce is thickened. Add vanilla.

Pineapple Sauce

NO CORN, EGG, MILK, WHEAT, OR GLUTEN

½ c. crushed, unsweetened
  pineapple

2 T. honey

Combine pineapple and honey. Cook until thickened, which will reduce the volume slightly. It should be warm, not hot.

Hawaiian Cake #2

NO CORN,* MILK, WHEAT, OR GLUTEN*
Servings: 12–14

2 c. brown rice flour, or 1 c.
  brown rice flour and 1 c.
  millet flour
⅔ c. sunflower seed meal
  (see page 15)
2 t. baking soda
1 t. arrowroot baking powder
  (see page 13)

1 c. honey
2 8-oz. cans crushed,
  unsweetened pineapple, juice
  included
1 egg, lightly beaten
½ c. shredded coconut

Combine all ingredients in a bowl and proceed as in recipe, page 78.

Variations: If you can use corn, you can substitute ¾ t. regular
baking powder for the arrowroot baking powder.

If you can use gluten but not wheat, you can substitute barley or oat
flour, or a mixture of the two, for the brown rice flour.

Pumpkin Cake

NO CORN,* EGG, OR MILK
Servings: 16

¼ c. corn-free vegetable
  shortening (see page 13)
½ c. honey
1 c. canned pumpkin puree
⅓ c. orange juice
1 t. grated orange rind
1 T. cornstarch or arrowroot
1½ c. less 1 T. whole wheat
  pastry flour

½ c. unbleached flour
1 t. cinnamon
1 t. nutmeg
1 t. baking soda
1¼ t. arrowroot baking
  powder (see page 13)
½ t. salt
2 T. honey (optional)

Cream shortening and honey together. Combine pumpkin, orange juice,
and rind. Set aside. Combine all dry ingredients. Add pumpkin mixture

and flour mixture alternately to the shortening mixture, mixing well. Pour into a greased 9-inch-square pan. Bake at 350° 45–50 minutes, or until a toothpick inserted in the center of the cake comes out clean. Remove pan to a wire rack to cool. Drizzle honey over top while still hot, or frost as desired (see pages 90–91).

Variations: If you can use corn, you can substitute 1 t. regular baking powder for the arrowroot baking powder.

Chopped nuts, sunflower seeds, or raisins may be added if desired.

Filbert Cake

NO CORN,* MILK, WHEAT, OR GLUTEN
Servings: 16–20

1½ t. arrowroot baking
   powder (see page 13)
2 c. finely ground filbert meal
   (see page 15; about 3 cups
   whole nuts ground to texture
   of fine cornmeal)

10 eggs, separated, at room
   temperature
1 c. sugar, divided
½ t. salt
2 t. vanilla

Mix the baking powder into the nut meal. Measure 1 cup unbeaten egg whites. Beat, adding ¼ cup of sugar, until whites are stiff and hold peaks. Without cleaning beaters, beat egg yolks until thick and lemon colored. Gradually beat in salt, ¾ cup of sugar, and the vanilla. Fold in the filbert mixture.

Gently fold egg white mixture into the yolk mixture. Spoon into a bundt or angel food pan which has been well buttered or greased and floured with ground nuts. Bake at 325° 1 hour. Turn off heat and let cake partially cool in oven. It should cool slowly. It will fall a little as it cools, but don't worry—it will still be as light as a feather and delicious.

Variation: If you can use corn, you can substitute 1 t. regular baking powder for the arrowroot baking powder.

Almond Pear Torte

NO CORN OR MILK
Servings: 12–14

2 c. finely chopped pears
  (2½–3 pears)
6 T. safflower oil
¾ c. honey or 1½ c. sugar
2 eggs
1 t. vanilla
½ t. almond extract

2 c. unsifted, unbleached flour
2 t. baking soda
1 t. cinnamon
½ t. nutmeg
¼ t. ground cloves
½ c. seedless raisins
½ c. chopped almonds

Peel, core, and chop the pears. Beat the oil and sugar together. Add eggs, one at a time. Beat mixture until light and fluffy. Blend in flavorings and pears. In a separate bowl, sift together dry ingredients. Add to pear mixture. Stir in raisins and nuts. Pour into a well-greased and floured (dusted), 2-quart tube pan. Bake at 350° 55–60 minutes, or until an inserted toothpick comes out clean. Turn out onto a wire rack. Cool thoroughly. Drizzle with Orange Glaze (see below) if you wish.

Orange Glaze

NO CORN, EGG, MILK, WHEAT, OR GLUTEN

1 c. confectioners sugar
½ t. grated orange peel

¼ t. almond extract
1 T. orange juice

Stir to combine.

Swedish Apple Cake

NO CORN* OR MILK
Servings: 8

3–4 Delicious apples
1 egg
½ c. honey
½ c. safflower oil
½ t. vanilla
¼ t. almond extract
½ c. whole wheat pastry flour

½ c. unbleached flour
¼ t. salt
1¼ t. arrowroot baking
  powder (see page 13)
2 T. sugar
¼ t. nutmeg
¼ t. cinnamon

Peel and core apples and slice into ¼-inch slices. Set aside. Beat egg until very light and fluffy. Slowly add honey, oil, and flavorings. Continue beating. Combine flours, salt, and baking powder and stir into honey-egg mixture. Spoon into greased 8-inch cake pan with removable bottom. Overlap the prepared apple slices in a spiral pattern to cover batter, using all the apples. Combine the sugar, nutmeg, and cinnamon and sprinkle mixture over apples. Bake at 350° 1 hour and 15 minutes, or until a toothpick inserted in the center of the cake comes out clean. Cool 5 minutes on a wire rack. Remove sides of pan. Serve warm with Lemon Sauce (see page 93) if allowed.

*Variation: If you can use corn, you can substitute 1 t. regular baking powder for the arrowroot baking powder.

Apple-Date Cake

NO CORN, EGG, OR MILK*
Servings: 12–16

*¼ c. corn-free margarine or
corn-free vegetable shortening
(see page 13)*
½ c. honey
1 t. vanilla
1 c. whole wheat pastry flour
1 t. baking soda

¼ t. salt
¼ t. nutmeg
1 t. cinnamon
1 c. peeled, grated apple
1 c. chopped dates
1 c. grated carrot

GLAZE:
½ c. confectioners sugar
1½ t. lemon juice

1 t. hot water

Blend margarine, honey, and vanilla. Sift together flour, soda, salt, and spices. Stir into shortening mixture; it will be stiff. Combine apple, dates, and carrots. Stir into flour mixture and blend well. Spoon into a well-greased 8-inch-square pan. Bake at 350° 40–50 minutes, or until a toothpick inserted in the center of the cake comes out clean. Place pan on a wire rack to cool. Combine confectioners sugar, lemon juice and hot water. While cake is warm, drizzle glaze over top. When cake is cool, remove from pan.

Variation: If you can use milk, you can substitute butter or margarine for shortening.

Wheat-Free Apple-Date Cake

NO CORN,* MILK, WHEAT, OR GLUTEN*

In preceding recipe, substitute ¼ c. safflower oil for the margarine or shortening, and 1¾ c. brown rice flour, or ¾ c. brown rice flour and 1 c. millet flour, for the wheat flour. Add 2 eggs; add 1¼ t. arrowroot baking powder to flour.

Beat eggs until light and lemon-colored. Beat in oil, honey, and vanilla and proceed as in Apple-Date Cake recipe.

Variations: *If you can use corn*, you can substitute 1 t. regular baking powder for the arrowroot baking powder.

If you can use gluten but not wheat, you can substitute a mixture of barley and oat flour.

Date-Nut Cake

NO CORN OR MILK
Servings: 12–16

1²⁄₃ c. whole wheat pastry
   flour
1 t. baking soda
½ t. salt
3 T. safflower oil
1 egg

1 t. vanilla
½ c. honey
½ c. water
1 c. chopped dates
½ c. chopped nuts

Combine all ingredients but dates and nuts in large bowl of electric mixer. Beat ½ minute at low speed to blend, scraping bowl. Increase speed to high and beat 3 minutes, scraping bowl occasionally. Stir in dates and nuts. Pour into a greased and floured 9 × 9 × 2-inch pan. Bake at 350° about 45 minutes, or until a toothpick inserted in the center of the cake comes out clean. Remove from pan and cool on wire rack. Serve plain, frosted, or with Lemon Sauce (see page 93) or Orange Sauce (see page 92).

Date-Nut Torte

NO CORN,* MILK, WHEAT, OR GLUTEN*
Servings: 6–8

2 eggs, separated, at room
   temperature
¼ c. honey
½ c. finely chopped nuts
½ T. lemon juice
½ t. grated lemon rind

¼ c. brown rice flour
⅛ t. salt
½ scant t. arrowroot baking
   powder (see page 13)
½ c. chopped dates

Grease a 5 × 9-inch loaf pan or a 7-inch-square pan well. Cut heavy brown paper to fit bottom and grease it well. Set aside. Beat egg whites until stiff peaks form. Set aside. Without cleaning beaters, beat egg yolks until thick and lemon colored. Slowly add honey, while continuing to beat at low speed. Stir in nuts, lemon juice, and lemon rind. Set aside. Combine flour, salt, and baking powder. Blend in dates. Add flour mixture to egg yolk mixture. Stir well. Gently fold flour mixture into egg whites. Pour into prepared pan. Bake at 325° 25–30 minutes, or until firm to the touch. Remove from oven. Turn out onto a wire rack and remove paper quickly. Let cool thoroughly. Serve plain or with Lemon Sauce (page 93).

*Variations: If you can use corn, you can substitute ¼ t. regular baking powder for the arrowroot baking powder.

If you can use gluten but not wheat, you can substitute a mixture of barley and oat flour.

Almond Torte

NO CORN,* MILK, WHEAT, OR GLUTEN
Servings: 8–10

4 t. finely chopped orange peel
4 T. honey, divided
2 T. water
4 eggs, separated
¾ t. arrowroot baking powder
   (see page 13)

¼ c. white wine or orange
   juice
1 c. ground almonds
½ c. ground, raw sunflower
   seeds

In a small saucepan, combine orange peel, 2 tablespoons of the honey, and the water. Bring to a boil and then simmer for several minutes until syrupy. Cool. In another bowl, beat egg whites until they hold stiff peaks. Set aside. Without cleaning beaters, beat egg yolks until lemon colored. Stir baking powder into almonds. Continue beating yolks and add the remaining honey and the wine, almonds, and seeds. Stir a small amount of egg whites into nut mixture. Then gently fold in the remaining egg whites. Use either a 9-inch pan with a removable bottom or a springform, or a 9-inch cake pan generously greased and covered with greased brown paper. Spoon batter into pan. Bake at 375° about 25 minutes, or until top is brown and center is firm. Cool slightly on a rack, then remove from pan.

   *Variation: If you can use corn, you can substitute ½ t. regular baking powder for the arrowroot baking powder.

Sponge Cake

NO CORN OR MILK
Servings: 14–16

4 eggs, separated, at room
   temperature
½ t. salt
6 T. sugar
2 t. vanilla

2 T. grated lemon peel
6 T. honey
1½ c. unbleached pastry flour,
   sifted

Grease the bottom of a 9 × 5-inch loaf pan and line with greased waxed paper. Beat egg whites at high speed of electric mixer 2–3 minutes.

Continue beating and gradually add salt and sugar. Set aside. Without cleaning beaters, beat egg yolks in a small bowl until thick and lemon colored. Continue beating as you add vanilla, lemon peel, and honey. Beat for 4 minutes. Gently fold the egg yolks and sifted flour alternately into the egg whites. Spoon batter into prepared pan. Bake at 325° 35–45 minutes, or until cake springs back when touched in center. Cool in pan 10 minutes. Remove from pan. Remove paper and finish cooling on a wire rack.

This can be served plain or with sauce of your choice. (If you can use milk, you could also serve with whipped cream.) Cake can also be cut horizontally with a serrated knife to make two layers and a filling of your choice put between the layers.

Fluffy Lemon Cheese Cake

NO CORN, WHEAT, OR GLUTEN
Servings: 6

An airy, low-calorie version to top off a heavy meal.

1 envelope plain gelatin
⅓ c. honey
Dash of salt
1 egg, separated
½ c. skim milk
2 t. grated lemon rind
1 c. dry low-fat cottage cheese
½ c. plain low-fat yogurt

¼ t. lemon flavoring
¼ c. nonfat, noninstant milk powder
¼ c. ice water
1 T. lemon juice
2 T. sugar
Wheat-free or gluten-free cookie crumbs or toasted coconut

In a double boiler, mix together gelatin, honey, salt, egg yolk, and skim milk. Cook over boiling water, stirring constantly, until gelatin is dissolved and mixture is slightly thickened, about 5 minutes. Add lemon rind. Set aside to cool to room temperature. Thoroughly chill a mixing bowl and beater in refrigerator. Place cottage cheese, yogurt, and lemon flavoring in blender, blending until smooth (or cheese can be forced through a fine sieve). Stir into cooled gelatin mixture and chill while continuing the preparation. In the prechilled bowl, sprinkle milk powder over the ice water. Beat until thickened. Add lemon juice. Continue beating until consistency of whipped cream. Fold into chilled cheese mixture. Beat egg white until frothy. Gradually add sugar. Continue beating until shiny peaks form. Fold into cheese mixture. Sprinkle a 9-inch, slip-bottom pan with cookie crumbs or toasted coconut. Turn mixture into pan. Sprinkle with more crumbs or coconut. Chill until firm, 2–3 hours.

Cherry Cheese Cake

NO CORN, EGG, WHEAT, OR GLUTEN
Servings: 8

1 Crumb Crust (see page 117), baked and cooled
1 8-oz. package cream cheese
2 T. cherry liqueur
6 T. sugar
1 t. lemon juice

1 c. sour cream (if less richness is desired, use sour half and half)
Fresh cherries
1 c. cherry jam (optional)
2–3 T. cherry liqueur (optional)

Make a crumb crust for an 8-inch pan with a removable bottom. Combine cream cheese, the 2 tablespoons cherry liqueur, and the sugar and lemon juice. Beat until smooth. Gradually add sour cream. Beat until smooth, the consistency of whipped cream. Spread over Crumb Crust. Cover and chill as long as 24 hours. Remove rim from pan. Garnish with fresh-stemmed cherries, if available. If you wish, add liqueur to jam and spread on top of cake, or pass in a separate serving bowl.

Variation: For Lemon Cheese Cake, replace cherry liqueur with lemon juice and add 1 T. grated lemon peel. Blueberry jam or marmalade can be substituted for the cherry jam. Add additional flavoring as desired.

Baked Cheese Cake

NO CORN, WHEAT, OR GLUTEN
Servings: 8–10

1 8-oz. package soft cream cheese
2 eggs
⅓ c. honey
2 t. vanilla, divided

1 Crumb Crust in a 9-inch pie pan (see page 117), baked and cooled
1 c. thick sour cream
2 T. sugar

Mash cheese with a fork. Add eggs. Blend in electric mixer until smooth. Very slowly add honey and 1 teaspoon of the vanilla. Blend until honey is completely incorporated. Pour into cooled shell and bake at 300° about

15 minutes. Blend sour cream, sugar, and the remaining vanilla until smooth. Pour over top of cheese cake. Return to oven and bake an additional 5 minutes at 300°. Remove from oven and cool. Chill in refrigerator for 24 hours before serving.

Apple Sponge Cake

NO CORN, MILK, WHEAT, OR GLUTEN*
Servings: 4–6

2 T. peanut flour (see page 15)
⅔ c. brown rice flour, or ⅓
*   c. brown rice flour and ⅓*
*   c. millet flour*
½ t. baking soda
¼ t. nutmeg
¾ t. cinnamon
¼ t. salt

½ c. chopped nuts
1 c. peeled, chopped apple
¼ c. honey
2 T. safflower oil
½ t. vanilla
2 large eggs, separated, at room
*   temperature*

Combine flours, baking soda, spices, salt, nuts, and apple. Stir in honey, oil, and vanilla. Set aside. Beat egg whites until stiff peaks form. Without cleaning beaters, beat yolks until frothy. Fold yolks gently into the whites, then fold egg mixture into flour mixture, very gently. Spoon batter into an oiled 6- or 7-inch-square baking dish. Bake at 350° 30–40 minutes, or until nicely browned and firm to the touch. Serve plain or with a sauce of your choice. Good with Mystery Sauce (page 94).

Variation: If you can have gluten but not wheat, you can substitute a mixture of ⅔ c. barley and oat flour.

SOME CAKE TOPPINGS

Carob Frosting
NO CORN, EGG, WHEAT, OR GLUTEN

2 T. butter
1/3 c. carob chips
2 T. honey
2 T. half and half
1/2 t. vanilla

1/3 c. noninstant, nonfat dry
   milk powder
1/4 c. chopped nuts or
   sunflower seeds

Melt together butter, carob chips, and honey. Cool *completely*. Stir in half and half, vanilla, and milk powder. Beat until smooth. Add nuts. This is sufficient for an 8- or 9-inch-square cake.

Cream Cheese Filling
NO CORN, EGG, WHEAT, OR GLUTEN

1 8-oz. package cream cheese at
   room temperature
1/3 c. sieved and packed
   confectioners sugar
Scant 1/3 c. half and half

1 t. vanilla or lemon juice, or
   1/2 t. almond or rum
   flavoring (or 1 T. thawed
   frozen orange juice and
   enough half and half to make
   1/3 c.)

Beat cheese until smooth and creamy. Gradually add sugar. Mix in half and half and flavoring. Enough for a 9-inch cake.

Creole Frosting

NO CORN, EGG, WHEAT, OR GLUTEN

*4 T. regular or decaffeinated hot
coffee*
*2 c. sieved and packed
confectioners sugar*
½ t. vanilla

¼ t. salt
*2 T. butter or corn-free vegetable
shortening*
*1 oz. bitter chocolate or ¼ c.
carob chips*

Pour coffee over sugar and stir until dissolved. Add vanilla and salt. Melt
butter or shortening and chocolate or carob over hot water. Add to sugar
mixture and beat until smooth and thick enough to spread. Enough for an
8- or 9-inch two-layer cake.

Cream Cheese Icing

NO CORN, EGG, WHEAT, OR GLUTEN

*1 3-oz. package cream cheese at
room temperature*
2½ T. milk
*1½ c. sieved and packed
confectioners sugar*

¼ t. salt
*1 t. vanilla or flavoring of your
choice*

Cream the cheese until soft and smooth. Add the remaining ingredients.
Beat until smooth. Use as a filling or frosting. (Top with chopped nuts if
desired.) Enough for an 8-inch two-layer cake.

Confectioners Icing

NO CORN, EGG, WHEAT, OR GLUTEN

Add 2 T. lemon juice or orange juice, or 2 T. milk or half and half, to
1 c. sifted, packed powdered sugar. (If milk is used, add ½ t. vanilla
or flavoring of your choice.)

Creamy Icing

NO CORN, EGG, WHEAT,* OR GLUTEN*

2 T. corn-free vegetable
  shortening
2 T. butter or margarine
1 T. tapioca flour or arrowroot
¼ t. salt

½ c. milk
3 c. sifted confectioners sugar
½ t. vanilla or flavoring of
  your choice

Melt shortening and butter. Remove from heat. Blend in thickener and salt. Slowly stir in milk. Bring to a boil, stirring constantly. Boil 1 minute. Remove from heat. Stir in the sugar and flavoring. Beat to spreading consistency. (Place pan in ice water while beating to hasten thickening). Enough for a 9-inch two-layer cake.

   *Variation: If you can have wheat or gluten, you can substitute 2½ T. flour for the tapioca flour or arrowroot.

Orange Sauce

NO CORN,* EGG, MILK, WHEAT, OR GLUTEN
Yield: 1¼ cups

2 T. honey
2½ t. arrowroot
1 c. boiling water

2 T. frozen orange juice
  concentrate, thawed
¼ t. grated orange rind

Combine honey and arrowroot in a saucepan. Stir in remaining ingredients. Cook over heat until clear and thickened.

   *Variation: If you can use corn, you can substitute 1 T. cornstarch for the arrowroot.

   Note: Arrowroot cannot be reheated because it loses its thickening consistency.

Cinnamon Sauce

NO CORN, EGG, WHEAT, OR GLUTEN
Yield: 1½ cups

1½ c. water
⅓ c. honey

2 T. butter
½ t. cinnamon

Combine all ingredients in a saucepan. Cook over moderate heat until slightly thickened.

Lemon Sauce

NO CORN,* EGG, MILK,* WHEAT, OR GLUTEN
Yield: 2 cups

½ c. honey
2 T. arrowroot
2 c. boiling water

3 T. lemon juice
1½ t. grated lemon rind
¼ t. salt

Combine honey and arrowroot. Gradually add boiling water. Stir until thoroughly mixed. Cook for 5 minutes, stirring. Remove from heat. Add lemon juice, rind, and salt. Blend thoroughly. Serve hot or cold. (Do not reheat if arrowroot is used.)

Variations: *If you can use corn*, you can substitute 2½ T. cornstarch for the arrowroot.

If you can use milk, add 2 T. melted butter with the lemon juice.

Mystery Sauce

NO CORN, EGG, MILK, WHEAT, OR GLUTEN
Yield: 2 cups

A lovely replacement for whipped cream.

1 c. ground raw cashews   *1 t. lemon juice*
3 medium-sized Delicious apples   *2 T. apple juice*

Grind or whirl the cashew nuts in blender or food processor with steel blade to make 1 cup. Set aside. Peel and core apples and cut into large chunks. Place in blender or food processor with steel blade. Add juices and puree. Add nuts to apple mixture. Blend. Any leftover sauce will freeze nicely.

Fruit Sauce

NO CORN,* EGG, MILK, WHEAT, OR GLUTEN
Yield: 1¾ cups

2 c. fruit juice   *Dash of salt*
2 T. lemon juice   *1½ T. arrowroot*
½ c. honey

Heat 1½ cups of the fruit juice and the lemon juice, honey, and salt in a saucepan. Stir arrowroot into the remaining ½ cup fruit juice. Stir arrowroot mixture into heated fruit juice and cook, stirring, over medium heat until clear and thickened. (Do not reheat if arrowroot is used.)
    *Variation: If you can use corn, you can substitute 2 T. cornstarch for the arrowroot.

Raisin Sauce

NO EGG, MILK, WHEAT, OR GLUTEN

¼ c. honey
1½ T. cornstarch
1 c. orange or apple juice, cider,
  or part juice and part sherry

½ c. plumped raisins

Stir honey and cornstarch together. Stir in liquid. Cook, stirring, over moderate heat until thickened. Add raisins. Serve hot.

Carob Sauce

NO CORN, EGG, WHEAT, OR GLUTEN

1 c. carob chips
Dash of salt
⅓–⅔ c. half and half,
  milk, or coffee

1 t. vanilla
1 T. butter (optional)

Combine carob, salt, and liquid. Heat to boiling and simmer gently, stirring, about 5 minutes. Remove from heat and add vanilla. Serve hot or cold.

Note: For a thick sauce use ⅓ c. liquid. For a thinner sauce, add more liquid as desired. Sauce thickens as it cools, which influences the amount of liquid you may want to add. Butter is optional but is a good addition when coffee is used as the liquid.

COOKIES

	NO CORN	NO EGG	NO MILK	NO WHEAT	NO GLUTEN
Coffee Squares	⊗	⊗	⊗		
Carrot Cookies	⊗		X		
Spicy Date Bars	⊗	X	X		
Shortbread Dainties	X	X		⊗	⊗
Applesauce Cookies	⊗	X	X	⊗	⊗
Chocolate Squares	X		X		
Chocolate Squares with Rice Flour	X		X	X	⊗
No-Bake Peanut Butter-Carob Cookies	X	X		X	X
Carob Delights	X	X		⊗	⊗
Apple-Coffee Cookies	X	X	X		
Ginger Cookies	X	X	X	⊗	⊗
Butterscotch Confections	X			X	
Oat Pastries	X	X	X		
Honey-Oatmeal Cookies	⊗	X	X		
Oatmeal-Fruit Cookies	⊗	⊗	X		
Peanut Butter Chewies	⊗	X		X	X
Peanut Butter Cookies	⊗		X		

⊗ means that the recipe includes instructions for adding that ingredient if allowed.

	NO CORN	NO EGG	NO MILK	NO WHEAT	NO GLUTEN
Refrigerator Peanut Butter Balls	X	X		⊗	X
Fruit Cake Cookie Cups	X		X		
Mixed Fruit Cookies	⊗			X	
Date-Nut Squares	⊗			X	
Banana Cookies	⊗	X	X		
Oatmeal Crisps		X		⊗	
Oat Shortbread	X	X	⊗	X	
Ginger Oatmeal Cookies	X		X		
Whole Wheat Cookies	⊗	⊗	⊗		
Spicy Cookies	X	X	X		

Coffee Squares

NO CORN,* EGG,* OR MILK*

Yield: 2–2½ dozen small squares

½ c. corn-free margarine or
   corn-free vegetable shortening
   (see page 13)
½ c. honey
1 t. vanilla
1 c. whole wheat flour
⅔ c. unbleached flour
½ t. soda

½ t. cinnamon
½ t. nutmeg
1½ t. arrowroot baking
   powder (see page 13)
½ t. salt
1 t. instant coffee
½ c. raisins
½ c. sunflower seeds

GLAZE (optional):
1⅓ c. sifted confectioners sugar
½ t. instant coffee
4 t. hot water

4 t. honey
½ c. chopped nuts (optional)

Cream together shortening, honey, and vanilla. Mix together dry ingredients. Stir into shortening mixture until well blended. Stir in raisins and

seeds. Pour into a greased and floured 9 × 13-inch pan. Bake at 350°
15–20 minutes, or until a toothpick inserted in center comes out clean.
Cool 5 minutes, and, if you wish, spread with glaze. To make a glaze,
combine all ingredients except nuts. Stir until smooth. Stir in nuts, if
desired. Finish cooling and cut into squares.

Variations: *If you can use corn*, you can substitute 1 t. regular baking
powder for the arrowroot baking powder.

If you can use egg, beat 1 egg into the shortening mixture and decrease
arrowroot baking powder to ¾ t. or regular baking powder to ½ t.

If you can use milk, you can substitute butter for the margarine or
shortening.

Carrot Cookies

NO CORN* OR MILK
Yield: 3 dozen

½ c. boiling water
½ c. raisins
2 T. safflower oil
2 T. corn-free vegetable
   shortening (see page 13)
½ c. honey
2 eggs
1 t. lemon extract
½ c. finely shredded raw
   carrot

1 c. whole wheat flour
½ c. unbleached flour
3 t. arrowroot baking powder
   (see page 13)
½ t. salt
2 T. wheat germ
2 T. sunflower seeds

Pour boiling water over raisins and let stand 5 minutes. Drain. Save water
for another use in making bread. Cream together oil and shortening. Beat
in honey, eggs, and extract. Stir in carrots and raisins. Combine dry
ingredients. Add to carrot mixture. Blend well. Drop by teaspoonfuls onto
a greased baking sheet. Bake at 375° 10–15 minutes.

Variation: *If you can use corn*, you can substitute 2 t. regular baking
powder for the arrowroot baking powder.

Spicy Date Bars

NO CORN,* EGG, OR MILK
Yield: 16 squares

⅔ c. honey
⅓ c. safflower oil
1¼ c. water
2 c. chopped dates
1 c. sifted whole wheat flour
1 c. sifted unbleached flour
½ t. salt
1½ t. arrowroot baking
  powder (see page 13)

1 t. baking soda
2 t. cinnamon
½ t. nutmeg
¼ t. ground cloves
½ c. chopped nuts or
  sunflower seeds

Combine honey, oil, water, and dates in a large saucepan. Bring to a boil and boil 3 minutes. Remove from heat and cool. Combine dry ingredients except nuts or seeds. Stir into cooled mixture. Blend well. Stir in nuts or seeds. Spread evenly in a greased and floured 7 × 12-inch pan or 9-inch-square pan. Bake at 350° 40–50 minutes, or until a toothpick inserted in the center comes out clean. Cool. Frost if desired (see pages 90–91). Store in tightly covered pan.

Variation: If you can use corn, you can substitute 1 t. regular baking powder for the arrowroot baking powder.

Shortbread Dainties

NO CORN, EGG, WHEAT,* OR GLUTEN*
Yield: 2½–3 dozen

½ c. butter
2 T. confectioners sugar
1 t. vanilla
½ c. potato flour (see page 15)

½ c. arrowroot
1 c. finely chopped nuts
Confectioners sugar

Cream together the butter and sugar. Add vanilla and stir until light and fluffy. Combine potato flour and arrowroot and blend into butter mixture.

Stir in the nuts. Form into a roll about 1 inch in diameter. Wrap in waxed paper and chill 1 hour. Cut into ½-inch slices; cut again into bite-sized pieces. Place on an ungreased cookie sheet. Bake at 300° 30–40 minutes, until lightly browned. Remove from pan and roll in confectioners sugar to coat. Let cool.

Variations: If you can use wheat and gluten, use 1 c. unbleached flour instead of the potato flour and arrowroot.

If you can use gluten but not wheat, substitute ½ c. barley flour and ¼ c. each potato flour and arrowroot.

Applesauce Cookies

NO CORN,* EGG, MILK, WHEAT,* OR GLUTEN*
Yield: 5 dozen

½ c. corn-free vegetable
    shortening (see page 13)
½ c. honey
1 c. tart applesauce (1½ t.
    lemon juice or vinegar can be
    added)
½ c. arrowroot
1¾ c. brown rice flour, or 1
    cup millet or garbanzo flour
    and ¾ c. brown rice flour

1¼ t. arrowroot baking
    powder (see page 13)
¼ t. baking soda
¼ t. ground cloves
¼ t. nutmeg
½ t. salt
1 t. cinnamon
1 c. chopped nuts or seeds
1 c. raisins

Cream together the shortening and honey. Add applesauce. Combine dry ingredients. Stir into applesauce mixture. Add nuts and raisins. Drop by teaspoonfuls onto a lightly greased cookie sheet. Bake at 400° about 10 minutes, or until lightly browned.

Variations: If you can use corn, you can substitute 1 t. regular baking powder for the arrowroot baking powder and ½ c. cornstarch for the arrowroot.

If you can use wheat and gluten, use 1⅛ c. whole wheat flour and 1⅛ c. unbleached flour instead of brown rice flour and omit arrowroot or cornstarch.

If you can use gluten but not wheat, you can use a mixture of barley and oat flour.

Chocolate Squares

NO CORN OR MILK
Yield: 20 squares

2 1-oz. squares unsweetened
    chocolate
½ c. safflower oil
2 eggs
¼ c. sugar

2 T. honey
½ t. vanilla
¼ t. salt
½ c. unbleached flour
½ c. chopped nuts

Place chocolate and oil into a small pan. Heat over low heat until chocolate is melted. Set aside. Beat eggs until light, adding sugar, honey, vanilla, and salt. Beat chocolate mixture into egg mixture. Stir in flour and nuts. Spread into a greased and floured 13 × 9-inch pan. Sprinkle with more chopped nuts if desired. Bake at 400° 15–20 minutes, or until a toothpick inserted in the center comes out clean. Cool slightly and cut into squares. Makes a wafer-type brownie.

Chocolate Squares with Rice Flour

NO CORN, MILK, WHEAT, OR GLUTEN*

Substitute ½ c. brown rice flour, or ¼ c. brown rice flour and ¼ c. millet or garbanzo flour, for the unbleached flour, and add ½ t. regular baking powder or ¾ t. arrowroot baking powder.

Proceed as for Chocolate Squares recipe above.

*Variation: If you can have gluten but not wheat, substitute ½ c. mixed barley and oat flour.

No-Bake Peanut Butter-Carob Cookies

NO CORN, EGG, WHEAT, OR GLUTEN
Yield: 12–16

Children of all ages love them.

½ c. honey
2 T. butter
2 T. milk
2 T. carob chips
⅓ c. chunky peanut butter

1½ t. vanilla
1¾–2 c. minute oats
Carob powder, sesame seeds, or
coconut

Combine honey, butter, milk, and carob in a saucepan. Bring to a full boil, stirring. Remove from heat. Stir in peanut butter, vanilla, and oats. Blend completely. The mixture should be stiff enough to handle. Using two teaspoons or your fingers, shape into balls. Place on waxed paper. Cool. Roll in carob powder, sesame seeds, or coconut.

Carob Delights

NO CORN, EGG, WHEAT,* OR GLUTEN*
Yield: 16 squares

½ c. carob powder
½ c. honey
½ c. peanut butter
¾ c. raw sunflower seeds

½ c. brown sesame seeds
½ c. chopped nuts or
unsweetened coconut

Combine all ingredients except nuts or coconut in food processor with steel blade. Whirl until well blended. (If you don't have a food processor, combine in batches in a blender and work together in a bowl.) Press into an 8- or 9-inch-square pan. Press in nuts or coconut. Cut into squares.

*Variation: If you can use wheat and gluten, decrease sunflower seeds to ½ c. and add ¼ c. raw wheat germ.

Apple-Coffee Cookies

NO CORN, EGG, OR MILK
Yield: 3 dozen

2 c. whole wheat flour
1 t. baking soda
¼ t. salt
2 c. peeled, cored, finely chopped apples
1 c. strong coffee
½ c. honey

1 c. raisins or chopped dates
1 t. cinnamon
¼ t. allspice
¾ t. nutmeg
⅓ c. safflower oil
1 t. vanilla
1 c. chopped nuts or seeds

Combine flour, baking soda, and salt. Set aside. Combine remaining ingredients except vanilla and nuts or seeds in a saucepan. Cover and simmer until apples are tender. Remove from heat. Cool. Add vanilla. Blend flour mixture into apple mixture. Add nuts or seeds. Drop by heaping teaspoonfuls onto an ungreased baking sheet. Bake at 375° about 12 minutes. Remove to wire racks to cool. These are very moist cookies and should be kept refrigerated or frozen if not used quickly.

Ginger Cookies

NO CORN, EGG, MILK, WHEAT,* OR GLUTEN*
Yield: 2½–3 dozen

½ c. safflower oil
½ c. molasses
⅓ c. honey†
1 t. ground ginger
¼ t. salt
1 t. baking soda, dissolved in 1 T. hot water

2⅔–3 c. brown rice flour, or 1 c. brown rice flour, 1 c. millet flour, and ⅔–1 c. garbanzo flour

Combine oil, molasses, honey, ginger, and salt in a saucepan. Stir to mix. Bring to a boil. Immediately remove from heat. Add baking soda dissolved in hot water immediately. While foaming, add flour. The dough should ball in the pan and be stiff enough to make into a roll on waxed paper. Slice ¼ inch thick and put onto a lightly greased cookie sheet. Bake at 350° about 10 minutes, or until lightly browned (*do not overcook*).

Variations: *If you can use wheat and gluten*, you can substitute wheat flour for the brown rice flour.

If you can use gluten but not wheat, you can substitute a mixture of barley and oat flour.

†For a less sweet cookie, use ¼ c. honey.

Butterscotch Confections

NO CORN OR WHEAT
Yield: 2 dozen

2 eggs
2 T. safflower oil
1 T. molasses
⅔ c. honey
2 t. vanilla
⅔ c. peanut flour (see page 15)

½ c. noninstant, nonfat milk powder
⅛ t. salt
3 T. oat flour (see page 15)
½ c. chopped walnuts

Beat eggs until light and thick. Add oil, molasses, honey, and vanilla. Combine dry ingredients and nuts in a bowl. Stir egg mixture into dry mixture. Spread evenly in a well-greased 9 × 12-inch pan. Bake at 350° about 30 minutes, or just until surface is firm to the touch. Cool on a wire rack before cutting.

Oat Pastries

NO CORN, EGG, OR MILK
Yield: 3 dozen

⅔ c. honey
½ c. corn-free vegetable
  shortening (see page 13)
½ c. safflower oil
1 t. vanilla
1 c. whole wheat flour
1 c. unbleached flour

¾ t. baking soda
1 t. salt*
2 T. water
3 c. quick or regular oats
1 c. unsalted sunflower seeds or
  chopped nuts

Cream together honey, shortening, and oil. Add vanilla. Sift together the flours, baking soda, and salt. Add flour mixture to creamed mixture. Add water, oats, and seeds. Work into a stiff dough. Separate into four parts. Refrigerate about 2 hours, or until well chilled. Roll out each fourth onto a floured board to ⅛-inch thickness. Cut into 3-inch squares. Place close together on an ungreased cookie sheet. Bake at 400° about 6 minutes, or until golden. Remove from pan and cool on wire rack.

*If seeds are salted, cut salt to ½ tsp.

Honey-Oatmeal Cookies

NO CORN,* EGG, OR MILK
Yield: 4 dozen

½ c. corn-free vegetable
  shortening (see page 13)
½ c. safflower oil
½ c. honey
2 t. vanilla
½ c. chopped raisins
½ c. chopped nuts or
  sunflower seeds
1 c. whole wheat flour

1 c. unbleached flour
¾ t. salt
¾ t. arrowroot baking powder
  (see page 13)
½ t. cinnamon
½ t. nutmeg
⅛ t. ground cloves
1 c. quick or regular oats

Cream together shortening, oil, and honey. Blend in vanilla, raisins, and nuts or seeds. Combine all dry ingredients, mixing thoroughly. Add the flour mixture to the creamed mixture. Blend well. Drop by teaspoonfuls onto a greased cookie sheet. Bake at 350° 10–12 minutes. Remove to wire rack to cool.

Variation: *If you can use corn*, you can substitute ½ t. regular baking powder for the arrowroot baking powder.

Oatmeal-Fruit Cookies

NO CORN,* EGG,* OR MILK
Yield: 4 dozen

¼ c. corn-free vegetable
  shortening (see page 13)
¼ c. safflower oil
⅔ c. honey
1 t. vanilla
1 c. whole wheat flour less 1 T.
¾ t. arrowroot baking powder
  (see page 13)
½ t. salt
½ t. baking soda
2 T. toasted wheat germ
1 c. rolled oats
½ c. chopped nuts or seeds, or
  a mixture
½ c. raisins
½ c. chopped dates

In electric mixer, cream the shortening, oil, and honey. Add vanilla. Beat until well blended. Combine flour, baking powder, salt, and baking soda. Add to creamed mixture. Blend well. Stir in wheat germ, oats, nuts or seeds, raisins, and dates. Blend thoroughly. Drop by teaspoonfuls about 2 inches apart on a greased baking sheet. Bake at 325° 8–10 minutes, or until brown. Cool on a wire rack.

Store in an airtight container.

Variations: *If you can use corn*, you can substitute ¾ t. regular baking powder for the arrowroot baking powder.

If you can use egg, add 1 egg with vanilla to the shortening mixture, decrease arrowroot baking powder to ¾ t. or regular baking powder to ½ t. and increase flour 1 T.

Peanut Butter Chewies

NO CORN,* EGG, WHEAT, OR GLUTEN
Yield: 2 dozen

1 c. peanut butter
½ c. brown sugar
2 T. honey

¼ c. undiluted evaporated
   milk
2½ t. arrowroot

Blend together all ingredients. Drop by teaspoonfuls onto an ungreased cookie sheet. Bake at 325° about 15 minutes (*don't overcook*). Cool 1–2 minutes on cookie sheet. Remove to a wire rack to finish cooling.

   Variations: If you can use corn, you can substitute 5 t. cornstarch for the arrowroot.

   Carob or chocolate chips can be added if allowed.

Peanut Butter Cookies

NO CORN* OR MILK
Yield: 2 dozen

¼ c. safflower oil
¾ c. honey
1 egg
¾ c. peanut butter
2 t. orange juice or water
½ t. vanilla

1⅔ c. whole wheat flour,
   sifted
1¼ t. arrowroot baking
   powder (see page 13)
¾ t. salt

Blend together oil, honey, and egg. Blend in peanut butter, orange juice, and vanilla. Mix in flour, baking powder, and salt. Shape into small balls and flatten with a fork dipped in flour. Bake on a greased cookie sheet at 350° 10 minutes, or until firm. Remove to wire rack to cool.

   Variation: If you can use corn, you can substitute 1 t. regular baking powder for the arrowroot baking powder.

Refrigerator Peanut Butter Balls

NO CORN, EGG, WHEAT,* OR GLUTEN
Yield: 12–16

1 c. chunky peanut butter
1 c. powdered dry milk
1 c. honey

Finely chopped sunflower seeds
or nuts, carob powder, or
coconut

Combine all ingredients. Mix well and roll into balls. Roll in seeds, nuts, carob, or coconut. Keep in refrigerator.

 *Variation: If you can use wheat, wheat cereal crumbs can be used for rolling the balls.

Fruit Cake Cookie Cups

NO CORN OR MILK
Yield: 1–1½ dozen

1 egg
3 T. safflower oil
¼ c. honey
½ t. vanilla
¾ c. combined whole wheat
 and unbleached flour
1 t. baking soda
⅛ t. allspice

⅛ t. ground cloves
⅛ t. nutmeg
⅛ t. cinnamon
¼ c. chopped sunflower seeds
½ c. chopped nuts
1 c. chopped moist dried fruit
 (raisins, dates, dried apricots,
 etc., or a mixture)

In small bowl of electric mixer, beat egg until thick and lemon colored. With mixer at high speed, slowly add the oil, then the honey and vanilla. Combine flour, baking soda, and spices. Stir half of flour mixture into creamed mixture. Combine the rest with the seeds, nuts, and fruit. Add to creamed mixture and blend well. Spoon batter into small paper baking cups, about 2 teaspoonfuls a cup, and place about 1 inch apart on a baking sheet, or drop by teaspoonfuls about 2 inches apart onto a lightly greased baking sheet. Bake at 300° 17–20 minutes, or until center springs back when touched. Cool on a wire rack.

Mixed Fruit Cookies

NO CORN* OR WHEAT
Yield: 3–3½ dozen

2 eggs
½ c. safflower oil
½ c. honey
1 t. vanilla
1 c. brown rice flour
½ c. oat flour (see page 15)
½ c. nonfat, noninstant milk
   powder

¾ t. salt
2 T. arrowroot
⅓ c. ground raw sunflower seeds
½ c. mixed dried fruit, finely
   chopped

In small bowl of electric mixer, beat eggs at high speed until thick and lemon colored. Slowly add oil, honey, and vanilla. Combine dry ingredients including seeds. Dredge fruit with the flour so it will be covered and separated. By hand, stir the flour into the egg mixture, blending well. Drop by teaspoonfuls onto a lightly greased cookie sheet. Bake at 350° about 15 minutes, or until edges are slightly browned and cookies are firm. Cool on a wire rack.

   *Variation: If you can use corn, you can substitute 2½ T. cornstarch for the arrowroot.

Date-Nut Squares

NO CORN,* OR WHEAT
Yield: 12–16 squares

½ c. brown rice flour
½ c. oat flour (see page 15)
¼ t. salt
2 eggs
½ c. carob powder
½ c. safflower oil

⅓ c. honey
1 t. vanilla
1 c. chopped dates
¼ c. ground almonds
½ c. chopped nuts

Combine flours and salt. Set aside. Beat eggs well. Combine carob and oil and add to eggs. Gradually stir in honey. Add vanilla. Stir in flour mixture. Combine dates, ground almonds, and nuts. Stir into egg mixture. Pour into a well-greased 8-inch-square pan. Bake at 325° 25–30 minutes, or until a toothpick inserted in the center comes out clean. Cool on a wire rack. Cut into squares.

Variations: *For a milk-free recipe, if you can use corn*, substitute ½ c. cocoa for the carob powder. *For milk-free and corn-free*, use ½ c. chocolate chips melted with the oil and cooled. Decrease flour by ½ T.

Banana Cookies

NO CORN,* EGG, OR MILK
Yield: 4 dozen

When bananas suddenly get too ripe too fast, this is a very good way to salvage them.

¼ c. chunky peanut butter
¼ c. corn-free vegetable shortening (see page 13)
½ c. honey
2 t. vinegar
1 c. mashed bananas (2–3 medium bananas)
1 c. whole wheat flour
1 c. unbleached flour

¼ c. raw wheat germ
1¼ t. arrowroot baking powder (see page 13)
½ t. baking soda
½ t. salt
1 t. cinnamon
1 c. chopped nuts, seeds, or raisins

Cream together peanut butter, shortening, and honey. Mix vinegar into mashed banana. Add to creamed mixture. Mix dry ingredients. Stir into banana mixture. Add nuts. Drop by teaspoonfuls onto a lightly greased cookie sheet. Bake at 375° about 10 minutes, or until lightly browned. Cool on a wire rack.

Variation: If you can use corn, you can substitute 1 t. regular baking powder for the arrowroot baking powder.

Oatmeal Crisps

NO EGG OR WHEAT*
Yield: 12–16

These are much like lace cookies. The batter is very thin.

5 T. butter
2 T. brown sugar
2 T. honey
2 T. light corn syrup
2 T. evaporated milk

½ c. regular or quick oats
½ c. brown rice flour
½ t. regular baking powder
⅛ t. salt

Melt butter in a heavy pan over moderate heat. Add sugar and honey. Stir until bubbly and blended. Remove from heat. Add remaining ingredients. Combine well. Drop by teaspoonfuls well apart on a greased baking sheet. Bake at 400° 7–8 minutes, or until edges are browned. Cool on sheet for 2–3 minutes. Transfer to a wire rack to finish cooling.

*Variations: If you can use wheat, you can substitute ⅓ c. whole wheat flour for the brown rice flour and decrease baking powder to ¼ t.

If you can use gluten but not wheat, you can use a ⅓ c. mixture of barley and oat flour.

Oat Shortbread

NO CORN, EGG, MILK,* OR WHEAT
Yield: 32 wedges

½ c. corn-free vegetable
   shortening (see page 13)
⅓ c. honey
½ t. vanilla

1½ c. plus 1 T. oat flour (see
   page 15)
¾ t. salt

Cream together shortening and honey. Add vanilla. Gradually add oat flour and salt. It will make a crumbly mixture. Press into a ball. Divide into four parts. On a lightly floured board, roll each fourth into a circle about 6 inches in diameter. Place circles about 4 inches apart on a lightly greased baking sheet. With a sharp knife, cut each circle into 8 wedges. Bake at 350° about 15 minutes, or until lightly browned. Carefully remove to wire rack to cool.

Variation: *If you can use milk*, you can use butter to replace all or part of the vegetable shortening.

Ginger Oatmeal Cookies

NO CORN OR MILK
Yield: 4 dozen

½ c. corn-free vegetable
  shortening (see page 13)
¼ c. safflower oil
½ c. honey
1 egg
¼ c. molasses
1½ c. whole wheat flour

2 t. baking soda
½ t. salt
1 t. cinnamon
¾ t. ground ginger
¼ t. ground cloves
2 c. rolled oats

Cream together shortening, oil, and honey. Beat in egg and molasses. Sift together all dry ingredients except oats. Stir into shortening mixture. Stir in oats. Blend all together. Drop by teaspoonfuls onto a lightly greased cookie sheet about 3 inches apart. Bake at 350° about 8 minutes, or until browned. Let cool on pan about 1 minute, then remove to a wire rack.

Whole Wheat Cookies

NO CORN,* EGG,* OR MILK*
Yield: 2½ dozen

¼ c. safflower oil
¼ c. corn-free vegetable
  shortening (see page 13)
⅔ c. honey
1¾ c. whole wheat flour
1 t. arrowroot baking powder (see
  page 13)

2 T. wheat germ
½ t. cinnamon
½ t. nutmeg
¼ t. salt

Cream oil, shortening, and honey together thoroughly in small bowl of electric mixer. Beat until light. Combine remaining ingredients. Stir into creamed mixture until well blended. Drop by teaspoonfuls onto an ungreased baking sheet. Bake at 350° 10–12 minutes, or until lightly browned. Cool on a wire rack.

Variations: *If you can use corn*, you can substitute ¾ t. regular baking powder for the arrowroot baking powder.

If you can use egg, beat one egg into the creamed mixture, increase the flour by 2 T., and omit the baking powder.

If you can use milk, you can substitute butter for the shortening.

Spicy Cookies

NO CORN, EGG, OR MILK
Yield: 2½–3 dozen

2 c. plus 2 T. whole wheat pastry
　flour
¼ t. ground ginger
¼ t. nutmeg
¼ t. cinnamon
¼ t. allspice
½ t. salt
¼ c. firmly packed brown
　sugar

2 T. honey
¼ c. safflower oil
½ c. molasses
½ t. baking soda
½ c. tart applesauce (1–2 t.
　lemon juice or vinegar can be
　added)

Combine flour, spices, salt, and sugar in a mixing bowl. Combine honey, oil, and molasses. Stir into flour mixture. Stir baking soda into applesauce. When it foams, stir into flour mixture. Blend well. The batter should be firm enough to use a teaspoon to drop onto cookie sheet. The appearance should be dry. (Since the consistency of applesauce varies, it may be necessary to add more flour.) Using two teaspoons, drop dough onto a greased cookie sheet. Bake at 350° about 15 minutes, or until tops are firm to the touch. Remove to a wire rack to cool.

PIES

	NO CORN	NO EGG	NO MILK	NO WHEAT	NO GLUTEN
Wheat Germ Pie Crust	X	X	⊗		
Whole Wheat Pie Crust	X	X	X		
Crumb Crust	X	X	⊗	⊗	⊗
Almond Pie Crust	X	X	⊗	X	
Barley and Oat Pie Crust	X	X	X	X	
Brown Rice Pie Crust	⊗		X	X	X
Cream Cheese Pastry	X	X			
Cranberry Pie		X		X	X
Harvest Pie	X	X	⊗	⊗	⊗
Banana Coffee Cream Pie	X	X		X	X
Coffee Cream Nut Pie	X	X		X	X
Raisin Pie	⊗	X	X	X	X
Fresh Pear Pie	X	X	X	X	X
Apple and Mincemeat Pie	X	X		X	X
Tofu Mincemeat Pie	X	X	X	X	X
Tofu Pineapple Cream Pie	X	X	X	X	X
Tofu Pumpkin Pie	X	X	X	X	X
Tofu Carob Pie	X			X	X
Tofu Cocoa Pie			X	X	X
Tofu Chocolate Pie	X		X	X	X
No-Bake Tofu Carob Pie	X	X		X	X

⊗ means that the recipe includes instructions for adding that ingredient if allowed.

115

PIE CRUSTS

Wheat Germ Pie Crust

NO CORN, EGG, OR MILK*
Yield: One 9-inch crust

½ c. wheat germ
½ c. whole wheat flour
⅛ t. salt
⅓ t. cinnamon

2 T. corn-free vegetable
  shortening (see page 13)
1 T. safflower oil
½ t. vinegar
1 T. ice water

Combine wheat germ, flour, salt, and cinnamon. Cut shortening into mixture. Add vinegar and oil to water. Stir into flour mixture. Press into a lightly oiled 9-inch pie plate. *For a no-bake filling*, bake at 325° 6–8 minutes, or until golden. *If filling is to be baked*, do not prebake crust.

*Variation: *If you can use milk*, substitute butter for shortening.

Whole Wheat Pie Crust

NO CORN, EGG, OR MILK
Yield: One 9-inch crust

If you are not ready for a 100 percent whole wheat crust, use half unbleached flour.

1⅓ c. whole wheat pastry
  flour
⅓ t. salt
½ c. chilled corn-free
  vegetable shortening (see
  page 13)

1 t. white vinegar
4 T. ice water

Combine flour and salt. Cut in shortening. Add vinegar to water. Sprinkle water over flour mixture to make a ball, working with hands if necessary. Chill. Roll out on a lightly floured pastry cloth or between two pieces of waxed paper dusted with flour. Press into a 9-inch pie plate and prick with a fork. *For a no-bake filling*, bake at 400° 10–12 minutes. *If filling is to be baked*, prebake 5 minutes.

Crumb Crust

NO CORN, EGG, MILK,* WHEAT,* OR GLUTEN*
Yield: One 8-inch crust

Oatmeal Crisps (see page 112) can be used to make wheat-free crumbs; Ginger Cookies (see page 104) for gluten-free. Graham crackers are good wheat crackers to use for crumbs.

1⅓ c. wheat-free, gluten-free crumbs (from cookies, cereals, or crackers)

⅓ c. melted corn-free margarine or corn-free vegetable shortening (see page 13)

Add melted shortening to crumbs and mix well. Pat firmly and evenly into 8-inch pie plate. Chill for several hours or bake at 350° 8–10 minutes (baking gives a firmer texture).

*Variations: *If you can use milk*, you can substitute butter for the margarine or shortening.

If you can use wheat and gluten, you can use wheat crumbs.

Almond Pie Crust

NO CORN, EGG, MILK,* OR WHEAT
Yield: One 9-inch crust

1 c. almond meal (see page 15)
⅔ c. oat flour (see page 15)
2 T. corn-free vegetable shortening (see page 13)

1 T. safflower oil
1 T. honey
2–3 T. ice water

Combine almond meal and oat flour. Cut in shortening. Add oil, honey, and ice water. Blend. Pat into a lightly oiled 9-inch pie plate. Bake at 400° 8–10 minutes for unbaked filling. (Do not prebake if filling is to be baked.)

*Variation: *If you can use milk*, substitute butter for shortening.

Barley and Oat Pie Crust

NO CORN, EGG, MILK, OR WHEAT
Yield: One 9-inch crust

This wheat-free but not gluten-free crust is easier to handle than the Brown Rice Pie Crust recipe (below). It is very good.

1 c. barley flour
⅔ c. oat flour (see page 15)
½ t. salt
4 T. corn-free vegetable
  shortening (see page 13)

1 T. safflower oil
4 T. ice water

Combine flours and salt. Cut in shortening. Combine and stir in oil and ice water. Form into a ball. Press into a 9-inch pie pan that has been lightly brushed with oil. (Roll out on pastry cloth first if you wish.) Bake at 400° 10–12 minutes for unbaked filling. (Do not prebake for a baked filling.)

Brown Rice Pie Crust

NO CORN,* MILK, WHEAT, OR GLUTEN
Yield: Two 9-inch pie shells, or one double crust

This gluten-free grain crust is difficult to handle. For that reason, the crumb or almond crust is preferable if compatible with your filling. If gluten is not a problem, the Barley and Oat Crust is definitely better.

¾ c. brown rice flour
1 c. millet flour
½ t. salt
2½ t. arrowroot baking
  powder (see page 13)

4 T. arrowroot
½ c. corn-free vegetable
  shortening (see page 13)
1 egg
Sugar (optional)

Combine flours, salt, baking powder, and arrowroot. Mix thoroughly. Cut in shortening. Beat egg and stir into mixture. No other liquid is used. Pat into a ball. Divide in two. This crust is very tender and cannot be picked up or treated like a regular pie crust without breaking. Roll pastry between two sheets of floured waxed paper. Carefully remove top sheet of paper. Place pie plate over crust and lift waxed paper, flipping crust onto pie plate. If the edges break, they can be pressed together again. If you like, sprinkle crust with sugar. Chill before baking. Bake at 425° about 10 minutes, or until delicately browned for unbaked filling. (Do not prebake if filling is to be baked.)

Variations: *If you can use corn*, use 2 t. regular baking powder instead of the arrowroot baking powder and 3 T. cornstarch instead of the arrowroot.

For egg-free, add 4–5 T. water instead of the egg.

Cream Cheese Pastry

NO CORN OR EGG

1 3-oz. package cream cheese, at room temperature
½ c. butter

1 c. unbleached flour
¼ c. sugar

Cream together cheese and butter. Add flour and sugar and blend well. Chill at least 2 hours.

For Cookies: **Yield: 1½ dozen**
Roll chilled dough to ¼-inch thickness on a lightly floured board. Sprinkle with sugar and cinnamon. Place on an ungreased cookie sheet. Bake at 350° about 15 minutes. Cool on wire rack.

For Tarts: **Yield: 12 tart cups**
Roll chilled dough to about ¼-inch thickness on a lightly floured board. Cut into circles to fit miniature muffin tins. Chill again before filling with filling of your choice, which can be anything from a meat to a pie filling. Bake at 350° 15–20 minutes until filling is done and crust is golden.

For Hors d'Oeuvres: **Yield: 12–16 pieces**
Omit sugar from pastry. Roll chilled dough to ¼-inch thickness on a lightly floured board. Cut into 2-inch squares. Place a spoonful of meat, cheese, mushroom, or other filling toward one corner. Fold pastry over, sealing edges. Bake at 350° 15–18 minutes. (For a meat filling, see Steamed Chinese Dumplings, page 204.)

PIE FILLINGS

Cranberry Pie

NO EGG, WHEAT, OR GLUTEN
Yield: Filling for one 9- or 10-inch pie crust

This is best served the day it is made.

½ t. plain gelatin
¾ c. evaporated milk, divided
¼ c. noninstant, nonfat milk
   powder
1 T. lemon juice

1 16-oz. can whole cranberry
   sauce
2 T. honey
¼ t. almond or orange extract
¼ c. chopped nuts (optional)

Put bowl and beater in refrigerator to chill thoroughly. Add gelatin to ¼ cup of the evaporated milk. Let sit for 5 minutes. Heat gently to dissolve gelatin. Slowly stir into remaining milk. Partially freeze. Whip the milk-gelatin mixture in a small, chilled bowl until partially thickened. Add milk powder and lemon juice. Whip until very stiff. Set aside. Mash the cranberry sauce with a fork. Add honey. Gradually spoon into the whipped milk, still beating in mixer. Add extract and chopped nuts. Spoon into a prepared 9- or 10-inch pie crust of your choice (see pages 116–19). Chill thoroughly.

Variation: For corn-free Cranberry Pie, use homemade cranberry sauce.

Harvest Pie

NO CORN, EGG, MILK,* WHEAT,* OR GLUTEN*
Yield: Filling for one 9-inch pie crust

This pie is very filling. It can be served plain, or with whipped cream or ice cream if milk is allowed. It is delicious if the wheat germ topping is allowed (see Variations).

1¾ c. unsweetened applesauce
1 c. chopped dates
½ c. seedless raisins
½ c. chopped, dried peaches
½ c. chopped, dried apricots
2–3 T. honey

2 T. grated lemon rind
1 c. chopped walnuts or a
mixture of chopped nuts and
chopped sunflower seeds
½ T. safflower oil

Combine applesauce, fruit, honey, and lemon rind in a saucepan. Simmer, uncovered, over low heat, stirring frequently, about 15 minutes. It should be very thick. Cool. Pour into an unbaked 9-inch pie crust of your choice (see pages 116–19). Sprinkle nuts over fruit. Bake at 375° 30 minutes, or until crust is baked and top is lightly browned.

Variations: If you can use milk, you can substitute 1 T. melted butter for the oil.

If you can use wheat and gluten, you can substitute ½ c. raw wheat germ for ½ c. of the nuts and add ½ T. safflower oil or 1 T. melted butter.

Prunes and dried figs are alternatives if peaches and apricots are unavailable or excessively expensive. They have more natural sugar than peaches and apricots and will take less honey.

Note: The quality of the dried fruit will determine the quality of the pie. Heavily sulfured or overly dry fruit will not be as good. Serve plain or with whipped cream or ice cream if allowed.

Banana Coffee Cream Pie

NO CORN, EGG, WHEAT, OR GLUTEN
Yield: Filling for one 8-inch pie crust

Be sure to chill mixer bowl and beaters in making these cream pie recipes.

1½ t. plain gelatin
1 5-oz. can evaporated milk,
    divided
2 t. regular or decaffeinated
    instant coffee
⅛ t. salt

¼ c. noninstant, nonfat
    powdered milk
¼ c. confectioners sugar
¼ t. vanilla
1–2 bananas

Pour gelatin into 2 tablespoons of the milk. Let sit for 5 minutes. Add coffee. Over low heat, stir until gelatin and coffee are dissolved. Stir in 2 more tablespoons milk and the salt. Stir until it is very smooth. Stir in remainder of milk. Pour into an icecube tray or a shallow pan. Place in freezer until nearly set. Remove from freezer. Beat at medium speed of electric mixer until almost doubled in bulk. Gradually add milk powder, sugar, and vanilla. Beat at high speed until stiff and more than doubled in bulk. Slice one large or two small bananas into a prebaked 8-inch pie crust of your choice (see pages 116–19). Cover with coffee filling. Chill for several hours before serving. (Serve same day it is made.)

Coffee Cream Nut Pie

NO CORN, EGG, WHEAT, OR GLUTEN
Yield: Filling for one 9-inch pie crust

1 T. plain gelatin
1½ c. evaporated milk, divided
2 T. regular or decaffeinated
    instant coffee
¼ t. salt

½ c. noninstant, nonfat dry
    milk powder
½ c. powdered sugar
½ t. vanilla
½ c. chopped nuts

Pour gelatin into 3 tablespoons of evaporated milk. Let sit 5 minutes. Add coffee. Over low heat, stir until gelatin and coffee are dissolved. Stir in

2 tablespoons of the evaporated milk and the salt. Stir until it is very smooth. Stir in remainder of milk. Pour into an icecube tray or shallow pan. Place in freezer until nearly set. Remove from freezer. Beat at medium speed of electric mixer until almost doubled in bulk. Gradually add milk powder, sugar, and vanilla. Beat at high speed until stiff and more than doubled in bulk. Stir in chopped nuts. Spoon into a prebaked 9-inch pie crust of your choice (see pages 116–119). Chill several hours before serving. Sprinkle more nuts on top if desired. (Serve same day it is made.)

Raisin Pie

NO CORN,* EGG, MILK, WHEAT, OR GLUTEN
Yield: Filling for one double-crust pie

This is a hearty dessert best served after a light meal. Enhance it with a dollop of hard sauce if allowed or warm Cinnamon or Lemon Sauce (see page 93). (Do not reheat arrowroot filling.)

2 c. seedless raisins	*2 T. sugar*
1¼ c. warm water	*Dash of salt*
Orange juice or port wine	*½ t. grated orange rind*
2 T. lemon juice	*½ t. grated lemon rind*
⅓ c. honey	*1 double pie crust for a 9-inch*
1¾ T. arrowroot	*pie tin (see pages 116–19)*

Cover raisins with water. Cook slowly over medium heat until fruit is plump. Drain off water into a small bowl and add enough juice or wine to it to make a total of ⅔ cup. Add lemon juice and honey. Combine arrowroot, sugar, and salt. Add juice mixture gradually to sugar mixture. Stir until smooth. Add grated rinds. Mix with raisins and cook gently until thickened. Cool slightly. Fill unbaked pie crust. Dot with butter, if allowed. Cover with top crust. Seal edges well. Make air vents and sprinkle lightly with sugar. Bake at 425° 30–40 minutes, or until filling is bubbly and crust is lightly browned.

Variation: If you can use corn, substitute 2½ T. cornstarch for the arrowroot.

Fresh Pear Pie

NO CORN, EGG, MILK, WHEAT, OR GLUTEN
Yield: Filling for one double-crust pie

Winter pears such as D'Anjou or Bosc are best for this pie. They should be ripe but firm.

5–6 pears
⅓ c. mild honey
1–2 T. lemon juice
2 T. quick-cooking tapioca
⅛ t. salt

⅛ t. ground ginger
½ t. cinnamon
1 double pie crust for a 9-inch
 pie tin (see pages 116–19)

Peel, core, and slice pears. Combine honey and lemon juice. Pour over pears quickly so pears will not discolor. Combine tapioca, salt, and spices. Combine with pears. Let stand 15 minutes. Fill unbaked pie shell with the pear mixture. Cover with top crust. Seal edges and make vents. Bake at 400° 10 minutes, then at 375° for an additional 30–40 minutes, or until tender.

Apple and Mincemeat Pie

NO CORN, EGG, WHEAT, OR GLUTEN
Yield: Filling for one 9-inch pie crust

3 oz. soft cream cheese
½ c. ground almonds
5–6 fresh apples, or 1 can apple
 slices
2 T. butter
1 T. lemon juice

1 t. grated lemon rind
½ c. honey
Arrowroot (optional)
1–1½ c. mincemeat
Chopped nuts

Mash cheese with a fork. Mix in almonds. Spread on bottom of cooled prebaked pie crust of your choice (see pages 116–19). Peel, slice, and core fresh apples to make 2 full cups. Melt butter in a large frying pan. Add apples, lemon juice, lemon rind, and honey. Sauté gently until apples are cooked and translucent. If there is juice, especially from canned apples, lift out the fruit carefully and thicken the juice with a little arrowroot.

Cool the apples. Then spread gently over cheese in pie crust. Mix the thickened juice into the mincemeat. Spread over apples. Top with chopped nuts. (If there is no juice, spread mincemeat as is.) Serve plain or with whipped cream if allowed.

Tofu

Many supermarkets as well as health-food stores, Oriental, and specialty markets carry tofu, the soybean cake used in so many Oriental dishes and now in our cuisine as well. It comes in soft, medium, and firm cakes. The soft is best for recipes requiring creaming although the others can be used. The firmer or medium cakes are good when the tofu is to be cut into pieces and keep its own identity. The recipes here are for desserts and use the soft.

Where milk and eggs present problems, tofu can be a welcome substitute. Interesting pies and puddings are possible. Tofu does have a soybean flavor but absorbs the flavors of the food with which it is combined. If there is still a distinguishable tofu flavor, add additional flavorings to taste. For example, use 2 teaspoons of vanilla instead of one, or more cinnamon, nutmeg, etc., or orange juice instead of water to make the difference. *To prepare tofu*, drain and rinse the cake in cold water. Split it in two horizontally and put the cakes side by side on 3 to 4 thicknesses of paper towel. Put more towels on top. Put a cutting board or something heavy on top to press out the excess moisture. Repeat if necessary. If too much moisture is removed, the tofu will be crumbly not creamy, and if not enough is removed, the filling will be runny. You will learn very quickly from working with it what the right consistency is.

Pat tofu dry. Put into a blender or food processor with steel blade and blend until creamy.

Tofu Mincemeat Pie

NO CORN, EGG, MILK, WHEAT, OR GLUTEN
Yield: Filling for one 9-inch pie crust

1 12-oz. cake soft tofu
2 t. plain gelatin
3 T. cold apple juice, orange
* juice, or water*

2 c. mincemeat
1 t. grated orange rind
½ c. chopped nuts
2–3 t. honey (optional)

Prepare tofu according to directions on page 125. When the tofu reaches the consistency of whipped cream, scrape into a large bowl. Set aside. Add gelatin to juice. Let sit 5 minutes, then warm gently to dissolve. Add 1–2 tablespoons creamy tofu to gelatin and blend thoroughly. Gradually return gelatin mixture to the prepared tofu. Transfer tofu to a bowl. Add mincemeat, rind and nuts. Mix thoroughly until blended. Taste, and if a sweeter filling is desired, stir in honey. Pour into prepared 9-inch pie crust of your choice (see pages 116–19). Refrigerate for several hours.

Variation: For Tofu Mincemeat Pudding, increase juice by 1 T., omit crust, and refrigerate in pudding bowls. Serves 6.

Tofu Pineapple Cream Pie

NO CORN, EGG, MILK, WHEAT, OR GLUTEN
Yield: Filling for one 9-inch pie crust

1 12-oz. cake soft tofu
2 t. plain gelatin
3 T. cold unsweetened pineapple
* juice*
⅓–½ c. honey (to taste)
1 t. grated lemon rind

1 t. vanilla, or ½ t. mint
flavoring
1½–2 c. well-drained,
* crushed, unsweetened*
* pineapple*

Prepare tofu according to directions on page 125. Add gelatin to pineapple juice. Let sit 5 minutes, then warm gently to dissolve. Add 1–2 tablespoons creamy tofu to gelatin and blend thoroughly. Gradually return mixture to creamy tofu. Add honey, rind, and flavoring. Process again, or beat until thoroughly blended. In a mixing bowl, combine tofu mixture and pineapple. Mix well. Pour into a prebaked 9-inch pie crust of your choice (see pages 116–19). Chill several hours.

Variations: Add ½ c. shredded coconut with the pineapple.

For Tofu Pineapple Cream Pudding, omit crust and refrigerate in pudding bowls. Serves 6.

Tofu Pumpkin Pie

NO CORN, EGG, MILK, WHEAT, OR GLUTEN
Yield: filling for one 9-inch pie crust

Here is a surprise filling without eggs or milk, but you wouldn't know it unless you were told. This is best served the day it is made.

1 12-oz. cake soft tofu	*½ t. ground ginger*
2 t. plain gelatin	*½ t. allspice*
3 T. frozen orange juice	*½ t. salt*
concentrate, thawed	*1 t. grated orange rind*
2 c. canned pumpkin puree	*½ c. honey*
1 t. cinnamon	*1½–2 t. vanilla*

Prepare tofu according to directions on page 125. When the tofu reaches the consistency of whipped cream, scrape into a large bowl. Set aside. Add gelatin to orange juice. Let sit 5 minutes, then warm gently to dissolve. Blend pumpkin, spices, salt, orange rind, honey, and vanilla. Spoon 1–2 tablespoons pumpkin mixture into warm gelatin and stir to give it a smooth texture. Return to rest of pumpkin. Mix well. Fold pumpkin mixture into tofu, blending thoroughly. Taste, and adjust flavors if necessary. (No tofu flavor should come through. If it does, more vanilla, cinnamon, or orange rind may be indicated.) Pile into prebaked 9-inch pie crust of your choice (see pages 116–19). Refrigerate for several hours.

Variation: *For Tofu Pumpkin Pudding*, omit crust and refrigerate in pudding bowls. Serves 6.

Tofu Carob Pie

NO CORN, WHEAT, OR GLUTEN
Yield: Filling for one 9-inch pie crust

Serve this the day it is made. Top with whipped cream or ice cream if desired.

1 c. carob chips
½ c. honey
1½ lb. soft tofu
1 T. vanilla

1 egg
½ t. cinnamon
¼ t. peppermint extract, or to
taste

Over low heat, melt carob chips with honey. Stir to prevent sticking. Remove from heat. Set aside. To prepare the tofu, rinse cake of soft or regular tofu, pat dry, removing all surface moisture. Whirl in a blender or food processor with steel blade until creamy. Add vanilla, egg, cinnamon, and extract. Continue blending while adding the honey-carob mixture. Pour into an unbaked 9-inch pie crust of your choice (see pages 116–19). Bake at 425° 15–20 minutes, or until crust is lightly browned and filling has a dull appearance. Let cool completely on a rack before cutting.

Variation: Sprinkle chopped nuts on top before baking.

Tofu Cocoa Pie

NO MILK, WHEAT, OR GLUTEN
Yield: filling for one 9-inch pie crust

This is an adaptation of the Tofu Carob Pie recipe, above.

Use ½ c. cocoa powder instead of carob chips. Proceed as directed in Tofu Carob Pie, except do not heat the honey-cocoa mixture.

Tofu Chocolate Pie

NO CORN, MILK, WHEAT, OR GLUTEN
Yield: filling for one 9-inch pie crust

This is an adaptation of the Tofu Carob Pie recipe, page 128.

Use 2 squares semisweet chocolate instead of carob chips. Melt chocolate with 1 T. water. Add the honey. Proceed as directed in Tofu Carob Pie.

No-Bake Tofu Carob Pie

NO CORN, EGG, WHEAT, OR GLUTEN
Yield: Filling for one 8-inch pie crust

Easy and good!

1 12-oz. cake soft tofu
1 t. plain gelatin
1 T. vanilla
1 c. carob chips

½ c. honey
½ t. cinnamon
1 T. half and half or evaporated milk

Prepare tofu according to directions on page 125 and blend until smooth and creamy. Set aside. Dissolve gelatin in vanilla. Set aside. Heat carob, honey, cinnamon, and half and half gently in a saucepan, stirring to prevent sticking. Add gelatin mixture to hot carob mixture. Stir to dissolve. Cool. Add carob mixture to tofu. Blend thoroughly. Spoon into a prebaked 8-inch pie crust of your choice (see pages 116–19).

OTHER DESSERTS

	NO CORN	NO EGG	NO MILK	NO WHEAT	NO GLUTEN
Carob Pudding	X	X		X	X
Cocoa Pudding		X	X	X	X
Chocolate Pudding	X	X	X	X	X
Peanut Pudding	X	X	X	X	X
Banana Pudding	X	X	X	X	X
Cranberry-Barley Pudding	X	X	X	X	
Whipped Farina Pudding	X	X	X		
Apricot Delight	X	X	X		
Baked Spiced Crumb Pudding	X	X			
Modified Danish Rice Pudding	X	X		X	X
Yam Peanut Pudding	X			X	X
Fruit Cobbler	X	X			
Mocha Poached Pears	⊗	X	X	X	X
Pears with Cream Cheese	X	X		X	X
Pear-Butterscotch Crisp	X	X	⊗		
Chocolate Mousse or Soufflé	X			X	X
Chocolate or Carob Peanut Butter Squares	X	X		⊗	
Sabayon	X		X	X	X
Kadaiff Phyllo Cream	⊗	X			
Phyllo Fingers	X	X			
Phyllo Apple Pastries	X	X			

⊗ means that the recipe includes instructions for adding that ingredient if allowed.

Tofu Pudding Base

12-oz. cake tofu
½–1 t. plain gelatin

2 T. water or juice

Prepare pressed tofu in a blender or food processor with steel blade and blend until smooth and creamy (see page 125). Set aside. Dissolve gelatin in water or juice. Let stand 5 minutes. Warm over low heat until gelatin is dissolved. Stir a small amount of the tofu into gelatin and mix, then add to remaining tofu and blend completely. This is your base.

Carob Pudding

NO CORN, EGG, WHEAT, OR GLUTEN
Servings: 4–6

Tofu base
½ c. carob chips
1–2 t. vanilla or ¼–½ t.
mint extract

Sugar or honey to taste,
if needed

Melt carob chips over hot water. Add vanilla or mint extract. Stir into prepared creamy tofu. Add honey, if desired, and adjust flavors to taste.

Cocoa Pudding

NO EGG, MILK, WHEAT, OR GLUTEN
Servings: 4–6

Substitute ½ c. cocoa for carob in preceding recipe. Add ¼ c. hot water and 2 T. honey or to taste. Heat to thicken. Proceed as above.

Chocolate Pudding

NO CORN, EGG, MILK, WHEAT, OR GLUTEN
Servings: 4–6

Substitute 2 oz. semisweet chocolate for carob and proceed as above.

Peanut Pudding

NO CORN, EGG, MILK, WHEAT, OR GLUTEN
Servings: 4–6

Tofu base
½–¾ c. peanut butter or to
taste
2 T. honey or to taste

½–1 t. vanilla (optional) or
to taste

Add peanut butter, honey, and vanilla to creamy tofu and blend in.

Banana Pudding

NO CORN, EGG, MILK, WHEAT, OR GLUTEN
Servings: 4–6

Tofu base
2–3 mashed bananas
1–2 t. vanilla or ½ t. almond
flavoring

2 T. thawed frozen orange juice
concentrate (instead of water)
1 T. honey, or to taste
¼–½ c. chopped nuts

Mash bananas. Add flavoring and juice. Add honey to taste. Stir into prepared tofu. Add chopped nuts.

Cranberry-Barley Pudding

NO CORN, EGG, MILK, OR WHEAT
Servings: 8–10

½ c. pearl barley
1 qt. boiling water
1 cinnamon stick, about 3 inches long
¼ t. salt

1 T. lemon juice
2 c. low-calorie cranberry juice cocktail
⅓ c. honey
¾ c. raisins

Rinse and drain barley. Place into a 3-quart saucepan with the boiling water, cinnamon, and salt. Cook slowly, about 30 minutes. Stir occasionally. Add juices, honey, and raisins. Continue cooking slowly until most of the moisture is absorbed and pudding is thick, about 30 minutes. Serve warm or cold. Pass Fruit Sauce (see page 94), or milk or cream, if allowed.

Whipped Farina Pudding

NO CORN, EGG, OR MILK
Servings: 6–8

2 c. apricot nectar
¼ c. farina or cream of wheat

Sugar or honey to taste
6–8 apricot halves

Bring nectar to a boil. Stir in farina. Reduce heat and cook about 3 minutes, stirring occasionally. Remove from heat, transfer to small bowl of an electric mixer. Beat at high speed about 10 minutes, or until mixture is doubled in volume. Sweeten to taste. Top each serving with an apricot half. Serve within 6 hours or pudding loses volume.

Variations: Instead of apricot nectar, use a 6-oz. can frozen orange, grape, lemon, or tangerine juice concentrate diluted with water to make 2 c. (or frozen lemonade concentrate, which is already sweetened, if preferred) or 2 c. unsweetened pineapple, apple, prune, or cranberry juice. Proceed as above. Serve topped with crushed pineapple, applesauce, chopped prunes, or mandarin orange sections, as desired.

Apricot Delight

NO CORN, EGG, OR MILK
Servings: 4

¾ c. bulgur
¾ c. water
¾ c. apricot nectar

¼ t. salt
2 T. honey
1 T. lemon juice

Combine all ingredients. Cover and cook over low heat until all juice is absorbed and bulgur is tender, about 30 minutes to 1 hour depending on altitude. For longer cooking, more juice may be needed. Stir occasionally. Serve warm or cold, with Fruit Sauce (see page 94).

Variation: Fold in ½ c. drained, crushed pineapple.

Baked Spiced Crumb Pudding

NO CORN OR EGG
Servings: 6–8

1 c. soft bread crumbs
1 c. buttermilk
3 T. safflower oil
½ c. honey
2 T. molasses
½ c. plus 1 T. sifted
    unbleached flour

½ t. salt
1 t. baking soda
½ t. cinnamon
¼ t. nutmeg
½ c. chopped raisins

Combine bread crumbs and buttermilk. Combine the oil, honey, and molasses and stir into the crumb mixture. Sift together the dry ingredients. Stir into crumb mixture. Add raisins. Pour into a greased 6½-inch-square or 5 × 8-inch baking dish. Bake at 350° 35–40 minutes.

Modified Danish Rice Pudding

NO CORN, EGG, WHEAT, OR GLUTEN
Servings: 10–12

1 qt. milk
¾ c. short-grain brown rice
⅛ t. salt
3 T. honey
⅔ c. evaporated milk
¾ c. chopped blanched
   almonds

¼ c. sherry
2 t. vanilla
¼ c. nonfat noninstant milk
   powder

Heat the 1 quart milk. Add the rice, salt, and honey. Stir to mix well. Simmer on top of stove about 20 minutes. Transfer to an ovenproof casserole, cover, and bake at 250° until rice is very tender, stirring occasionally and adding more milk if necessary. This will take several hours.

While the rice is baking, put the evaporated milk in a small pan in the freezer to partially freeze. Chill a bowl and beaters. When rice is tender, pour immediately into a shallow bowl to cool quickly in refrigerator. When cool, add almonds, sherry, and vanilla. Whip milk in the chilled bowl until stiff. Add milk powder. Whip until very stiff. Fold into the cooled rice mixture. Turn into a serving bowl and chill thoroughly. Serve the same day.

Yam Peanut Pudding

NO CORN, WHEAT, OR GLUTEN
Servings: 8–10

3–4 yams
¼ c. honey
½ t. nutmeg
¼ c. butter or corn-free
   margarine, melted

3 eggs
½ c. crunchy peanut butter
2½ c. milk
Chopped nuts (optional)

In a blender or food processor, whirl peeled, cut-up yams until coarsely chopped (to make 4 cups). Stir in honey, nutmeg, and butter. Beat together eggs, peanut butter, and milk. Stir into potato mixture and blend. Pour into a well-greased, shallow 2-quart baking dish. Bake at 350° 45 minutes, or until potatoes are tender and custard is set. Sprinkle top with chopped nuts if desired. Serve warm or cold.

Fruit Cobbler

NO CORN OR EGG
Servings: 6–8

5–6 peaches, or 3 large pears
Juice of ½ lemon
4 T. sugar, divided
¾ c. unbleached flour
¼ c. raw wheat germ
¼ t. salt

¼ c. butter or corn-free
*   vegetable shortening*
*   (see page 13)*
½ t. baking soda
1 t. water
½ c. plain yogurt

Peel, core, and slice peaches or pears to make 2 cups of fruit. Place in a 7-inch baking dish. Sprinkle with lemon juice and 2–3 tablespoons of the sugar. Combine flour, wheat germ, salt, and the remaining 1 tablespoon sugar. Cut in butter as for pie crust. Dissolve baking soda in the 1 teaspoon water. Stir into yogurt. Stir yogurt mixture into flour mixture. Pour over fruit. Bake at 375° 40–50 minutes, or until fruit is soft and top is brown.

Mocha Poached Pears

NO CORN,* EGG, MILK, WHEAT, OR GLUTEN
Servings: 6

½ c. honey
2 T. ground semisweet chocolate
2 t. regular or decaffeinated
*   instant coffee*
1 stick cinnamon, about 2 inches
*   long*

2 whole cloves
1½ c. water
6 large, firm D'Anjou, Bosc, or
*   Bartlett pears*
1 t. arrowroot (optional)

Combine first 6 ingredients in a large pan. Bring to a boil. Remove core from blossom end of pears, leaving stem in place, and peel. Put pears gently into boiling syrup, reduce heat, cover, and let cook until pears pierce easily with a fork, about 10–20 minutes depending on the ripeness of the pears. Turn pears in syrup as they cook if syrup does not cover them. When cooked, remove pears gently to individual serving dishes. If the syrup seems too thin, let it cook down or thicken it with arrowroot. Pour the syrup over the pears. Serve at room temperature or cold. Sour cream or whipped cream can be passed if allowed.

Variation: *If you can use corn,* cocoa can be substituted for the semisweet chocolate and 2 t. cornstarch for the arrowroot.

Pears with Cream Cheese

NO CORN, EGG, WHEAT, OR GLUTEN
Serving: 1

1 ripe Comice or D'Anjou pear
Lemon juice in water, or
  pineapple juice
1 T. soft cream cheese
Chopped nuts, seeds, or
  chocolate or carob bits

1 T. mild honey
Sour cream, sweet wine, or
  liqueur

Peel, half lengthwise and core one pear per serving. Dip halves into lemon water or pineapple juice to prevent discoloring. Add nuts, seeds, or bits to taste to cream cheese. Spread on pear halves and press together. Spoon honey over pears in individual dishes and pass sour cream, sweet wine, or liqueur such as crème de cacao or Triple Sec.

Pear-Butterscotch Crisp

NO CORN, EGG, OR MILK*
Servings: 6–8

6–8 pear halves, fresh or canned
Lemon juice in water or
    pineapple juice
½ c. brown sugar
½ c. unbleached flour

¼ t. salt
¼ t. cinnamon or nutmeg
¼ c. corn-free vegetable
    shortening (see page 13)

For fresh pears, peel, cut in half lengthwise, remove core, and dip into lemon juice in water or pineapple juice to prevent discoloring. Drain canned pears. Place pear halves cut-side-down in a greased casserole. Combine dry ingredients and cut in shortening as for pie crust. Pat mixture on top of pears. Bake at 350° about 20–30 minutes or until fresh pears are tender and top is bubbly and slightly browned. Serve warm or cold.

*Variation: If you can use milk, you can substitute butter for the shortening.

Chocolate Mousse or Soufflé

NO CORN, WHEAT, OR GLUTEN
Servings: 4–6

Super delicious. Shamefully rich.

4 oz. semisweet chocolate
4 eggs, separated, at room
    temperature

4 T. butter

Place chocolate in a small pan, cover with hot tap water, and let stand until soft enough for point of knife to penetrate. Pour off water. Add egg yolks to chocolate and whisk until thoroughly blended. Add butter. Stir over low heat until butter is melted, but do not cook the egg yolks. Transfer to a mixing bowl. Beat egg whites until stiff peaks form. Gently fold whites into chocolate mixture. *For mousse*, place into a glass bowl and refrigerate overnight. *For soufflé*, scrape mixture into a buttered, confectioners-sugar-dusted, 1-quart baking dish or soufflé mold. Place in oven so lower part of dish is just below mid-oven. Bake at 475° about 2 minutes, or until top is just set and it has begun to rise. Reduce temperature to 425° and continue baking about 5 minutes or until center is soft but outer surface is firm (*Do not overcook*.) Serve immediately. Use soft inside as sauce.

Chocolate or Carob Peanut Butter Squares

NO CORN, EGG, OR WHEAT*
Servings: 9

A make-ahead winner!

1 c. evaporated milk
¼ c. plus 1 T. butter or margarine
1 c. chocolate or carob bits, divided
1½ c. rolled oats
⅔ c. peanut butter

1 c. low-fat cottage cheese
¼ c. honey
1 t. vanilla
3 T. noninstant, nonfat milk powder
¼ c. chopped nuts (optional)

Chill a small mixing bowl and beaters in freezer. In a small pan, partially freeze the evaporated milk while preparing rest of filling. Heat together just until melted the butter and ¼ cup of the chocolate or carob bits. Stir in the oats. Press into the bottom of a greased 8 × 8-inch pan. Chill thoroughly. In a small pan over low heat, combine the remaining ¾ cup carob bits and the peanut butter. Stir until melted. Cool slightly. Combine cottage cheese, honey, and vanilla in small bowl of electric mixer or in food processor with steel blade. Blend until creamy and fluffy. Beat in peanut butter mixture. (It will be quite stiff.) Remove evaporated milk from freezer. Transfer to the very cold bowl. Beat in electric mixer at high speed until doubled in volume. Slowly add the milk powder and beat until very thick. Fold whipped milk into peanut mixture. Spoon into prepared crust. Sprinkle top with chopped nuts if desired. Cover and chill thoroughly. If not used the day it is made, freeze it; remove from freezer ½ hour before serving.

Variations: *If you can use wheat*, substitute graham cracker crumbs for the oats, omit 1 T. butter or margarine, and use ¼ c. chocolate or carob bit for crust.

For a firmer texture, gelatin can be added to the evaporated milk. Stir ½ t. plain gelatin into 2 T. of the milk and let sit 5 minutes. Heat gently until dissolved. Slowly stir in 1–2 T. more milk; then add remaining milk. Put in freezer. Proceed as above.

Sabayon

NO CORN, MILK, WHEAT, OR GLUTEN
Servings: 4–5

½ T. plain gelatin
¼ c. water
2 eggs, separated, at room
   temperature

¼ c. honey
¾ c. sherry
⅛ t. salt
¼ c. sugar

Stir gelatin into cold water. Set aside. Combine egg yolks with honey, sherry, and salt. Cook in double boiler, stirring constantly, until slightly thickened. Add softened gelatin to hot mixture. Stir to dissolve. Set aside to cool. Beat egg whites until fluffy. Slowly add sugar. Beat until a stiff meringue. Slowly stir into cooled yolk mixture. Spoon into serving dishes. Cool thoroughly.

Kadaiff Phyllo Cream

NO CORN* OR EGG
Servings: 8–9

Packages of phyllo sheets without corn or egg are available. Check package ingredients. This dessert is a delectable praise-getter. It can be made a day ahead.

1½ T. sugar
1 T. arrowroot
1¼ c. half and half
½ t. vanilla
½ t. grated orange rind
½ lb. phyllo sheets (corn- and egg-free)

¼ lb. butter (½ c.)
½ c. honey
¼ c. water
1 T. lemon juice

Blend sugar and arrowroot in a saucepan. Gradually add half and half, stirring. Continue stirring and cooking over medium heat until thickened slightly. Remove from heat. Stir in vanilla and orange rind. Cover and set aside. Roll phyllo sheets up like a jelly roll. Cut crosswise in ⅛-inch strips. Shake strands apart. Melt butter in a large frying pan. Add phyllo and toss with a fork to blend. Pat a little over half of the phyllo into the bottom of a 5 × 9-inch greased glass baking dish. Stir the lukewarm sauce and spoon evenly over phyllo. Top with remaining phyllo. Bake on lowest rack of oven at 375° about 30 minutes, or until a deep golden brown. Be sure bottom is also browned (if baking dish is opaque, lift phyllo gently with a spatula to inspect).

While phyllo bakes, bring honey and water quickly to a boil. Stir until clear. Remove from heat. Let stand until tepid. Add lemon juice. Remove phyllo from oven when done and pour lemon syrup evenly over top.

*Variation: If you can use corn, 1½ T. cornstarch can be substituted for the arrowroot.

Phyllo Fingers

NO CORN OR EGG
Yield: 16–20 fingers

1–1½ c. mixed chopped nuts, sunflower seeds, and raisins; plus coconut if desired
2 T. honey (approx.)
¼ c. butter

4–5 phyllo sheets (corn- and egg-free)
Cinnamon-sugar or nutmeg
Confectioners sugar (optional)

Combine nut mixture with honey for filling, using just enough honey to hold ingredients together. Melt butter without stirring. Skim off foamy top. Discard foam. Lay phyllo sheets flat. From the long side, cut each sheet into four equal strips. With a pastry brush, paint butter onto each strip in thin streaks. It should cover at least half the strip. Fold one of the short ends of each piece over about 1 inch. Spread 2–3 teaspoons of filling just below the fold. Sprinkle with cinnamon-sugar or nutmeg. Roll firmly but not tightly. Place seam-side-down on an ungreased baking sheet ½ inch apart. Cover with a tea towel while preparing remaining fingers. Bake at 350° about 20 minutes, or until lightly golden. Cool on a wire rack. Confectioners sugar may be sprinkled on after 5 minutes if desired.

Note: Keep sheets covered with waxed paper or a damp cloth while working to prevent drying.

Phyllo Apple Pastries

NO CORN OR EGG
Servings: 16

3–4 apples
2 T. lemon juice
2 T. honey
Dash of salt
1 t. cinnamon

1 c. chopped nuts or raisins
15 phyllo sheets (corn- and egg-
  free)
½–⅔ c. melted butter

HONEY SYRUP:
3 T. sugar
2 T. honey
1 T. lemon juice

1 cinnamon stick,
  about 2 inches long

Peel, core, and slice apples very thin to make 4 cups. Mix lemon juice, honey, salt, and cinnamon. Pour over apples. Add nuts or raisins. Cut phyllo sheets in half. Cover half with waxed paper or a damp cloth. Brush top sheet lightly with melted butter. Lift carefully into a buttered, 9-inch-square pan. Fold in the long sides. Brush second sheet with butter and place in pan so long ends go the opposite direction. Fold in. Repeat until first half of sheets are used. Carefully layer the apples over the sheets. Using the second half of the sheets, repeat buttering and layering but fold the overlap under. Brush top with butter. With a sharp knife, cut through the top layers making squares or diamonds. Bake on low rack of oven at 350° 1 hour, or until golden brown and apples are tender.

While baking, prepare syrup. Combine syrup ingredients in a saucepan. Bring to a boil. Boil gently until thickened. Partially cool.

Remove pastry from the oven and cool on a wire rack for 10 minutes. Spoon syrup over the top. Finish cooling. To serve, cut through bottom layer of phyllo sheets and lift squares out with a spatula.

MEATLESS DISHES AND MEAT EXTENDERS

	NO CORN	NO EGG	NO MILK	NO WHEAT	NO GLUTEN
Navy Beans with Rice	X	X	X	X	X
Baked Lentils and Cheese	X	X		X	X
Sweet and Sour Soybeans	⊗	X	X	X	X
Soybean Curry	⊗	X	⊗	⊗	⊗
Soybean Casserole	X	X	X	X	X
Black-Eyed Peas	⊗	X	X	X	X
Brown Rice with Cheese Sauce	X	X		⊗	⊗
Broccoli-Tofu Soufflé	⊗	X		⊗	⊗
Tofu Squares	X	X	⊗	X	X
Tofu Casserole	X		⊗	⊗	⊗
Carrot Loaf	X	X		⊗	⊗
Chick Pea Patties	X	⊗	X	⊗	⊗
Mushroom Sauce	X	X	⊗	⊗	⊗
Lentil Loaf	X	⊗	⊗	⊗	⊗
Lentil-Carrot Loaf	X	⊗	X	⊗	⊗
Meat Ball and Garbanzo Bean Stew	⊗	X	X	X	X
Cranberry Bean and Pork Casserole	⊗	X	X	X	X

⊗ means that the recipe includes instructions for adding that ingredient if allowed.

	NO CORN	NO EGG	NO MILK	NO WHEAT	NO GLUTEN
Barley-Mushroom Casserole	X	X	⊗	X	
Sweet Basil Pasta	X	⊗			
Wheat-Free Noodles	X		X	X	

Navy Beans with Rice

NO CORN, EGG, MILK, WHEAT, OR GLUTEN
Servings: 4–6

This is excellent as either a meat substitute or a meat extender.

1 c. navy beans
1 medium-sized onion, finely chopped
1 green pepper, finely chopped
3 T. safflower oil
1 t. oregano
1 clove garlic, minced
1 T. chopped fresh parsley

1 c. tomato sauce
1 c. reserved bean-cooking liquid
2 t. sugar
1 t. vinegar
1 t. salt
1 T. molasses
1 small bay leaf

AS A MEAT EXTENDER:
½ lb. ground beef or other ground or finely chopped meat of your choice
Salt

Pepper
Onion powder

Soak beans overnight. Drain. Cover with fresh water and cook ½ hour. Drain, cover again with water, and cook until tender.* Drain, reserving 1 cup of the cooking liquid. Sauté the onion and pepper in oil until onions are golden. Lower heat. Add oregano, garlic, and parsley. Cook about 3 minutes, or until spices are well incorporated. Add tomato sauce, bean liquid, sugar, vinegar, salt, molasses, and bay leaf. Simmer 5 minutes. Remove bay leaf. Serve as a meat substitute over cooked brown rice. (The combination of the beans and the brown rice makes a complete protein— replacing meat, see pages 2–3.)

As a Meat Extender:
Brown the beef or meat of your choice. Season with salt, pepper, and onion powder. Stir into cooked bean mixture. Serve over brown rice.

Variation: Kidney beans can be used instead of navy beans.

*This method of cooking substantially reduces or eliminates the problem of flatulence. There is a little loss of vitamins, which can be replaced by adding about 1 t. brewer's yeast for each ½ c. dry beans to the sauce.

Baked Lentils and Cheese

NO CORN, EGG, WHEAT, OR GLUTEN
Servings: 6−10

This is an excellent main dish to serve with a crispy salad and an interesting bread. It is a complete protein. To make a heartier meal, the salad can be chicken, fish, or meat.

1¾ c. rinsed lentils*	1 1-lb. can stewed tomatoes, broken up
1 t. salt	
⅛ t. marjoram	2 c. water
⅛ t. whole thyme, crumbled	¾ c. thinly sliced celery
⅛ t. whole sage	2 c. thinly sliced carrots
1 large bay leaf	1 green pepper, seeded and chopped
¼ t. pepper	
2 large onions, chopped	2 T. finely chopped fresh parsley
2 cloves garlic, minced	3 c. grated sharp cheddar cheese

In a shallow baking dish, about 9 × 13 inches, mix together lentils, salt, marjoram, thyme, sage, bay leaf, pepper, onions, garlic, tomatoes, and water. Let stand 20 minutes, then cover tightly and bake at 375° 30 minutes. Uncover. Stir in celery, carrots, and green pepper. Return to oven, covered, and bake another 40 minutes, or until vegetables are tender. Remove bay leaf. Stir in parsley and cheese. Bake uncovered 5 more minutes, or until cheese is melted.

*Lentils do not need to be presoaked.

Sweet and Sour Soybeans

NO CORN,* EGG, MILK, WHEAT, OR GLUTEN
Servings: 6–8

This dish provides complete protein when served with brown rice. It can also be fortified with bits of cooked chicken, veal, or pork.

1 c. soybeans
3 c. cold water
2½ t. arrowroot
¼ c. honey
¼ t. ground ginger
1 T. soy sauce
3 T. sherry
2–3 T. vinegar, depending on acidity
¼ c. reserved bean-cooking liquid or drained pineapple juice (see below)

2 T. safflower oil
1 large onion, cut into 1-inch squares
2 large carrots, cut into ¼-inch slices
1 clove garlic, minced
1 green pepper, seeded and cut into 1-inch squares
1 c. drained pineapple chunks
2 small tomatoes, cut into 1-inch cubes (optional)

Pick over soybeans. Soak overnight in the water. Discard any loose skins. Put into large pot, adding enough more water to completely cover beans. Cover and simmer 3 hours, or until beans are tender to bite. Stir occasionally to prevent sticking. Add more water if necessary. When beans are done, drain any excess liquid and save for the sauce. Pick over beans again, discarding loose skins. Set aside.

To make the sauce,† stir together the next seven ingredients. Set aside. In a large frying pan, heat oil. Add onion, carrots, and garlic. Cook, stirring about 3 minutes, or until vegetables are slightly cooked but crisp. (You may wish to precook the carrots by steaming or boiling for a few minutes; otherwise they will be almost raw.) Add green pepper. Cook 1 minute. Add pineapple and tomatoes (if desired). Add soybeans and sweet and sour sauce. Cook, stirring, until mixture boils and everything is coated with sauce, about 2 minutes. Serve with steamed brown rice. Excellent with a tomato aspic salad and Carrot-Corn Bread (see page 58) or muffins.

*Variation: If you can use corn, you can substitute 1 T. cornstarch for the arrowroot.

†The sauce amounts can be doubled if desired. Do not reheat if arrowroot is used (3 t. tapioca flour can be substituted).

Soybean Curry

NO CORN,* EGG, MILK,* WHEAT,* OR GLUTEN*
Servings: 8–10

Unusual and very good.

1⅓ c. soybeans
4 c. water
2½ c. thinly sliced carrots
¼ c. safflower oil
1 t. curry powder
⅓ t. ground ginger
1 large onion, thinly sliced
½ lb. mushrooms, sliced,
  washed, trimmed, and dried

1½ T. potato flour
1½ c. reserved bean-cooking
  liquid
1 c. drained and sliced water
  chestnuts
1 Delicious apple, cored and
  sliced
Salt and pepper
Bean sprouts

Soak soybeans overnight in the water. Put beans in a large pan, adding enough more water to cover. Cover and simmer 3–4 hours, or until tender to bite. Add more water if necessary. Discard the loose skins. Drain, saving the liquid and adding more if necessary to make 1½ cups. Set beans aside. Steam or boil carrots until partially cooked. In a large pan, heat oil. Stir in curry powder and ginger. Cook about 1 minute. Add carrots, onion, and mushrooms. Cook, stirring until onion is limp. Stir in the flour. Gradually add the reserved cooking liquid and cook, stirring, until bubbly. Add water chestnuts and soybeans. Cover and simmer until carrots are tender. Stir in the apple. Add salt and pepper to taste. Simmer, covered, about 5 minutes. Serve over bean sprouts that have been immersed in boiling water and drained. Pass an assortment of condiments such as raisins, chutney, unflavored yogurt, salted peanuts, sliced bananas, or shredded coconut.

Variations: If you can use corn, you can substitute 1½ T. cornstarch for the potato flour.

If you can use milk, you can substitute butter for the oil.

If you can use wheat and gluten, you can substitute 3 T. unbleached flour for the potato flour.

If you can use gluten but not wheat, you can substitute a mixture of 3 T. barley and oat flour for the potato flour.

Soybean Casserole

NO CORN, EGG, MILK, WHEAT, OR GLUTEN
Servings: 6–8

2 stalks celery, chopped
¼ green pepper, chopped
3 medium carrots, grated
8–10 mushrooms, washed, trimmed, dried, and sliced
½ onion, chopped, or 1 t. onion powder (added to spices)
2 T. safflower oil
2 c. cooked soybeans (see page 148)

1¼ t. dry mustard
1¼ c. tomato juice
2 T. soy sauce
¼ c. sherry
2 T. molasses
½ t. salt
¼ t. sweet basil or 1 T. fresh, chopped
¼ t. ground coriander

Sauté the vegetables in the oil. Add to cooked soybeans. Mix mustard with a little water or tomato juice and combine with the remaining liquid. Stir into bean and vegetable mixture. Add remaining ingredients. Blend well. Spoon into a greased casserole. Bake at 350° 30–40 minutes. Serve with steamed brown rice with green peas and chopped nuts or sunflower seeds. Or, serve with hot muffins and baked squash. This supplies complete protein. A mixed green salad or sliced cucumber gives a crisp contrast.

Black-Eyed Peas

NO CORN,* EGG, MILK, WHEAT, OR GLUTEN
Servings: 6

1 c. black-eyed peas
2 c. water
¼ t. mace or coriander
¼ t. nutmeg
2 t. honey or brown sugar

1 t. dry mustard
3 T. tomato sauce
2 T. molasses
½ t. salt

Presoak peas 6–8 hours. Drain. Place peas in a large pan, add water, cover, and cook until nearly done and water is nearly absorbed, about 1–

1½ hours. Combine remaining ingredients and mix well. Add to the peas and simmer until sauce is almost absorbed. Peas should still be very moist. Serve as a vegetable, or with Brown Rice with Cheese Sauce (if allowed; see below) as a main dish.

Variation: *If you can use corn*, you can substitute catsup for the tomato sauce.

Brown Rice with Cheese Sauce
NO CORN, EGG, WHEAT,* OR GLUTEN*
Servings: 3–4

This combination is a complete protein and can be served as the main dish or with crisp bacon or sausages. You can also add ½–¾ cup small cooked shrimp or crab meat to the sauce or bits of meat or chicken. A hearty vegetable salad adds zest.

4 T. butter or safflower oil
4 T. brown rice flour
½ t. salt
2 c. milk

½–1 c. grated sharp cheddar
* cheese (to taste)*
2 c. cooked brown rice

Heat butter or oil in a saucepan. Stir in flour and salt. Add the milk, stirring and cooking until thickened and smooth. Stir in the cheese. Cook just until cheese is melted. Blend in hot, cooked brown rice.

Variations: *If you can use wheat and gluten*, you can substitute wheat flour for the brown rice flour; *if you can use gluten but not wheat*, you can substitute barley or oat flour.

Broccoli-Tofu Soufflé

NO CORN,* EGG, WHEAT,* OR GLUTEN*

Servings: 4–6

½ lb. broccoli
1 12-oz. package soft tofu,
  prepared as directed on
  page 125
2 T. lemon juice
1½ t. mixed spices
1 c. grated cheese
½ t. salt

1¼ t. arrowroot baking
  powder (see page 13)
2 T. butter
2 T. brown rice flour
½ c. chicken broth
  (see page 7)†
½ c. milk†

Cut broccoli into 1-inch pieces, peel tough skin, and cook until tender. Process tofu in blender or food processor with steel blade until creamy. Add broccoli and continue processing until thoroughly blended. It should be quite stiff. Scrape into a bowl. Add lemon juice, spices, cheese, salt, and baking powder. Blend. Make a cream sauce using the butter, flour, chicken broth, and milk. Stir into tofu mixture. Spoon into a greased ovenproof casserole. Bake at 325° 40–45 minutes. Serve immediately. This is very nice with baked fish and steamed carrots.

*Variations: If you can use corn, you can add 1½ t. A-1 Sauce with the lemon juice and substitute 1 t. regular baking powder for the arrowroot baking powder.

If you can use wheat and gluten, you can substitute whole wheat flour for the brown rice flour.

If you can use wheat but not gluten, you can substitute barley or oat flour.

†1 c. milk can be used instead of milk and broth combination.

Tofu Squares

NO CORN, EGG, MILK,* WHEAT, OR GLUTEN
Servings: 6

This is an excellent meat substitute. The addition of brown rice, chicken, or fish makes this a complete protein.

1 14–16 oz. package firm tofu,
prepared as directed on
page 125
¼ c. soy sauce
2 t. grated fresh ginger, or 1 t.
ground ginger

3 T. vinegar
¼ t. dry mustard
2 medium garlic cloves, crushed
or minced
1 T. honey
2 T. safflower oil

Cut tofu into 1-inch squares. Combine remaining ingredients except oil. Marinate tofu squares about 1 hour, turning once after 30 minutes. Heat oil in a large skillet. Sauté tofu, turning pieces until browned on all sides. Serve plain with remaining marinade, or with sautéed mushrooms or Peanut Sauce (see page 185). Accompany with brown rice (see page 14–15).

*Variations: If you can use milk, substitute 1 T. butter for 1 T. of the oil.

Marinate bite-sized pieces of chicken or fish with the tofu. When tofu pieces are about half cooked, add chicken or fish and sauté along with the tofu squares.

Tofu Casserole

NO CORN, MILK,* WHEAT,* OR GLUTEN*
Servings: 4–5

1 stalk celery, finely chopped
½ green pepper, finely
    chopped
½ c. minced onion
2 T. safflower oil
1 12-oz. package soft tofu,
    prepared as directed on
    page 125

1 egg, beaten
2 T. brown rice flour
1 T. soy sauce
¼–½ t. curry powder
1 T. peanut butter
Ground sunflower seeds
Parsley or wheat germ

Combine celery and green pepper with onion and sauté in oil until soft.
Process tofu until creamy in a blender or food processor with steel blade.
Add beaten egg, flour, soy sauce, and curry powder to tofu. Mix thoroughly. Stir in vegetables and peanut butter. Spoon into a greased oven-proof casserole. Sprinkle on ground sunflower seeds mixed with chopped parsley or wheat germ. Bake at 350° about 45 minutes, or until set. Serve with Peanut Sauce (page 185). Mixed vegetables and hot bread make good accompaniments.

*Variations: If you can use milk, you can substitute ½ c. grated cheese for the curry powder.

If you can use wheat and gluten, you can substitute whole wheat flour for the brown rice flour.

If you can use gluten but not wheat, you can substitute barley or oat flour.

Cheese Sauce (see page 15) is also good on this, if milk is allowed.

Carrot Loaf

NO CORN, EGG, WHEAT,* OR GLUTEN*
Servings: 8

This is a complete protein.

*½ green pepper, finely
   chopped*
2 stalks celery, finely chopped
1 onion, finely chopped
3 T. oil or butter
*½ c. diced mushrooms,
   washed, trimmed, and dried*
½ c. fresh parsley, snipped
*4 large carrots, ground or finely
   chopped*
*2 c. cooked brown rice or
   Japanese-style rice noodles*

½–1 c. chopped walnuts
*2 t. mixed spices (see pages
   17–18)*
½ t. sweet basil
4 T. brown rice flour
4 T. melted butter or safflower oil
*2 c. chicken stock (see page 7) or
   a combination of stock and
   milk*
1 c. diced cooked chicken
1 c. grated sharp cheese

Sauté pepper, celery, and onion in the 3 tablespoons oil. Add mushrooms, parsley, and carrots. Sauté until carrots are nearly cooked. Add rice, nuts, spices, and basil. Set aside. For the sauce, stir flour into melted butter or oil. Stir in chicken stock or milk. Cook, stirring, until thickened. Add chicken and cheese. Pour about half the sauce into carrot mixture. Blend well. Spoon into a greased 5 × 9-inch loaf pan. Bake at 350° 25–30 minutes. Reheat remaining sauce and pass at the table.

*Variations: If you can use wheat and gluten, you can substitute cooked whole wheat macaroni for the brown rice and wheat flour for the brown rice flour.

If you can use gluten but not wheat, you can use barley or oat flour.

Chick Pea Patties

NO CORN, EGG,* MILK, WHEAT,* OR GLUTEN*
Servings: 4

1 c. chick pea flour (see page 15)
2 T. brown rice flour
1 t. onion powder
1 T. chopped fresh parsley
¼ t. baking soda
¾ t. ground coriander
1 t. mixed herbs

½ t. salt
2 t. lemon juice
⅓ c. water
1½ T. safflower oil
*⅓ c. grated raw zucchini or
carrot*

Mix together the dry ingredients. Stir in lemon juice, water, and oil. Add zucchini or carrots. Form patties with a large spoon or your hands coated with arrowroot. Heat enough oil in a large pan to cover bottom generously. Brown patties in oil, turning once. Drain on paper towels to remove any excess oil. Keep warm in oven until all are cooked. Serve with Mushroom Sauce (see below). This is not a complete protein unless used with brown rice, cheese sauce, or some other complementary protein.

Variations: If you can use egg, beat 1 large egg white until stiff and fold gently into zucchini or carrot mixture before forming patties.

If you can use wheat and gluten, you can substitute whole wheat flour for the brown rice flour.

If you can use gluten but not wheat, you can substitute barley or oat flour.

Cheese Sauce is also very good on these patties, if milk is allowed.

Mushroom Sauce

NO CORN, EGG, MILK,* WHEAT,* OR GLUTEN*
Yield: 1½ cups (approx.)

½ lb. mushrooms
2 T. safflower oil
2 T. brown rice flour

*1 c. beef broth or stock (see
page 7)*
¼ c. sherry (optional)

Wash, trim, dry, and slice mushrooms. Pat dry. Sauté mushrooms in oil 4–5 minutes. Stir in flour. Add beef broth and sherry. Stir until thickened.

Variations: *If you can use milk*, you can substitute butter for the oil.

If you can use wheat and gluten, you can substitute whole wheat flour for the brown rice flour.

If you can use gluten but not wheat, you can substitute barley or oat flour.

Lentil Loaf

NO CORN, EGG,* MILK,* WHEAT,* OR GLUTEN*
Servings: 4–6

½ onion, minced
1 clove garlic, minced
2 T. safflower oil
¼ lb. mushrooms, washed, trimmed, dried, and chopped
½ c. rinsed lentils†
⅛ t. thyme
¼ c. chopped nuts

⅛ t. ground cloves
⅛ t. nutmeg
¾ c. tomato juice
¼ c. dry sherry
2 T. chopped sunflower or sesame seeds
1 T. molasses
2 T. brown rice flour or tapioca flour

Sauté onion and garlic in oil until onion is almost soft. Add mushrooms. Cook about 5 minutes. Grind the raw lentils or put through food processor with steel blade. Combine with remaining ingredients. Stir into onion-mushroom mixture. Blend all together. Put into a well-greased ovenproof casserole. This much can be done ahead. Bake at 350° about 30 minutes, or until lightly browned and moisture is absorbed. (If it dries out too quickly, add more tomato juice.) Serve with Mushroom Sauce (see page 156), Cheese Sauce (see page 151), or a tomato sauce, depending on your diet limitations and preferences. The sunflower seeds, brown rice flour, and egg make this a complete protein. If egg is omitted, increase the sunflower seeds to ¼ cup.

Variations: *If you can use egg*, add 1 well-beaten egg to the ground lentils and combine with remaining ingredients.

If you can use milk, you can substitute butter for the oil.

If you can use wheat and gluten, you can substitute wheat germ for the seeds.

If you can use gluten but not wheat, you can substitute barley or oat flour.

†Lentils do not need to be presoaked.

Lentil-Carrot Loaf

NO CORN, EGG,* MILK, WHEAT,* OR GLUTEN*
Servings: 8

This combination of lentils and rice makes a complete protein in one dish.

1 c. rinsed lentils†
3–3½ c. water.
2 c. grated carrots (5–6 medium-sized)
½ c. chopped celery
¼ c. chopped green pepper
½ c. chopped onion
3 T. safflower oil
1 c. cooked brown rice
1 c. cooked green peas (optional)
1 t. salt
1 c. wheat- or gluten-free bread crumbs (see page 13)

½ c. raw sunflower seeds
1 t. mixed spices (see pages 17–18)
¼ t. sweet basil
¼ t. ground coriander
1 T. chopped fresh parsley
2 T. brown rice flour
½ c. reserved bean-cooking liquid, vegetable stock, or chicken broth (see page 7)
1 T. vinegar
Sesame seeds

Cook lentils in the water until tender, about 1 hour. If water is not absorbed, drain off and retain ½ cup. Sauté carrots, celery, pepper, and onion in the oil. Mix with the lentils, rice, peas, salt, crumbs, sunflower seeds, spices, herbs, and parsley. Stir flour into the ½ cup liquid. Add vinegar. Combine with lentil mixture. Mix thoroughly. Spoon into a well-greased ovenproof casserole or loaf pan. Sprinkle generously with sesame seeds. Cover and bake at 350° 30 minutes. Uncover and bake 10 minutes longer. Serve with a tomato sauce, Cheese Sauce (if allowed; see page 151), or Mushroom Sauce (see page 156), or with creamed fish or chicken, if allowed. Fruit salad and hot bread go well with this.

*Variations: If you can use egg, mix 1 well-beaten egg into the lentil mixture before putting in casserole.

If you can use wheat and gluten, you can substitute whole wheat bread crumbs and add ½ c. wheat germ.

If you can use gluten but not wheat, you can substitute wheat-free bread crumbs.

†Lentils do not need to be presoaked.

Meat Ball and Garbanzo Bean Stew

NO CORN,* EGG, MILK, WHEAT, OR GLUTEN
Servings: 6–8

1½ lb. lean ground beef
½ t. salt
½ t. oregano
1 T. safflower oil
1 c. sliced mushrooms
1 16-oz. can stewed tomatoes, undrained and chopped
2 c. canned or precooked garbanzo beans (chick peas), drained

1 t. onion powder
½ t. garlic powder
2 t. beef bouillon stock (see page 7)
½ c. tomato sauce
2–3 medium-sized zucchini
Salt
Pepper

Combine beef, salt, and oregano. Mix thoroughly and shape into balls a little larger than a walnut. Brown in oil in a Dutch oven. Add mushrooms. Cook about 5 minutes. Remove any excess grease. Add tomatoes, beans, and all remaining ingredients except zucchini. Cover and simmer about 15 minutes. This much can be done ahead. Peel and cut zucchini into ⅛-inch slices. Add to simmering bean mixture. Cook until squash is tender, 5–10 minutes. Add salt and pepper to taste. Remove solids to a serving dish. Thicken juice with a little brown rice flour if desired. Pour juice over mixture.

*Variation: If you can use corn, you can substitute catsup for the tomato sauce and beef bouillon base or cubes for the beef stock.

To extend the meat to about 12 servings, garbanzos may be increased to 4–6 c.

Cranberry Bean and Pork Casserole

NO CORN,* EGG, MILK, WHEAT, OR GLUTEN
Servings: 6–8

1½ c. dried cranberry beans
1 qt. water
2 lb. boneless pork loin or cooked roast pork
2 T. olive oil
1 medium-sized onion, finely chopped
1½ c. water

2 cloves garlic, minced
1 bay leaf
½ t. thyme
3 beef bouillon cubes (see page 7)
1 T. tomato paste
1 peeled carrot studded with 3 whole cloves
½ t. salt

Soak beans overnight in the 1 quart water. Drain. Cover with fresh water. Cook until tender. Cut pork into bite-sized pieces. Brown in olive oil (if cooked roast pork is used, do not brown). Remove pork to a 3-quart baking dish. Sauté onion in pan drippings. Pour the 1½ cups water into pan and scrape up pan drippings, then pour over meat. Add remaining ingredients and the beans to the meat. Cover and bake at 350° 1½ hours, stirring occasionally. Liquid should about be absorbed. Add more water if needed. Discard carrot and bay leaf before serving.

Variation: If you can use corn, you can substitute 1T. beefstock base.

Barley-Mushroom Casserole

NO CORN, EGG, MILK,* OR WHEAT
Servings: 4–6

1 small onion, finely chopped
2 stalks celery, finely chopped
1 clove garlic, finely chopped
½ lb. mushrooms, sliced
2 T. safflower oil

⅓ c. minced fresh parsley
1 bay leaf
1 c. medium-sized pearl barley
2 c. chicken or beef broth (see page 7), divided

Sauté onion, celery, garlic, and mushrooms in oil. Add parsley, bay leaf, and barley. Cook and stir until barley begins to turn golden. Remove from heat and stir in 1 cup of the broth. Put in an ungreased ovenproof casserole with a tight cover. Bake at 350° 30 minutes. Stir in the remaining cup broth. Bake 30 minutes more. Barley should be cooked but chewy. Remove bay leaf before serving.

Variation: *If you can use milk*, you can substitute butter for the safflower oil.

Sweet Basil Pasta

NO CORN or EGG*
Servings: 4–6

¼ c. minced fresh basil, or 2
   T. dried basil
2 T. minced fresh parsley
   (optional)
1 clove garlic, minced
3 T. hot water, divided
1 T. butter

¼ c. olive oil
¼ t. salt
¼ t. nutmeg
Dash of chili powder
2 T. Parmesan cheese
8 oz. cooked pasta of your choice

Mash basil, parsley, and garlic in 1 tablespoon of the water. Place in a saucepan. Mix and add butter, oil, salt, nutmeg, and chili. Add 2 tablespoons of the hot water. Heat over low heat. Add Parmesan cheese. Pour sauce over cooked pasta. Pass more Parmesan cheese.

Variation: *If you can use egg and wish to have a wheat-free dish*, serve on Wheat-Free Noodles. If Wheat-Free Noodles are used, this is a complete protein.

Wheat-Free Noodles

NO CORN, MILK, OR WHEAT
Yield: 3–6 servings

1¼ c. barley flour
½ c. brown rice flour
¼ c. oat flour (see page 15)
½ t. salt

2 eggs
½ c. water
1–2 T. safflower oil

Combine dry ingredients. Mix thoroughly. Make a well in center of mixture. Break eggs into well and add water. Beat until mixture is well blended. It should be a dough stiff enough to handle and roll with a rolling pin. Add more flour if necessary.

Pat onto floured waxed paper or pastry cloth. Use covered rolling pin, or cover dough with flour-dusted waxed paper. Roll very thin and cut into narrow strips. Drop strips a few at a time into gently boiling water. When they rise to the top, lift out with a slotted spoon. Put into a pan of cold water to prevent them from sticking together. When all are cooked, drain in a colander and rinse with more cold water.

If noodles are to be used quickly, sauté in oil in medium-hot frying pan until well coated. Sprinkle with parmesan cheese, if allowed, or minced parsley or other seasoning of your choice. *To hold for later use*, put in an oiled casserole, mixing oil into noodles and keep them warm in a 300° oven. Good served with stews, meatballs, in casseroles, with fish steaks, with fillets baked on top, or a tomato and meat sauce. Best used the day they are made.

FISH

	NO CORN	NO EGG	NO MILK	NO WHEAT	NO GLUTEN
Florentine Red Snapper	⊗	X	X	X	X
Sea Bass with Celeriac	X	X	⊗	⊗	⊗
Broiled Fillet of Sole	X	X		⊗	
Sautéed Scallops	⊗	X	X	⊗	⊗
Baked Sole with Mushrooms	⊗	X	⊗	⊗	⊗
Salmon Loaf with Garbanzo Beans	X	X	X	X	X
Salmon Mousse	X	X	X	X	X
Salmon Roll or Pie	X	X	X		
Caper Sauce	X	X	⊗	⊗	⊗
Tofu-Tuna Casserole #1	X	X		X	X
Tofu-Tuna Casserole #2	X	X		⊗	⊗
Tuna Casserole	X	X	⊗	⊗	⊗
Fish and Rice Ramekins	X	X	⊗	⊗	⊗
Fillet of Sole with Yogurt Sauce	X	X		⊗	⊗
Sautéed Sesame Fish	X	X	⊗	⊗	⊗
Fish Fillets with Shrimp	⊗	X	⊗	⊗	⊗

⊗ means that the recipe includes instructions for adding that ingredient if allowed.

Florentine Red Snapper

NO CORN,* EGG, MILK, WHEAT, OR GLUTEN
Servings: 2

1 large stalk celery, finely
   chopped
½ medium-sized green pepper,
   seeded and finely chopped
½ medium-sized onion, finely
   chopped, or 1 t. onion powder
¼ c. chopped fresh parsley, or
   1 T. dried parsley
2 T. olive oil
¼ t. garlic powder

2 T. brown rice flour, or 1 T.
   potato flour
1 c. tomato juice
½ t. salt
4 t. lemon juice, divided
½ t. sugar
½ 10-oz. package frozen
   spinach, thawed
½ lb. red snapper fillet
Salt

In a medium-sized frying pan sauté celery, pepper, onion, and parsley in
the olive oil until vegetables are just slightly crisp. Stir in garlic powder
and flour. Mix well into vegetables. Add tomato juice. Cook, stirring,
until thickened to a sauce. If too thick, add more tomato juice. Stir in salt,
2 t. lemon juice, and sugar. Taste and adjust seasoning if desired. Drain
thawed spinach. Put in bottom of a lightly greased baking dish. Lay snapper
on top of spinach. Salt lightly and spoon remaining lemon juice over the
fish. Top with the tomato sauce. Bake at 325° 15–20 minutes, or until
fish flakes with a fork.

Variation: If you can use corn, add ¼ t. A-1 Sauce or Worcestershire sauce with the lemon juice and sugar and, if desired, substitute 3
t. cornstarch for the brown rice flour.

Sea Bass with Celeriac

NO CORN, EGG, MILK,* WHEAT,* OR GLUTEN*
Servings: 4

*1 medium-sized celeriac (celery
   root), about ¾ lb.*
*1 c. chicken stock or broth (see
   page 7)*

2 T. lemon juice
*1 small onion, chopped, or 1 t.
   onion powder*
4 sea bass fillets

SAUCE:
2 T. oil
2 T. brown rice flour
1 c. reserved cooking liquid
¼ c. dry white wine

¾ t. thyme
1 c. small shrimp (optional)
Salt

Peel and grate celeriac. (A food processor makes this task easy.) Combine
with chicken stock, lemon juice, and onion. Mix thoroughly. Spoon into
one large ovenproof casserole or four individual ones. Top with four
serving-sized pieces of sea bass fillets. Sprinkle with more lemon juice.
Cover casserole tightly. Bake at 400° about 25 minutes, or until fish flakes
with a fork. Hold top(s) on casserole(s) and drain cooking liquid into a
pan. There should be a full cup.

Keep fish warm while making sauce. Melt oil in a saucepan. Stir in
flour. Stir in fish liquid, wine, and thyme. Keep stirring until sauce thickens. Add shrimp if desired and salt to taste. Spoon sauce generously over
fish. Serve with brown rice, baked potato, or Gnocchi (if allowed; see
page 203) and salad.

*Variations: *If you can use milk*, you can substitute butter for the oil
and half and half for the wine.

If you can use wheat and gluten, you can substitute wheat flour for the
brown rice flour.

If you can use gluten but not wheat, you can substitute barley or oat
flour.

Broiled Fillet of Sole

NO CORN, EGG, OR WHEAT*
Servings: 4–5

1½ lb. thin sole fillets
Salt
¾ c. grated sharp cheddar
cheese
2 c. fine, dry wheat-free bread
crumbs (see page 13)

2 T. minced fresh parsley, or 1
T. dried parsley
¼ t. curry powder
⅓ c. butter
Lemon wedges

Arrange sole in a single layer in a shallow, buttered baking dish. Sprinkle with salt. Combine cheese, crumbs, parsley, and curry powder. Melt butter and mix into crumb mixture. Spread mixture over fish. Broil 3–4 inches from heat under preheated broiler 5–7 minutes, or until fish flakes with a fork. Serve with lemon wedges.

*Variations: If you can use wheat and gluten, you can use dry wheat bread crumbs.

If you cannot use gluten, you can substitute crumbs made from crisp dry rice cereal mixed with sunflower seed meal.

Sautéed Scallops

NO CORN,* EGG, MILK, WHEAT,* OR GLUTEN*
Servings: 3–4

1 lb. scallops
2 T. olive oil
½ t. tarragon
⅛ t. basil
⅛ t. oregano

½ c. dry white wine
1 T. mild or rice vinegar
2 t. brown rice flour
1 T. cold water
Salt

Dry scallops between paper towels. Sauté in oil over high heat 3–4 minutes, depending on size of scallops. Turn carefully. Combine herbs wine, and vinegar. Pour over scallops, reduce heat, simmer 5 minutes. Lift out scallops and keep warm. Mix flour in cold water. Add to pan liquid and stir until it thickens. Salt to taste. Spoon sauce over scallops and serve immediately.

Variations: If you can use corn, you can substitute 1–1½ t. cornstarch for the flour.

If you can use wheat and gluten, you can substitute wheat flour for the brown rice flour.

If you can use gluten but not wheat, you can substitute barley or oat flour or 1½ t. cornstarch.

Baked Sole with Mushrooms

NO CORN,* EGG, MILK,* WHEAT,* OR GLUTEN*
Servings: 4

8 small fillets of sole, of equal
    size
Salt
1 small onion, finely chopped
¼ c. chopped fresh parsley or
    1 T. dried parsley
3 T. safflower oil

1 c. chopped mushrooms,
    washed, trimmed, and dried
¼ c. dry white wine
1 T. brown rice flour
½ c. chicken broth
    (see page 7)
Paprika

Oil baking dish as near the size of half of the fillets as possible. Place four fillets in the dish, not touching. Salt lightly. Set aside. Sauté onion and parsley in oil. Add mushrooms. Cook about 5 minutes longer. Spread mushroom mixture on fillets. Place remaining four fillets on top of matching sizes. Add salt. Pour on dry white wine. Bake at 350° 15 minutes, uncovered. While fish is baking, stir flour into chicken broth and wine. Cook over medium heat, stirring until thickened. Remove fish from oven. Pour off wine and juices and stir them into the sauce. Pour sauce over the fish, return to oven, and bake 5 minutes longer. Sprinkle with paprika. Serve garnished with sprigs of fresh parsley and thin orange slices.

Variations: If you can use corn, you can substitute 1½ t. cornstarch for the flour.

If you can use milk, sprinkle ½ c. grated jack or cheddar cheese on the mushroom mixture and substitute half and half or a combination of half and half and chicken broth for the broth and wine combination if desired.

If you can use wheat and gluten, you can substitute wheat flour for the brown rice flour.

If you can use gluten but not wheat, you can substitute barley or oat flour for the brown rice flour.

Salmon Loaf with Garbanzo Beans

NO CORN, EGG, MILK, WHEAT, OR GLUTEN
Servings: 6–8

2 1-lb. cans or 2½–3 c.
cooked garbanzo beans (chick
peas), drained
1 16-oz. can salmon and juice
¾ c. ground sunflower seeds
½ t. tarragon

¾ t. onion powder
½ t. salt
3 T. lemon juice
½ t. chervil
½ t. mixed spices (optional,
see pages 17–18)

Whirl drained beans in blender or food processor with steel blade. In a
bowl, mix beans with remaining ingredients. Blend thoroughly. Spoon
into a greased ovenproof casserole. Bake at 350° about 30 minutes. Serve
with a dill or mustard sauce.

Salmon Mousse

NO CORN, EGG, MILK, WHEAT, OR GLUTEN
Servings: 8–10

1 12–16 oz. cake soft or medium
tofu, prepared as directed on
page 125
1 1-lb. can salmon
2 T. lemon juice
1 t. plain gelatin
1 t. onion powder

1 t. garlic powder
1 t. Dijon-style mustard
1 t. tarragon
1 t. sweet basil
1 t. celery seed
2 T. chopped fresh parsley

Whirl tofu in blender or food processor with steel blade until creamy.
Drain salmon, reserving juice (there should be ⅓–½ cup). Pick out
any black skin and bones from salmon. Sprinkle with the lemon juice.
Add salmon juice to gelatin. Let sit 5 minutes. Heat to dissolve gelatin.
Stir 1–2 tablespoons of tofu into gelatin, then return mixture to rest of
tofu along with salmon and remaining ingredients. Blend thoroughly in
food processor with steel blade or in a blender. (In a blender, this will
have to be done in several batches.) When all is smooth, taste for seasoning

and adjust if needed. Pour into an oiled 1½ or 2-quart mold and refrigerate several hours. This makes a very smooth-textured mousse.

Serve on crisp greens, plain or topped with a caper or dill dressing or the dressing of your choice.

Variations: For variety and texture, stir in chopped celery, seeded and chopped green pepper, sliced olives, finely chopped onion instead of onion powder, chopped cucumber, or whatever pleases you; then pour into mold.

Salmon Roll or Pie

NO CORN, EGG, OR MILK
Servings: 4–6

½ c. sliced mushrooms
    washed, trimmed, and dried
½ c. finely chopped celery
½ green pepper, seeded and
    finely chopped
¼ c. finely chopped onion
3 T. safflower oil

1 16-oz. can salmon, drained
2 T. lemon juice
2 T. chopped fresh parsley
½ t. tarragon
1 recipe Whole Wheat Pie Crust
    (see page 116–17)

Sauté mushrooms, celery, pepper, and onion in the oil. Pick over salmon, discarding any black skin or bones. Sprinkle with lemon juice. Add parsley and tarragon. Mix all together. Prepare pie crust dough and roll out into a rectangle for the roll, a round for the pie.

For the roll, spread salmon mixture evenly over crust. Roll as a jelly roll. Tuck in ends. Place on a lightly greased baking sheet. Bake at 400° 30 minutes, or until crust is baked. Serve with Caper Sauce (see below) or a sauce of your choice.

For the pie, lightly grease an ovenproof casserole or a 7- or 8-inch pie tin. Spoon salmon mixture into container. Top with crust. Prick top. Bake at 400° 25–30 minutes, or until crust is baked and filling is hot. Pass Caper Sauce (see below) or a sauce of your choice.

Variation: *For wheat- and gluten-free diets*, Brown Rice Pie Crust (see page 118) can be used, but since it is hard to handle, it is advisable to make the pie, not the roll. Barley oat pie crust can also be used.

Caper Sauce

NO CORN, EGG, MILK,* WHEAT,* OR GLUTEN*

3 T. corn-free vegetable
  shortening (see page 13)
2 T. brown rice flour
1 c. fish stock or chicken broth
  (see page 7)

1 T. lemon juice
1 T. capers, or to taste
Salt

Heat shortening, blending in flour. Slowly stir in stock and lemon juice. Cook, stirring, until thickened.

*Variations: If you can use milk, you can substitute butter for the shortening.

If you can use wheat or gluten, you can substitute unbleached flour for the brown rice flour.

If you can use gluten but not wheat, you can substitute barley flour for the rice flour.

Tofu-Tuna Casserole #1

NO CORN, EGG, WHEAT, OR GLUTEN
Servings: 4–6

1 stalk celery, finely chopped
½ green pepper, seeded and
  finely chopped
3 T. safflower oil
1 c. thinly sliced mushrooms,
  washed, trimmed, and dried
1 c. cooked brown rice

6–8 oz. firm tofu, prepared as
  directed on page 125
1 7-oz. can water-packed tuna,
  drained
2–3 T. grated Parmesan cheese
¼ c. grated cheddar cheese
¾ c. milk

Sauté celery and pepper in oil. Add mushrooms. Stir and cook until moisture is absorbed. Add rice. Stir and cook about 2 minutes. Cut tofu into cubes and add to rice mixture. Stir and cook about 2 minutes. Add tuna. Stir all together. Spoon into a well-greased ovenproof casserole. Sprinkle with grated Parmesan cheese. Spread grated cheddar cheese over all. Pour milk over all. Bake at 350° 20–30 minutes, or until milk is absorbed and cheese is melted. Serve with a tossed green salad and hot bread for a very satisfactory, economical meal.

Tofu-Tuna Casserole # 2

NO CORN, EGG, WHEAT,* OR GLUTEN*
Servings: 4–6

This excellent, economical entrée is also good cold.

1 large stalk celery, finely chopped
2 T. safflower oil
1 c. thinly sliced mushrooms
1 T. dry parsley, or ¼ c. chopped fresh parsley
½ t. tarragon
2 t. brown rice flour
2 T. dry sherry
1 7-oz. can water-packed tuna, drained
1 12-oz. package soft tofu, prepared as directed on page 125

½ c. plain yogurt
¼ t. dry mustard
½ t. grated ginger
2 T. tamari or soy sauce
⅛ t. nutmeg
2 t. lemon juice
¼ c. chopped, stuffed olives (optional)
½ c. grated sharp cheddar cheese
Salt
Sugar (optional)

Sauté celery in the oil. Add mushrooms, parsley, and tarragon. Cook until moisture is absorbed. Add flour and sherry. Stir and cook until flour is thoroughly mixed. Add drained tuna. Set aside. Blend tofu in a blender or food processor with steel blade until creamy. Add remaining ingredients, except sugar, and continue processing. Combine tuna mixture and tofu mixture and thoroughly blend. Taste and adjust seasoning. If too tart, add a little sugar. Put mixture into a greased ovenproof casserole. Bake at 350° 30–40 minutes, or until it looks dry and edges are slightly browned. This is nice served with broccoli, asparagus, or a salad and hot bread.

Variations: If you can use wheat and gluten, you can substitute whole wheat flour for the brown rice flour.

If you can use gluten but not wheat, you can substitute barley or oat flour.

Tuna Casserole

NO CORN, EGG, MILK,* WHEAT,* OR GLUTEN*

Servings: 4–6

2 T. brown rice flour
¼ t. salt
¼ t. garlic powder
½ t. mixed spices (see
  pages 17–18)
2 T. safflower oil
1 c. soybean milk (see
  page 16)
½ t. Dijon-style mustard

2 t. lemon juice
1 7-oz. can water-packed tuna,
  drained
1 c. cooked fresh or frozen peas
½ c. sliced or chopped ripe
  olives
½ c. sliced water chestnuts
¼ c. finely chopped nuts or
  sunflower seeds

Mix together the flour and spices. Stir into oil in a medium saucepan over low heat. Add soybean milk and mustard. Stir until thickened and flour is cooked. Sprinkle lemon juice over tuna. Stir into white sauce along with peas, olives, and chestnuts. Stir until well mixed. Pour into a small oven-proof casserole. Sprinkle on nuts or sunflower seeds. Bake at 350° 20–25 minutes, or until bubbly and seeds are lightly browned.

  *Variations: If you can use milk, you can substitute butter for the oil, milk for the soybean milk, and Parmesan cheese for the nuts or crumbs.

  If you can use wheat and gluten, you can substitute unbleached flour for the brown rice flour and buttered bread crumbs for nuts or seeds.

  If you can use gluten but not wheat, you can substitute barley or oat flour for the brown rice flour.

Fish and Rice Ramekins

NO CORN, EGG, MILK,* WHEAT,* OR GLUTEN*
Servings: 4

1 c. cooked brown rice
3 T. safflower oil plus 2 t.,
   divided
1 t. onion powder
1/8 t. marjoram
3/4 c. sliced mushrooms
1 T. dry sherry
1 1/2 T. brown rice flour
1 c. soybean milk (see page 16)

1/4 t. salt
1/4 t. marjoram
1 1/2 c. prepared fish (any
   cooked white fish, including
   leftovers, or drained, water-
   packed tuna or salmon; a few
   added shrimp are always good)
Ground nuts or sunflower seeds

Combine rice, 1 tablespoon of the oil, and the onion powder and marjoram. Pat into four oiled ramekins and up the sides as a pie crust. Set aside. Sauté mushrooms in 2 teaspoons of the oil until moisture is evaporated. Add sherry and heat until nearly evaporated. Set aside. Make a white sauce: Blend flour into the remaining 2 tablespoons oil. Stir in soybean milk. Add salt and marjoram. Stir until smooth and thickened. Have fish ready. Stir mushrooms and fish into white sauce. Spoon into the ramekins. Top with finely chopped or ground nuts or seeds. Bake at 350° about 20 minutes, or until bubbly.

Variations: *If you can use milk*, sauté the mushrooms in 2 t. butter instead of oil, use 2 T. butter in the white sauce instead of oil, and substitute milk for the soybean milk and grated Parmesan cheese for the ground nuts or seeds.

If you can use wheat and gluten, you can substitute unbleached flour for the brown rice flour.

If you can use milk and wheat and gluten, you can substitute buttered bread crumbs for the ground nuts or seeds.

If you can use gluten but not wheat, you can substitute barley or oat flour.

Fillet of Sole with Yogurt Sauce

NO CORN, EGG, WHEAT,* OR GLUTEN*
Servings: 3–4

1 lb. sole fillets
2 t. rice flour plus enough to
    dust fillets
⅔ c. plain yogurt
¼ t. salt

½ t. onion powder
1 t. dried parsley
1 t. Dijon-style mustard
2 t. finely chopped capers
½ t. sugar

Butter or oil a shallow baking dish large enough to hold the fish in a single layer. Dust fillets with flour. Spread fish in greased dish. Mix the 2 t. flour into the yogurt. Add remaining ingredients. Mix thoroughly. Spread on top of fish, covering completely. Bake at 350° 15 minutes, or until fish flakes with a fork.

*Variations: If you can use wheat and gluten, you can substitute un-bleached wheat flour for the rice flour.

If you can use gluten but not wheat, you can substitute barley flour for the rice flour.

Sautéed Sesame Fish

NO CORN, EGG, MILK,* WHEAT,* OR GLUTEN*
Servings: 4

1 lb. rockfish, red snapper fillets,
    or halibut steaks
Rice flour
Soybean milk (see page 16)
⅓ c. sesame seeds and wheat-
    free, gluten-free crumbs

3–4 T. olive oil
2 T. lemon juice
2 T. chopped fresh parsley
½–1 c. small, cooked shrimp,
    canned or fresh†

Cut fish into four pieces. Dust with flour. Dip in soybean milk. Coat evenly with a mixture of sesame seeds and crumbs. Heat oil in a large frying pan (it should cover the bottom of pan generously). Add fish and sauté, turning once, until fish flakes with a fork, about 6–10 minutes depending on thickness of fish. Put lemon juice, parsley, and shrimp into a small pan. Stir and heat just to warm. Spoon over fish.

Variations: *If you can use milk*, substitute milk for the soybean milk.

If you can use wheat and gluten, you can substitute unbleached flour for the rice flour and wheat bread crumbs for the wheat-free, gluten-free crumbs.

If you can use gluten but not wheat, you can substitute barley flour for the rice flour.

†You may omit the shrimp and stir in ¼ c. finely chopped green onion.

Fish Fillets with Shrimp

NO CORN,* EGG, MILK,* WHEAT,* OR GLUTEN*

Servings: 4–6

4 large or 6 small fillets of sole, red snapper, turbot, or other white fish
¼ c. white wine
Salt
2 c. hot water
2 T. lemon juice
2½ T. safflower oil
3 T. brown rice flour

1 T. minced onion
1 T. seeded and minced green pepper
1½ T. chervil
1 c. shrimp
1 c. wheat-free, gluten-free crumbs toasted in 1–2 T. safflower or sesame oil

Marinate fish in wine. Transfer to a frying pan, salt lightly, and cover with hot water and lemon juice. Simmer 5 minutes, or until about half cooked. Transfer fish to a greased baking dish. Mix together the oil and flour. Add to the liquid remaining in the pan. Add onion, green pepper, chervil. Cook, stirring, until thickened and smooth. Salt to taste. Mix in shrimp. Spread ½ cup of the crumbs on fish. Cover with sauce. Sprinkle on the remaining ½ cup crumbs. Bake at 350° about 15 minutes, or until fish flakes with a fork. If crumbs are not browned, slip dish under broiler. Serve garnished with lemon wedges and parsley.

Variations: *If you can use corn*, you can substitute 1½ T. cornstarch for the flour.

If you can use milk, you can substitute 3 T. butter for the oil.

If you can use wheat and gluten, you can substitute wheat flour for the brown rice flour and wheat bread crumbs for the wheat-free, gluten-free crumbs.

If you can use milk and wheat and gluten, you can substitute buttered bread crumbs for the crumbs toasted in oil.

If you can use gluten but not wheat, you can substitute crumbs from barley, oat, or rye flour breads, and barley or oat flour for the rice flour.

CHICKEN

	NO CORN	NO EGG	NO MILK	NO WHEAT	NO GLUTEN
Baked Chicken	X	X		⊗	⊗
Orange-Glazed Roast Chicken	⊗	X	⊗	⊗	⊗
Chicken with Tofu	⊗	X	X	X	X
Assyrian Chicken	X	X	X	X	X
Parmesan Chicken	X	X		⊗	⊗

⊗ means that the recipe includes instructions for adding that ingredient if allowed.

Baked Chicken

NO CORN, EGG, WHEAT,* OR GLUTEN*
Servings: 4–6

1 3–3½ lb. broiler/fryer
    chicken, cut into serving-sized
    pieces
1 lemon
2 cloves garlic, minced
1 t. tarragon
½ t. thyme
¼ t. salt
2 T. plus 1½ t. olive oil,
    divided
2 T. butter

¼ c. brown rice flour
1 14-oz. can chicken broth or
    1¾ c. homemade chicken
    stock (see page 7)
¼ c. dry vermouth, dry sherry,
    or milk
¾ c. milk
1 c. Parmesan cheese, divided
½ c. sliced, pitted olives
1 2-oz. jar sliced, drained
    pimiento

Rub all surfaces of chicken with cut lemon. Blend garlic, herbs, salt, and 1½ teaspoons of the olive oil. Spread skin sides of chicken with marinade. Cover and refrigerate for several hours. In a large frying pan, heat butter and the remaining 2 tablespoons oil. Brown chicken pieces well, a few at a time. Place skin-side-up in a single layer in a shallow baking dish about 9 x 12 inches. Reserve 2 tablespoons fat in frying pan. Discard rest. Blend in flour. Gradually add chicken broth, wine, and milk. Cook, stirring, until thickened. Simmer, uncovered, about 10 minutes, stirring occasionally. Blend in ½ cup of the Parmesan cheese. Sprinkle chicken with olives and pimiento. Cover with sauce. Top with the remaining ½ cup Parmesan. Bake, uncovered, at 350° 30 minutes, or until chicken is tender.

    *Variations: If you can use wheat and gluten, you can substitute unbleached flour for the brown rice flour.

    If you can use gluten but not wheat, you can substitute barley flour for brown rice flour.

Orange-Glazed Roast Chicken

NO CORN,* EGG, MILK,* WHEAT,* OR GLUTEN*
Servings: 4–6

1 3-lb. broiler/fryer chicken
½ t. salt
½ t. garlic powder
½ t. tarragon
1 T. safflower oil

⅓ c. frozen orange juice
concentrate, thawed
¾ c. plus ⅓ c. chicken
broth (see page 7)
4 t. brown rice flour

Rub chicken inside and out with salt, garlic powder and tarragon, then oil. Place in bottom of roasting pan and roast at 400° 20 minutes. Spoon orange juice over chicken. Reduce heat to 375° and continue roasting about 40 minutes longer, or until tender. Remove to platter and keep warm. Pour the ¾ cup chicken broth into drippings and heat, stirring until blended. Mix the ⅓ cup broth with the flour. Stir into pan and simmer, stirring, until thickened. Serve chicken with rice mixed with raisins and chopped nuts or seeds. Pass sauce.

Variations: *If you can use corn*, you can substitute 2 t. cornstarch for the flour.

If you can use milk, you can substitute butter for the oil.

If you can use wheat and gluten, you can substitute wheat flour for the brown rice flour.

If you can use gluten but not wheat, you can substitute barley or oat flour.

Chicken with Tofu

NO CORN,* EGG, MILK, WHEAT, OR GLUTEN
Servings: 3–4

Buy a whole 3–3½-pound chicken, cut out the breast for this recipe, and use the rest for other things—soup, salads, etc. Chicken breasts can be purchased alone, but are much more expensive.

2½ t. arrowroot (see page 14)
⅓ c. dry sherry
1 T. vinegar
3 T. soy sauce
3 T. safflower oil
1 whole chicken breast, boned and cut into small cubes
1 clove garlic, minced
1 T. grated fresh ginger
½ t. ground coriander
1 c. quartered small mushrooms
1 onion, cut into 1-inch squares, or 1 t. onion powder

1 c. thinly sliced carrots, partially cooked if desired
½ c. sliced water chestnuts
1 c. frozen peas or edible pea pods
1 12–16 oz. package firm tofu, prepared as directed on page 125 and cut into ½-inch cubes
1–2 T. sesame seeds or as many as you wish

This is a stir-fry and all ingredients should be prepared before any cooking is done. To make sauce, blend arrowroot, sherry, vinegar, and soy sauce over medium heat until sauce boils and thickens. Set aside. Heat oil in a large frying pan, electric skillet, or wok. Add chicken. Cook and stir for 1 minute. Add garlic, ginger, onion, and coriander. Stir 1 more minute. Add mushrooms, carrots, and water chestnuts and cook and stir 1 more minute. Stir in peas or pods, tofu, and sauce. Cook 1 more minute or just enough to heat sauce. Turn into a serving dish. Sprinkle with sesame seeds. Serve over brown rice.

*Variation: If you can use corn, you can substitute 1 T. cornstarch for the arrowroot.

Assyrian Chicken

NO CORN, EGG, MILK, WHEAT, OR GLUTEN
Servings: 4

1 onion, thinly sliced
1 large garlic clove, minced or
  mashed
2 T. lemon juice
½ t. turmeric

¼ t. salt
4 half chicken breasts, or a
  combination of breasts and
  thighs

Combine first five ingredients. Marinate chicken several hours or overnight. Turn once or twice. Broil in a preheated broiler 10–15 minutes. Serve with brown rice and a vegetable of your choice—broccoli or glazed carrots go well. This recipe can be doubled or tripled.

Note: If thighs need longer cooking, remove breasts and keep warm in covered pan in lower part of oven if there is room under your broiler.

Parmesan Chicken

NO CORN, EGG, WHEAT,* OR GLUTEN*
Servings: 6

2 fryer chickens, or 3 whole
  breasts, cut into serving-sized
  pieces
⅓–½ c. butter, melted
2 c. crisp wheat-free, gluten-free
  crumbs (see page 13)
¾ c. Parmesan cheese

¼ c. chopped fresh parsley, or
  1 T. dried parsley
1 clove garlic, minced, or ¼ t.
  garlic powder
1½ t. salt
Butter (optional)

Dip each piece of chicken into melted butter. Combine next five ingredients. Dip buttered chicken pieces into crumb mixture to completely cover. Arrange in a single layer, not touching, in a shallow baking dish. Dot with additional butter if desired. Bake at 350° 45 minutes to 1 hour, or until chicken is tender and browned.

*Variation: *If you can use wheat and gluten*, you can substitute wheat bread crumbs for the wheat-free, gluten-free crumbs.

BEEF

	NO CORN	NO EGG	NO MILK	NO WHEAT	NO GLUTEN
Indian Beef with Peanut Sauce	X	X	X	⊗	⊗
Peanut Sauce	X	X	⊗	X	X
Teriyaki Meat Loaf	X	X	X	⊗	⊗
Beef Curry on Raisin Rice	X	X	X	⊗	⊗
Oyster Beef with Tofu	⊗	X	X	X	X
Greek Shish Kebab	X	X	X	X	X
Dutch Oven Beef	⊗	X	X	⊗	⊗
Braised Beef Provençal	X	X	X	⊗	⊗
Sauerbraten Beef	X	X	X	⊗	⊗
Swedish Pot Roast	⊗	X	⊗	⊗	⊗
Flank Steak Oriental	⊗	X	X	⊗	⊗
Stuffed Flank Steak	X	X		⊗	⊗
Parisian Beef Stew	X	X	X	⊗	⊗
Spiced Pot Roast	⊗	X	X	X	X
Creamed Dried Beef with Artichoke Hearts	X	X		⊗	⊗
Beef and Eggplant Casserole	X	X		X	X
Pot Roast of Veal	X	X	X	⊗	⊗

⊗ means that the recipe includes instructions for adding that ingredient if allowed.

Indian Beef with Peanut Sauce

NO CORN, EGG, MILK, WHEAT,* OR GLUTEN*
Servings: 4

1 lb. flank steak, round steak, or
    other beef of your choice
2 T. safflower oil
1/3 c. chopped onion
1 clove garlic, minced
1 c. grated, peeled apple or
    unsweetened applesauce

1 T. brown rice flour
1 c. condensed beef broth or
    homemade stock (see page 7)
1/2 c. dark, seedless raisins
1/2 t.–1 T. curry powder
2 T. chopped chutney

Open flank steak so it is flat. Partially freeze meat and then cut into thin slices on the diagonal. Heat oil in a large frying pan. Brown meat in three or four batches (remove to bowl as it is done and replace with more). When it is all browned, set aside. In the same pan, sauté the onion, garlic, and fresh apple until apple is just soft; return meat to pan. (If you are using applesauce, add it just before meat.) Stir in flour. Add remaining ingredients. Stir until well blended and mixture comes to a boil. For flank steak, about 5 minutes cooking is enough, just to blend flavors. If less tender cuts of meat are used, longer cooking is recommended, up to 30 minutes. Serve over brown rice. Sprinkle with shredded coconut if desired. Pass Peanut Sauce (see below).

Variations: If you can use wheat and gluten, you can substitute unbleached flour for the brown rice flour.

If you can use gluten but not wheat, you can substitute barley flour for the brown rice flour.

Peanut Sauce

NO CORN, EGG, MILK,* WHEAT, OR GLUTEN
Yield: ½–⅔ cups

¼ c. creamy peanut butter
1 T. safflower oil
2 T. soy sauce
1 T. honey

1 T. sesame oil
¼ t. minced garlic
2 T. coconut milk† (optional)

Combine peanut butter and oil. Add remaining ingredients. Blend well.
Cover and chill if made ahead. Serve at room temperature or slightly warm.

   *Variation: If you can use milk, you can substitute milk for the 3 cups
water used to make coconut milk.

   †To make coconut milk, soak 2 cups shredded unsweetened coconut in
3 cups water. Bring to a boil. Remove from heat and let stand 30 minutes.
Pour through dampened cheesecloth into a bowl, squeezing out all liquid.
Canned coconut milk is also available.

Teriyaki Meat Loaf

NO CORN, EGG, MILK, WHEAT,* OR GLUTEN*
Servings: 10–12

1 lb. lean ground beef
¾ lb. mild bulk sausage or
   ground pork
½ c. cooked brown rice
1 t. onion powder
½ c. chopped seeded green
   pepper

3 T. soy sauce, divided
2 T. lemon juice
1 T. honey
1 garlic clove, minced
½ t. ground ginger
1 T. honey

Mix all ingredients except the honey and 1 tablespoon of the soy sauce
together thoroughly. Shape into a loaf. Put into a 9 × 5-inch loaf pan.
Bake at 350° about 1 hour, or until pork is cooked. When loaf is half
cooked, blend the 1 tablespoon soy sauce with honey. Spoon over loaf.
Use a meat thermometer or cook until juices run clear and meat has lost
its pinkness.

   *Variation: If you can use wheat and gluten, you can substitute wheat
germ for the rice.

Beef Curry on Raisin Rice

NO CORN, EGG, MILK, WHEAT,* OR GLUTEN*
Servings: 4

2 T. brown rice flour
1 t. salt
1 lb. beef chuck, cut into ¾-inch cubes
2 T. safflower oil
1 t. onion powder
1 clove garlic, pressed or minced
½ t. basil

¼–1 t. curry powder
1 c. beef broth or homemade stock (see page 7)
½–1 c. tomato juice
2–3 c. steamed brown rice
¼–½ c. each seedless raisins and slivered almonds

Put flour and salt into a paper bag. Shake meat cubes in bag to cover well. Heat oil in a heavy skillet. Brown meat on all sides. Add onion powder, garlic, basil, curry powder, and broth. Cover and simmer until meat is tender, stirring occasionally. Add tomato juice to desired consistency. Serve on steamed brown rice mixed with raisins and almonds.

Variations: If you can use wheat and gluten, you can substitute whole wheat flour for the brown rice flour.

If you can use gluten but not wheat, you can substitute barley or oat flour for the brown rice flour.

Oyster Beef with Tofu

NO CORN,* EGG, MILK, WHEAT, OR GLUTEN
Servings: 4–5

1 12–16-oz. package firm tofu,
  prepared as directed on
  page 125
¾ lb. flank or top round steak
2 T. soy sauce
2 t. oyster sauce
2 t. dry white wine
2½ t. arrowroot or 3½ t.
  potato flour, divided

½ t. sesame or safflower oil
1 t. sugar
1 T. safflower oil
2–3 T. water
½ c. beef stock (see page 7)
Alfalfa sprouts (optional)

Cut the tofu into ½–1-inch pieces. Set aside. Partially freeze steak for easier slicing. Cut on diagonal into thin slices. Combine soy and oyster sauces, wine, 2 teaspoons of the arrowroot (or 2½ teaspoons of potato flour), and the sesame oil and sugar. Stir into the meat and mix until meat is well coated with sauce. Heat the safflower oil until very hot. Sauté the meat in several batches until browned. Remove to a serving bowl. Keep warm. Add the water to the cooking pan, loosen the bits, and mix with the meat drippings. Add the tofu pieces and lightly brown them. Lift tofu with a slotted spoon and put over the meat. Dissolve the remaining ½ teaspoon arrowroot (or 1 teaspoon potato flour) in the beef stock. Add to pan, stir until slightly thickened and smooth. Pour over meat and tofu. Garnish with sprouts if desired. Serve with baked squash and a quick hot bread.

*Variation: If you can use corn, you can substitute 3 t. cornstarch for the arrowroot.

Greek Shish Kebab

NO CORN, EGG, MILK, WHEAT, OR GLUTEN
Servings: 6

½ c. olive oil
3 T. vinegar
¼ t. oregano
2 T. finely chopped carrot
2 T. finely chopped celery
2 T. finely chopped onion

1½ lb. round steak, cut into
    1-inch cubes
Chunks of onion, green pepper,
    eggplant, or vegetables of your
    choice

Combine the first six ingredients. Marinate the meat about 3 hours in the mixture. Thread onto skewers with the vegetable chunks of your choice. Cook under broiler or on a grill to desired doneness.

Dutch Oven Beef

NO CORN,* EGG, MILK, WHEAT,* OR GLUTEN*
Servings: 8

1–2 cloves garlic, slivered
3–4 lb. chuck, rump, or top
    round roast
1 t. salt
1 t. allspice
1 T. brown sugar
½ c. red wine vinegar, or half
    red wine and half mild vinegar

2 T. safflower oil
1 c. chopped carrots
1 c. chopped celery
1 c. chopped onions
1½ c. strong regular or
    decaffeinated coffee
3 T. brown rice flour
¼ c. water

Insert garlic slivers into tiny cuts in the roast. Put meat in a bowl. Combine salt, allspice, sugar, and wine vinegar. Pour over meat and marinate 4 hours to overnight, turning meat several times. Drain, reserving marinade. In a Dutch oven, brown the meat in the oil. When meat is browned, add chopped vegetables, coffee, and reserved marinade. Reduce heat, cover, and cook slowly until meat is tender, 2½–3 hours. Remove meat to a warm platter. Skim off fat. Transfer cooking liquid and vegetables to a blender or food processor with steel blade and puree, or mash through a sieve. Put liquid into a saucepan. Combine flour and water and stir into the liquid. Cook, stirring, until it thickens. Pour over meat.

Variations: If you can use corn, add 1 T. Worcestershire sauce with the wine vinegar.

If you can use wheat and gluten, you can substitute unbleached flour for the brown rice flour.

If you can use gluten but not wheat, you can substitute barley or oat flour for the brown rice flour.

Braised Beef Provençal

NO CORN, EGG, MILK, WHEAT,* OR GLUTEN*
Servings: 8

1 large onion, cut in ½-inch slices

4 medium carrots, cut in ½-inch slices

1 large green pepper, seeded and cut in chunks

½ lb. mushrooms (leave whole if small; if large, cut in 2–3 pieces)

1 c. whole pitted black olives

3–4 lb. cross rib, chuck, or rump roast

1 clove garlic, mashed

1 t. thyme

Salt

½ c. dried wheat-free, gluten-free crumbs

2 c. beef broth (see page 7)

2 c. red wine (or omit and use 4 c. broth)

Place vegetables in bottom of a Dutch oven. Add olives. Place meat on top. Mix together the garlic, thyme, salt, and crumbs. Sprinkle over meat. Pour wine and broth around meat. Seal pan tightly with foil, then cover with a tight lid. Bake at 375° 10 minutes, then reduce heat to 275° and bake about 5 hours longer, or until meat is very tender.

Variations: If you can use wheat and gluten, you can substitute wheat bread crumbs for the wheat-free, gluten-free crumbs.

If you can use gluten but not wheat, you can substitute barley, oat, or rye bread crumbs for the wheat-free, gluten-free crumbs.

Sauerbraten Beef

NO CORN, EGG, MILK, WHEAT,* OR GLUTEN*
Servings: 8

4 lb. rolled and boned top sirloin
   or rump roast
Salt
1 pt. vinegar
1 pt. water
2 large onions, sliced
3 bay leaves
6 celery tops
6 peppercorns
1 large carrot, sliced
1/4 t. thyme

1/4 t. garlic powder
5 whole cloves
2 T. brown sugar
Brown rice or potato flour
2 T. safflower oil
1/3 c. seedless raisins
1/4 t. ground ginger and 1/4
   c. wheat-free, gluten-free
   crumbs, or 2 T. brown rice
   flour

Rub roast with salt and place in a large bowl. Combine vinegar, water, onions, bay leaves, celery tops, peppercorns, carrot, thyme, garlic, cloves, and brown sugar. Pour over meat, cover with plastic wrap, and marinate in refrigerator for three days, turning meat about twice a day. When ready to cook, lightly dust the meat with flour. Brown the meat quickly on all sides in the oil. Add marinade and vegetables, cover, and simmer until tender, about 3 hours. Lift meat out onto a platter and keep warm in a low oven. Strain the juices. Add 3–4 tablespoons of the juices to brown rice flour to make a paste. Stir into pan juices. Add the raisins and ginger-crumbs, and cook, stirring constantly, until smooth and thickened. Pour part of sauce over the meat and pass the remainder. Traditionally this dish is served with potato pancakes and tiny beets.

*Variations: *If you can use wheat and gluten*, you can substitute wheat flour for the rice or potato flour, and use 5 gingersnaps, crumbled, instead of the ginger and wheat-free or gluten-free crumbs.

If you can use gluten but not wheat, you can substitute barley, oat, or potato flour for the brown rice flour and use 2 T. more flour instead of crumbs.

Swedish Pot Roast

NO CORN,* EGG, MILK,* WHEAT,* OR GLUTEN*
Servings: 8–10

3–4 lb. chuck or rump roast
1 t. salt
1 t. allspice
3 T. safflower oil
2 medium-sized onions, sliced
1 t. anchovy paste

2 bay leaves
2 T. vinegar
2 T. molasses
4 T. brown rice flour
½ c. water

Rub roast on all sides with salt and allspice. Brown on all sides in oil. Halfway through, add onions. Stir in anchovy paste, bay leaves, vinegar, and molasses. Reduce heat, cover, and simmer until meat is tender, 2–2½ hours. Remove meat to a warm platter. Blend flour into the ½ cup water to make a paste. Stir into pan juices and cook until slightly thickened. Serve with roast.

*Variations: If you can use corn, you can substitute 2 T. cornstarch for the flour.

If you can use milk, you can use 1 c. sour cream or yogurt instead of water.

If you can use wheat and gluten, you can use whole wheat flour instead of brown rice flour.

If you can use gluten but not wheat, you can substitute barley or oat flour for the brown rice flour.

Flank Steak Oriental

NO CORN,* EGG, MILK, WHEAT,* OR GLUTEN*
Servings: 4–5

1 flank steak, about 1¼ lb.
½ lb. mushrooms, sliced
(about 2½ c.)
1 c. diagonally sliced celery
1 10-oz. package frozen peas
¾ c. water
2 T. brown rice flour

2 T. water
¼ c. dry sherry
2 T. soy sauce
2 t. grated ginger, or ¼ t.
ground ginger
¼ t. garlic powder
3 T. safflower oil

Partially freeze flank steak. Cut in half lengthwise and slice each half into ¼-inch strips. Place vegetables in a large, heavy pan. Add the ¾ cup water. Cover, bring to a boil, and boil 5 minutes over high heat until celery is tender but still crisp. Drain, reserving liquid. Place vegetables in an uncovered bowl. Add 2 tablespoons water to the flour. Stir in sherry, soy sauce, ginger, and garlic. Set aside. Brown meat quickly in the oil. Reduce heat, return vegetables and soy mixture to pan, and cook about 1 minute, stirring constantly until sauce is thickened. Blend in about ⅓ cup of the reserved vegetable liquid for a thinner sauce. Serve with steamed brown rice or Chinese noodles.

Variations: If you can use corn, you can substitute 1 T. cornstarch for the flour.

If you can use wheat and gluten, you can substitute whole wheat flour for the brown rice flour.

If you can use gluten but not wheat, you can substitute barley or oat flour for the brown rice flour.

Stuffed Flank Steak

NO CORN, EGG, WHEAT,* OR GLUTEN*
Servings: 4–5

⅓ c. chopped onion
2–3 T. safflower oil, divided
1 t. salt
½ t. basil, thyme, or
   marjoram
1 T. dried parsley

½ c. shredded raw carrot
1½ c. cooked brown rice
About 1½ lbs. flank steak
2 c. buttermilk
2 T. brown rice flour
¼ c. water

Sauté onion in 1 tablespoon of the oil until soft. Add next 5 ingredients and spread over flank steak. Roll from one of long sides and fasten with skewers or string. Brown on all sides in 1–2 tablespoons more oil. Place meat in a deep baking dish. Pour buttermilk over it. Cover and bake at 350° 1½ hours, or until tender. Remove from pan. The buttermilk will look curdled. Strain liquid into a pan and whip well or put into the blender and blend until smooth. Return to pan. Combine flour and water. Stir into buttermilk. Cook, stirring, until thickened. Pour part over meat and pass the remainder.

Variations: *If you can use wheat and gluten*, you can use 2 c. soft bread crumbs, loosely packed, instead of the rice, and wheat flour instead of the brown rice flour.

If you can use gluten but not wheat, you can substitute barley or oat flour for the brown rice flour.

Parisian Beef Stew

NO CORN, EGG, MILK, WHEAT,* OR GLUTEN*
Servings: 4

3 strips bacon
1 lb. chuck, top round, or
sirloin, cut into 1½-inch
cubes
Brown rice flour or potato flour
½ c. beef broth (see page 7)
½ c. Burgundy wine (or omit
and use 1 c. broth)

½ t. garlic powder
1 t. salt
¼ t. marjoram
⅛ t. thyme
1 T. dried parsley
3 carrots, cut into 1-inch pieces
3 medium potatoes, quartered
8 peeled pearl onions

Cook bacon until crisp. Set aside. Dredge meat in flour. Brown in bacon fat in a Dutch oven. Add beef broth, wine, garlic, salt, marjoram, thyme, and parsley. Stir all together. Cover tightly. This may be simmered on top of the stove or put into a 300° oven. You may have to add more beef broth as the gravy thickens. Add vegetables to oven-cooked roast after about 1½ hours, or to roast cooked on top of stove after about 2 hours. Simmer until meat is tender and vegetables are cooked, about 1 hour in oven or 30–40 minutes on top of stove.

*Variations: *If you can use wheat and gluten*, you can substitute wheat flour for the rice or potato flour.

If you can use gluten but not wheat, you can substitute barley or oat flour for the brown rice flour or potato flour.

Spiced Pot Roast

NO CORN,* EGG, MILK, WHEAT, OR GLUTEN
Servings: 8–10

1 t. salt
½ t. mace
½ t. ground cloves
3 lb. chuck roast
1 large onion, chopped
2 stalks celery with leaves,
   chopped
¼ c. safflower oil

¼ c. vinegar
½ t. chervil
¼ t. thyme
1 T. safflower oil
About 4 c. beef broth
   (see page 7)
2 T. tomato sauce (see page 268)
2 c. sliced peeled carrots

Mix together the salt, mace, and cloves. Rub into meat. Put into a large bowl. Combine onion, celery, ¼ cup oil, vinegar, chervil, and thyme, and mix together. Pour over meat and marinate several hours or overnight, turning meat at least once. Remove meat and save marinade. In a Dutch oven, brown meat on all sides in 1 tablespoon hot oil. Add enough beef broth to barely cover meat. Cover pot tightly and simmer about 2 hours, adding more broth if needed. Add the marinade, tomato sauce, and carrots. Simmer until meat and vegetables are tender, about 40 minutes longer.

   Variation: *If you can use corn*, you can substitute catsup for the tomato sauce.

Creamed Dried Beef
with Artichoke Hearts

NO CORN, EGG, WHEAT,* OR GLUTEN*
Servings: 4

¼ lb. dried beef
Boiling water to cover
1 can artichoke hearts
2 T. safflower oil

2 T. brown rice flour
½ t. onion powder
1½ c. milk

Tear beef into small pieces. Pour boiling water over to cover and let stand 5 minutes, then drain thoroughly. Drain artichoke hearts and cut in half lengthwise. Heat oil in a frying pan. Add beef and cook, stirring, until edges are frizzled. Stir in flour and onion powder. The beef should be evenly coated with the flour. Cook, stirring, about 1 minute. Gradually stir in the milk. Cook, stirring, until thickened. If a thinner consistency is desired, add more milk. Carefully stir in the artichoke hearts. Cover and simmer just until artichokes are heated through.

Variations: *If you can use wheat and gluten*, you can substitute whole wheat flour for the brown rice flour.

If you can use gluten but not wheat, you can substitute barley or oat flour for the brown rice flour.

Omit artichokes and add sliced avocado and a few slices of pimiento-stuffed olives.

Beef and Eggplant Casserole

NO CORN, EGG, WHEAT, OR GLUTEN
Servings: 6

1 large eggplant, peeled and
    sliced into ½-inch slices
Safflower oil for brushing
    eggplant slices
1 lb. lean ground beef
1 medium-sized onion, chopped
1 clove garlic, minced
¼ lb. mushrooms, sliced

2 T. safflower oil
1 15-oz. can tomato sauce
¾ t. basil
¾ t. oregano
Salt
1½ c. mozzarella cheese
½ c. Parmesan cheese

Brush eggplant slices with oil, arrange on a baking sheet, and bake, uncovered, at 450°, turning once, until lightly browned and very soft, about 30 minutes. Brown the beef and drain off fat. Remove beef to a bowl. Sauté the onion, garlic, and mushroom in the 2 tablespoons oil until soft. Add tomato sauce, basil, and oregano. Simmer sauce, uncovered, about 10 minutes. Add beef. Season to taste with salt. In a 1½-quart ovenproof casserole, layer half of the eggplant, cover with half of the sauce, followed by ¾ cup mozzarella and ¼ cup Parmesan. Repeat the layering. Bake at 350° about 25 minutes, or until hot and bubbly.

Variation: Mushroom soup instead of the tomato sauce is also good if ingredients are allowed (check label) or homemade soup is used.

Pot Roast of Veal

NO CORN, EGG, MILK, WHEAT,* OR GLUTEN*
Servings: 6–8

This is a comparatively economical dish because you start with a breast of veal.

1 3–4-lb. breast of veal
1 small onion
Dash of salt
¼ t. thyme
¼ t. marjoram
½ t. curry powder
½ t. basil
½ t. salt
2 medium carrots, peeled and
sliced lengthwise

Brown rice or potato flour
2 T. safflower oil
1–1½ c. veal-bone broth
2 cloves garlic, minced
1 onion, cut into pieces
1 large apple, peeled, cored, and
cut into pieces

Spread out veal and carefully cut off the rib bones, leaving a flat piece of meat. Cover the bones with water, add the small onion and salt, and cook over low heat to make a broth. Remove bones and onion. Skim fat and reserve broth for the roast. Mix spices and salt. Rub into the meat. Place carrots at one end of meat. Roll meat tightly around carrots and tie with a string. Dredge with flour, rubbing it in well. Heat oil in a Dutch oven. Brown meat on all sides, turning carefully. Add reserved broth, garlic, onion, and apple. Cover and simmer about 2 hours, or until meat feels tender when pierced with a fork. Turn roast frequently as it cooks. Lift out onto a platter and keep warm. Puree broth and vegetables in a blender or food processor with steel blade, or mash through a sieve. Thicken, if desired, with brown rice flour. Cut strings on roast. Pass gravy.

*Variations: *If you can use wheat and gluten*, you can substitute unbleached wheat flour for the brown rice flour.

If you can use gluten but not wheat, you can substitute barley or oat flour for the brown rice flour.

Instead of using carrots in the roll, extend the meat with 1½–2 c. bread or rice stuffing.

PORK

	NO CORN	NO EGG	NO MILK	NO WHEAT	NO GLUTEN
Chutney-Glazed Leftover Roast Pork	X	X	X	X	X
Baked Eggplant with Pork	X	X	⊗	X	X
Baked Pork Chops with Fruit	⊗	X	X	⊗	⊗
Curried Cranberry Pork Chops	⊗	X	X	X	⊗
Ham Rolls	X	X	X	X	X
Gnocchi with Meat Sauce	X	X	X		
Wheat-Free Gnocchi	X		X	X	
Meat Sauce	X	X	X	⊗	⊗
Steamed Chinese Dumplings in Broth	X	X	X		
Fillings for Dumplings	⊗	X	⊗	⊗	⊗
Potlickers	X	X	X		
Dip for Potlickers	X	X	X	X	X
Fillings for Potlickers:					
Pork	⊗	X	X	⊗	⊗
Ginger-Beef	X	X	X	X	X

⊗ means that the recipe includes instructions for adding that ingredient if allowed.
Note: See also Cranberry Bean and Pork Casserole, page 160.

Chutney-Glazed Leftover Pork Roast

NO CORN, EGG, MILK, WHEAT, OR GLUTEN
Servings: 4

¼ c. chutney
1 T. soy sauce
1½ T. frozen orange juice
   concentrate, thawed
¼ t. ground ginger

¼ t. garlic powder
3 c. cold roast pork, cut into 1 x
   1½-inch cubes, all fat
   trimmed off

Combine first five ingredients. Puree in blender or food processor, or chop chutney very fine before adding to other ingredients. Combine with pork in a medium-sized skillet and sauté over medium-low heat until pork is thoroughly hot and glazed with the sauce. Serve over brown rice or wheat-free noodles or with baked sweet potatoes or yams.

Baked Eggplant with Pork

NO CORN, EGG, MILK,* WHEAT, OR GLUTEN
Servings: 4

2 small eggplant, about 1½ lb.
Lemon juice
Salt
Safflower oil
1 lb. ground sausage, or 2 c.
   leftover pork roast trimmed
   and ground

½ c. minced onion, or 1½
   t. onion powder
½ c. ground nuts
2 T. minced fresh parsley
½ t. oregano
3 large fresh tomatoes

Trim and peel eggplant. Cut crosswise into ½-inch slices. Rub the slices with lemon juice and sprinkle with salt. Let sit on paper towels 30 minutes, then drain and pat dry. Sauté the slices on both sides in hot oil until they are softened and browned. Drain on paper towels, removing any excess fat. Set aside. In the same pan, cook the sausage or warm the roast with the onion. Drain any fat from the pan. Combine the nuts, parsley, and oregano. Peel and cut tomatoes in thin slices. In a lightly oiled ovenproof casserole, alternate layers of eggplant, meat, nut mixture, and tomatoes, ending with tomatoes. Sprinkle on more nuts. Bake at 375° about 40 minutes, or until bubbly and top is golden. Skim off any fat from top.

Variation: *If you can use milk*, you can substitute grated Parmesan cheese for the ground nuts.

Baked Pork Chops with Fruit
NO CORN,* EGG, MILK, WHEAT,* OR GLUTEN*
Servings: 4

4 pork chops, ½ inch thick	*1 12-oz. can apricot nectar*
½ t. dry mustard	*1–2 c. moist, mixed dried fruit*
2 t. vinegar	*Brown rice flour (optional)*

Trim excess fat from chops. Rub a large frying pan with some of the fat until it is lightly greased. Discard the fat. Brown chops well on both sides. Remove to a large ovenproof casserole or pan in a single layer as they are browned. Combine mustard, vinegar, and nectar. Add to frying pan, stirring to loosen any bits stuck to pan. Arrange dried fruit around meat. Pour sauce over all. Cover and bake at 325° about 1 hour, or until meat is tender. Transfer meat to a warm serving platter. Arrange fruit around chops. If you desire a thicker sauce, thicken with a little brown rice flour moistened in water and stirred until thickened and desired consistency. Pour over chops or reserve some to pass at the table. Serve with baked yams or brown rice and Zucchini Fingers (see page 230) or Scalloped Turnips (see page 238).

Variations: *If you can use corn*, you can thicken sauce with cornstarch instead of flour.

If you can use wheat and gluten, you can thicken sauce with wheat flour instead of brown rice flour.

If you can use gluten but not wheat, you can substitute barley or oat flour for the brown rice flour.

Curried Cranberry Pork Chops

NO CORN,* EGG, MILK, WHEAT, OR GLUTEN*
Servings: 4

2 t. curry powder
¼ t. ground ginger
4 thick pork chops
¼ c. brown rice flour
1 T. safflower oil

2 c. homemade whole cranberry
    sauce†
¼ c. dry white wine
½ t. grated lemon rind
½ t. salt

Combine curry powder and ginger. Rub into both sides of pork chops. Dredge chops in flour. Brown in oil. Place in an ovenproof casserole. Drain off fat in frying pan. Mix remaining ingredients and add to pan. Heat, stirring, until simmering. Pour over chops. Bake at 350° about 1 hour.

Variations: If you can use corn, you can use a 1-pound can whole cranberry sauce instead of the homemade.

If you can use gluten but not wheat, you can substitute barley or oat flour for the brown rice flour.

†Pick over a 12-ounce package fresh or frozen cranberries. Follow directions on package for making sauce, or, for a thicker sauce, put ½ cup of water in the bottom of a pan, add cranberries and 1½ cups of sugar. Bring gently to a boil, stirring to dissolve sugar, and cook until berries pop. Test for sweetness. You may want more sugar.

Ham Rolls

NO CORN, EGG, MILK, WHEAT, OR GLUTEN
Serving: 1

1–2 slices ham
2 t. chutney, chopped

2 T. chopped nuts
½ c. cooked brown rice

Have ready as many thin slices of ham as desired, allowing one or two per serving depending on their size. Mix chutney and chopped nuts with the rice. Place some of mixture on each slice. Make a roll of the ham slices. Put seam-side-down in a baking dish. Bake at 325° just until heated through, 20–30 minutes depending on size. Serve with Mushroom Sauce (see page 156) or a raisin sauce.

Variations: Add water chestnuts, sliced almonds, chopped celery, chopped chicken, raisins, and, if milk is allowed, cottage cheese, or grated cheese to the brown rice stuffing.

Ham rolls are also good served with Cheese Sauce (see page 15), if allowed.

Gnocchi (Italian Potato Dumplings) with Meat Sauce

NO CORN, EGG, OR MILK
Servings: 4

2–3 potatoes (enough for 2 c. mashed or riced)

1 c. unbleached flour plus more flour for dredging

Cook potatoes and mash or rice without added liquid. While warm, gradually mix in the flour. Form mixture into long rolls, ½–¾ inch in diameter. Cut into 1½-inch pieces. Roll in flour. Have ready a pot of salted boiling water. Carefully lower rolls into water. They will sink but should rise to the top after about 5 minutes. Boil gently another 5 minutes. Serve with Meat Sauce (see below).

Variations: Gnocchi are also good served with a cheese or fish sauce or plain with butter and a sprinkle of Parmesan cheese, if allowed.

Wheat-Free Gnocchi

NO CORN, MILK, OR WHEAT
Servings: 4

2–3 potatoes (enough for 2 c. mashed or riced)
1 egg, lightly beaten

1 c. oat flour (see page 15) plus more flour for dredging

Cook potatoes and mash or rice. Lightly beat 1 egg and stir into potatoes. Knead in the oat flour. Proceed as in recipe for Gnocchi above.

Variation: Gnocchi are also good served with a cheese or fish sauce or plain with butter and a sprinkle of Parmesan cheese, if allowed.

Meat Sauce

NO CORN, EGG, MILK, WHEAT,* OR GLUTEN*

1 lb. pork sausage
½ lb. mushrooms, sliced
2–3 T. dry white wine or beef stock (see page 7)

2 T. brown rice flour
1 c. beef stock (see page 7)
Salt (optional)

Brown sausage. Break it up with a fork. Lift out onto paper towels to drain all excess fat. Leave 1 tablespoon fat in pan. Discard the rest. Sauté the mushrooms for 1 minute. Add wine or broth. Simmer until mushrooms are cooked. Stir in flour. Mix well. Add the 1 cup beef stock. Stir until mixture thickens. Add more stock if too thick. Add sausage. Mix well. The broth is salty, so the use of more salt is optional. Taste for seasoning. Spoon over gnocchi.

Variations: If you can use wheat and gluten, you can substitute unbleached wheat flour for the brown rice flour.

If you can use gluten but not wheat, substitute barley or oat flour.

Steamed Chinese Dumplings in Broth

NO CORN, EGG, OR MILK
Servings: 8–10

The dough for these dumplings is made without egg, in contrast to the traditional won ton skins, which contain egg. (Won ton skins, available at many supermarkets as well as Oriental or specialty stores, can be used in the same way if egg is no problem.) These dumplings have a different texture and are very good.

2 c. unsifted, unbleached flour
1 c. boiling water
Safflower oil
2–3 qt. chicken broth (see page 7)

1–2 slices fresh ginger (optional)
2 t. crushed coriander (optional)

Measure flour into a bowl. Stir in the boiling water. Blend quickly and thoroughly with a fork and shape into a ball. Knead on a lightly floured board until smooth and velvety, about 10 minutes. Cover with a cloth and let rest 20 minutes. While dough is resting, prepare your choice of one or more dumpling fillings (see below). ˜

Divide dough into two parts and cover part not to be used immediately. Roll first part into a log about 1 inch in diameter. Cut off a slice about ½ inch thick. Roll it out thin. It should make a 3-inch circle. Proceed to cut and roll the rest of the log, covering each circle as you go to keep it from drying out. When all are cut, put a spoonful of filling in the center of each circle and pinch dough up around the filling, leaving the center open and the filling exposed there. Continue until all are filled. Brush lightly with safflower oil. Keep covered and cold until ready to steam. Repeat with second half of dough, using the same filling or a different one. To differentiate a different filling, pinch dough over filling to make a half circle. Stand dumpling up and press to flatten the bottom. Brush with oil. Cover rack of steamer with well-perforated foil to prevent moisture accumulation. Oil the foil. Place dumplings on rack so they do not touch or they will stick together. Have enough water (1–2 inches) in the steamer to last the 15 minutes the dumplings cook. Cover tightly to steam. If dumplings are to be done in several batches, remove each group as it is done and keep warm until all are steamed. Add more water if necessary.

In a large kettle, heat chicken broth. Add fresh ginger and crushed coriander if desired. Add cooked dumplings and heat gently until dumplings are good and hot. Spoon them into soup bowls and cover with broth.

Dumplings may be made ahead, steamed, and then reheated or frozen for later use. Spread out on rack or in pan to freeze before bagging for storing. They should not touch each other while freezing or thawing. Do not keep frozen for more than a month or refrigerated for more than a day.

Pork Filling for Half of Dumpling Dough

NO CORN,* EGG, MILK,* WHEAT,* OR GLUTEN*
Yield: 1½–2 cups

½ c. diced celery	1½ t. grated fresh ginger, or
½ c. chopped mushrooms	⅓ t. ground ginger
¼ c. minced green onion	⅓ c. chopped water chestnuts
2 T. safflower oil	2 T. brown rice flour
1 lb. lean ground pork	3 T. soy sauce
½ t. ground coriander	

Sauté celery, mushrooms, and onion in the oil for 5 minutes. Celery and onion should still be crispy. Remove to a bowl and set aside. Sauté pork until pink is almost gone. Remove any excess fat. Add coriander and ginger. Return celery mixture to pan. Add water chestnuts. Mix flour with soy sauce. Stir into meat mixture. Cook and stir another minute or two. Set aside.

Chicken Filling for
Half of Dumpling Dough

Substitute 2 c. chopped chicken for the pork. Omit the onion. If chicken is precooked, prepare other ingredients and stir in chicken last.

Shrimp Filling for
Half of Dumpling Dough

Substitute 2 c. finely chopped cooked shrimp for the pork. Prepare other ingredients as above, stirring in shrimp at the end.

Variations: *If you can use corn*, you can substitute 1½ T. cornstarch for the flour in the fillings.

If you can use milk, you can substitute butter for the oil.

If you can use wheat and gluten, you can use wheat flour instead of brown rice flour.

If you can use gluten but not wheat, you can substitute barley or oat flour for the brown rice flour.

Potlickers

NO CORN, EGG, OR MILK
Servings: 8–10

Usually served as an hors d'oeuvre.

1 recipe Steamed Chinese
Dumpling dough (see page
204)

Peanut or safflower oil
¼ c. regular-strength beef
broth (see page 7)

Proceed as for dumpling half circles. While dough is resting, prepare one or both of the potlicker fillings (see below). Pinch dough closed over filling starting at ends and work toward the center as you go. When completely closed, set potlickers down, seam-side-up, and flatten bottoms. To cook, brush a large frying pan with peanut or safflower oil and place over medium heat. Set potlickers in pan without touching each other, seam-side-up. Cook until bottoms are brown but do not burn, about 5 minutes. For a 10–12-inch frying pan of dumplings, pour in ¼ cup beef broth. Cover tightly immediately and steam about 10 minutes. Remove from pan with spatula. If there is more than one batch to cook, keep prepared ones warm in a slow oven. Serve hot with dipping sauce (see below). Potlickers may be made ahead and frozen. Allow 15 minutes for steaming frozen ones. Follow directions for freezing given for Chinese Dumplings (page 205).

Dip for Potlickers

NO CORN, EGG, MILK, WHEAT, OR GLUTEN
Yield: 1½ cups

½ c. grated daikon (Japanese
radish) or regular radish
½ c. soy sauce
¼ c. sesame oil

1 T. white wine
1 T. vinegar
½ c. regular strength beef
broth (see page 7)

Put grated daikon in individual dipping cups. Combine remaining ingredients and pour over daikon.

Pork Filling for Potlickers

NO CORN,* EGG, MILK, WHEAT,* OR GLUTEN*
Yield: 1½ cups for half of potlickers recipe

2 T. soy sauce
1 T. honey
1 t. garlic powder
⅓ c. minced green onion
1–1¼ lb. lean pork, cut into
⅓-inch cubes

1 T. safflower or sesame oil
4 t. brown rice flour
2 T. sherry
¼ c. regular-strength beef
broth (see page 7)
Salt

Stir together soy sauce, honey, garlic powder, and onion. Brown meat in oil over high heat. Stir together flour and sherry. Combine soy mixture and sherry mixture and stir into pork mixture. Cook until mixture boils and thickens. Taste for seasoning. Add salt to taste.

Variations: *If you can use corn*, you can substitute 2 t. cornstarch for the brown rice flour.

If you can use wheat and gluten, you can substitute wheat flour for the brown rice flour.

If you can use gluten but not wheat, you can substitute barley or oat flour for the brown rice flour.

Ginger-Beef Filling for Potlickers

NO CORN, EGG, MILK, WHEAT, OR GLUTEN
Yield: 2½ cups

1 T. sesame or safflower oil
¾ lb. lean ground beef
1 T. minced fresh ginger root

1 onion, finely chopped
1 c. chopped bean sprouts
1 T. soy sauce

Heat oil in a large frying pan. Combine remaining ingredients and sauté until meat is cooked.

LAMB

	NO CORN	NO EGG	NO MILK	NO WHEAT	NO GLUTEN
Chutney-Grilled Lamb Chops	X	X	X	X	X
Lamb Shanks with Grapes	⊗	X	⊗	X	⊗
Greek Lamb in Phyllo	X	X			
Sweet and Sour Lamb	⊗	X	X	⊗	⊗
Lebanese Pastries	X	⊗	⊗		
Fillings for Pastries					
Lamb	X	X	X	X	X
Spinach	X	X	X	X	X
Stuffed Chayote Squash	⊗	X	⊗	⊗	⊗
Lamb Stroganoff	⊗	X		⊗	⊗

⊗ means that the recipe includes instructions for adding that ingredient if allowed.

SAVE MONEY,
BONE A LEG OF LAMB

Faced with the inflated prices of meat, it is important to know how to get the most possible for our dollars. Even though the price of a whole leg of lamb may seem staggering, it is cheaper to buy lamb that way and cut it up yourself than to buy steaks, cubes, and ground lamb prepared and packaged by the butcher.

It is not difficult to bone a leg of lamb. Position lamb with the shin bone on the top side. Cut along the shin bone with a sharp knife, trimming around it as you go, clear to the joint. Then, from the large end, cut around the larger bone and follow it down to the joint. Lift out the bones, and there you have material for the soup pot or to make stock, a marinade for kabobs, etc.

You now have a rather large piece of meat which can be trimmed to use as a small roast or cut into steaks. There are also pieces for kabobs or stews, and the smaller bits and pieces (including where the cut was not just perfect) are great for ground lamb. Since you can remove the excess fat and some of the heavy tendons and gristle before grinding, home-ground lamb is a better quality than ground lamb from the market. Divide the meat according to how you plan to use it. Wrap and freeze what you do not need immediately.

Chutney-Grilled Lamb Chops
NO CORN, EGG, MILK, WHEAT, OR GLUTEN
Servings: 4

½ c. finely chopped chutney
2 t. lemon juice
¼ t. curry powder

⅛ t. ground ginger
4 lamb chops or lamb steaks

Combine the first four ingredients and brush some on both sides of chops. Broil 4–5 inches from heat for about 5 minutes. Brush with more of the chutney mixture and continue broiling another 5 minutes. Turn chops.

Spread with more sauce, using about half in both brushings, and continue broiling until done. Pass the remaining sauce.

Variation: Broil eggplant at the same time. It makes a fine combination (see Broiled Marinated Eggplant, page 227).

Lamb Shanks with Grapes

NO CORN,* EGG, MILK,* WHEAT, OR GLUTEN*
Servings: 4

1 medium-sized onion, finely
   chopped
2 T. safflower oil, divided
4 lamb shanks
2 cloves garlic, minced
3/4 t. salt
1 c. chicken broth (see page 7)
1/2 c. dry white wine (or omit
   and use 1 1/2 c. broth)

3 c. cooked brown rice
2 T. potato flour or 3 T. brown
   rice flour
2 T. cold water
1/4 lb. mushrooms, sliced
1 c. washed, fresh seedless
   grapes, or 1 8-oz. can grapes,
   drained

Sauté onions in a Dutch oven in 1 tablespoon of the oil. When golden, remove from pan with a slotted spoon. Brown the lamb in the same pan. Add garlic, salt, broth, wine, and onion. Cover and simmer until tender, about 2 hours. Put cooked rice in a serving dish. Arrange lamb on top. Keep warm. Mix flour with water. Bring pan juices to a boil. Stir in the thickening, cooking until smooth and thickened. Reduce heat to low. Sauté mushrooms in the remaining 1 tablespoon oil. Add mushrooms and grapes to sauce. Heat. Spoon part over lamb and pass the rest.

*Variations: *If you can use corn*, you can substitute 2 T. cornstarch for the potato or brown rice flour.

If you can use milk, stir 1/3 c. sour cream into the sauce after lowering the heat.

If you can use gluten but not wheat, you can substitute barley flour for the potato or brown rice flour.

Greek Lamb in Phyllo

NO CORN OR EGG

Yield: 4–6 large squares, or 10–12 small squares

These are delicious. Select lean lamb, preferably home-ground from a leg of lamb. (See page 210.) Corn-free and egg-free phyllo sheets are available commercially—check the ingredient list on the label.

Safflower oil
¾ lb. ground lamb
½ t. onion powder
½ t. chervil
½ t. tarragon
½ t. salt
¼ t. garlic powder
1 T. dried parsley or ¼ c.
chopped fresh parsley

2–4 t. lemon juice or to taste
½ package frozen chopped
spinach, thawed, well drained
8 phyllo sheets (corn- and egg-free)
About ½ c. melted butter
Mozzarella and Parmesan cheese

In a lightly oiled frying pan, brown meat over moderate heat. Combine onion powder, chervil, tarragon, salt, garlic powder, and parsley. Add to meat. Add enough lemon juice to enhance the flavor. This is important. Taste and adjust seasonings. It may need more tarragon and chervil. Mix spinach into meat. Set aside. Take one phyllo sheet at a time and brush on melted butter, putting one sheet on top of another until there are eight sheets. Keep sheets not in use covered with plastic wrap or a damp towel; they dry out very quickly. Cut phyllo into either large or small squares depending on whether they are to be used as a main course or as hors d'oeuvres. Spoon the lamb mixture onto center of each square. Sprinkle generously with grated mozzarella and Parmesan cheese. Fold phyllo over filling to make a triangle. Lift onto an ungreased cookie sheet. Bake at 400° until golden brown, 15–20 minutes depending on size. Serve hot.

For a dinner entrée, serve Mushroom Sauce with Greek Lamb.

Mushroom Sauce

*½ lb. mushrooms, washed and
    sliced*
2 T. dry white wine

*2 T. wheat, barley, or potato
    flour*
1–1½ c. milk or stock

Sauté mushrooms in wine until cooked. Stir in flour; then stir in milk or stock and cook until thickened.

Variation: If you can use canned mushroom soup, dilute with cream or chicken stock for a quick sauce.

Sweet and Sour Lamb

NO CORN,* EGG, MILK, WHEAT,* OR GLUTEN*
Servings: 3–4

1 lb. cubed lamb
3 T. safflower oil
*1 medium-sized onion, cut into
    1-inch squares*
*1 medium-sized green pepper,
    seeded and cut into strips*
*1 9-oz. can pineapple chunks
    with juice*

2 T. brown rice flour
½ t. salt
1 T. honey
2 T. rice vinegar
Chicken stock (see page 7)

Sauté lamb in the oil. Brown on all sides. Add onion and pepper to meat. Cook, stirring, until onion is transparent. Drain pineapple, saving juice. Blend flour with salt, honey, pineapple juice, vinegar, and enough chicken stock to make 1 cup. Add to lamb along with pineapple chunks. Stir until thickened. Reduce heat. Simmer 25–30 minutes, or until meat is tender. Stir frequently. Serve on brown rice or bulgur pilaf if allowed.

*Variations: *If you can use corn*, you can substitute 1 T. cornstarch for the flour.

If you can use wheat and gluten, you can substitute wheat flour for the brown rice flour.

If you can use gluten but not wheat, you can substitute barley or oat flour for the brown rice flour.

Lebanese Pastries

NO CORN, EGG,* OR MILK*
Servings: 6

1 T. dry yeast
1 c. warm water
1 t. sugar
1 t. salt
¼ c. olive oil
¼ c. raw wheat germ

1½ c. whole wheat pastry
   flour, unsifted
1 c. unbleached flour (approx.),
   divided
Sesame or poppy seeds

In large bowl of electric mixer, combine yeast, water, and sugar. Let stand 5 minutes. It will be bubbly. Add salt, oil, and wheat germ. Gradually mix in the pastry flour. Beat at medium speed for 5 minutes. Stir in ½ cup of the unbleached flour. Turn out onto a pastry cloth sprinkled with some of the unbleached flour. Knead until smooth and satiny, about 10 minutes, using up to another ½ cup unbleached flour. Put dough in a greased bowl, turning to grease top, cover with a cloth, and let rise in a warm place until almost doubled in bulk, about 1 hour. Punch down dough. Remove to a pastry cloth. Divide into twelve equal-sized balls. Cover balls and let rest about 30 minutes. While dough is resting, prepare one or both of the fillings (see below). Roll out each ball into a 5 or 6-inch circle. Place 2 tablespoons filling in center of each circle. Pinch edges into a three-cornered hat over filling. Place about 1 inch apart on a lightly greased baking sheet. Cover lightly and let rise in a warm place until puffy, about 30 minutes. Brush lightly with oil and sprinkle with sesame or poppy seeds. Bake at 400° until golden brown, about 20 minutes.

   Variation: *If you can use egg and milk*, beat 1 egg with 1 T. milk and brush pastries with mixture before baking.

Lamb Filling for Pastries

NO CORN, EGG, MILK, WHEAT, OR GLUTEN
Yield: 1½–2 cups

1 onion, finely chopped, or 1 t.
*   onion powder*
1 garlic clove, finely chopped, or
*   ½ t. garlic powder*
1 T. olive oil
1 lb. lean ground lamb
1 T. lemon juice

½ t. cinnamon
½ t. allspice
¾ t. salt
1 c. thawed frozen spinach,
*   chopped, or 2 T. minced*
*   parsley*

Sauté onion and garlic in oil just until barely soft. Stir in lamb, and brown until crumbly. Skim fat. (If garlic powder and onion powder are used, add at this point.) Stir in remaining ingredients. Cool before using.

Spinach Filling for Pastries

NO CORN, EGG, MILK, WHEAT, OR GLUTEN
Yield: 1–1¼ cups

3 T. pine nuts or blanched
*   almonds*
3 T. olive or safflower oil
1 large onion, finely chopped
1 small clove garlic, minced
1 10-oz. package frozen chopped
*   spinach, thawed, well drained*

¼ c. raisins
¾ t. salt
¼ t. nutmeg
2 T. lemon juice

Lightly brown nuts in the oil. Remove nuts and set aside. Add onion and garlic to pan. Cook until onion is limp. Add spinach, raisins, salt, and nutmeg. Cook, stirring, until spinach is heated through and any moisture is evaporated. Add lemon juice and nuts. Cool.

Stuffed Chayote Squash

NO CORN,* EGG, MILK,* WHEAT,* OR GLUTEN*
Servings: 4

A nice variation of stuffed eggplant or zucchini.

2 chayote squash
Salted water
1 T. safflower oil
½ c. chopped onion, or 2 t.
* onion powder*
¾ lb. lean ground lamb
2 T. wheat-free, gluten-free bread
* crumbs*

2 t. dried mint leaves
½ c. seedless raisins
¼ c. tomato sauce
1 clove garlic, minced or mashed
Chopped pine nuts (optional)

Wash squash well and cut in half lengthwise. Simmer in small amount of salted water until tender, 40–50 minutes. Drain and cool. Scoop out pulp and seeds, leaving a ¼-inch shell. Chop pulp and seeds and set aside. Heat the oil in a large frying pan. Sauté onion until golden. (Eliminate this step if onion powder is used.) Add the lamb. Sauté lamb in the oil until just pink. Remove from heat and add crumbs, mint leaves, raisins, tomato sauce, garlic, and the chopped chayote pulp. Mix thoroughly and mound in the chayote shells. Sprinkle with pine nuts if desired. Put squash into shallow baking dish, add ¼ inch water, and bake, uncovered, at 350° about 30 minutes, or until mixture is cooked and lightly browned.

*Variations: If you can use corn, you can substitute catsup for the tomato sauce.

If you can use milk, you can substitute grated Parmesan cheese for the nuts.

If you can use wheat and gluten, you can substitute wheat bread crumbs for the wheat-free, gluten-free crumbs.

Lamb Stroganoff

NO CORN,* EGG, WHEAT,* OR GLUTEN*
Servings: 4

2 T. olive oil
1 lb. boned lamb, cubed
1 onion, diced
1 clove garlic, minced
½ c. dry sherry or lamb or
    chicken broth (see page 7)
1 c. sliced mushrooms

¼ c. sweet cherry peppers,
    seeded and sliced
⅓ c. drained, sliced ripe olives
½ t. salt
2 t. brown rice flour
1 c. unflavored yogurt

Heat oil in a large frying pan. Brown meat on all sides. Add onion and garlic. Cook until onion is transparent. Add sherry or broth. Cover and simmer until lamb is tender, 1–1½ hours. Add mushrooms, peppers, olives, and salt. Cook about 10 minutes. Stir flour into yogurt. Add to meat mixture. Simmer very gently 2–3 minutes, just to warm it through. Serve over Wheat-Free Noodles (see page 162), brown rice, or mashed potatoes.

*Variations: If you can use corn, you can substitute 1 t. cornstarch for the flour.

If you can use wheat and gluten, you can substitute unbleached wheat flour for the brown rice flour.

If you can use gluten but not wheat, you can substitute barley flour for the brown rice flour.

Lamb Stroganoff is also good served over spaghetti (if wheat and gluten are allowed).

VEGETABLES

	NO CORN	NO EGG	NO MILK	NO WHEAT	NO GLUTEN
Baked Mushrooms and Cheese	X	X		⊗	
Sautéed Mushrooms	X	X	X	⊗	⊗
Mushrooms au Gratin	⊗	X		⊗	
Vegetables à la Grecque	X	X	X	X	X
Celeriac Salad	X	X		X	X
Baked Squash with Apple	X	X	⊗	X	X
Eggplant "Cannelloni"	X	⊗		⊗	⊗
Sautéed Eggplant Slices	X	X	X	⊗	⊗
Eggplant with Nuts	⊗	X		⊗	⊗
Broiled Marinated Eggplant	X	X	X	X	X
Parmesan Baked Eggplant	X	X		X	X
Eggplant Supreme	X	X		X	X
Butternut Squash Casserole	⊗	⊗		X	X
Parsnips with Pears	X	X	⊗	X	X
Zucchini Fingers	X	X	⊗	⊗	⊗
Zucchini-Spinach Casserole	X	X	⊗	X	X
Baked Zucchini with Seasoned Crumbs	X	X	X	X	
Seasoned Crumbs	X	X	X	⊗	
Zucchini Casserole	⊗	X		⊗	
Zucchini and Rice Casserole	⊗	X		⊗	⊗

⊗ means that the recipe includes instructions for adding that ingredient if allowed.

	NO CORN	NO EGG	NO MILK	NO WHEAT	NO GLUTEN
Curried Squash Bake	⊗	X		⊗	⊗
Yam Casserole	X		⊗	⊗	⊗
Lima Bean Casserole	X	X		⊗	⊗
Baked Lima Beans	⊗	X	⊗	X	X
Lima Beans with Curry Sauce	⊗	X		⊗	⊗
White Sauce with Mushrooms	X	X		X	X
Scalloped Turnips	X	X		⊗	⊗
Chayote Squash with Yogurt Sauce	⊗	X		⊗	⊗

Baked Mushrooms and Cheese

NO CORN, EGG, OR WHEAT*
Servings: 4

1 lb. fresh mushrooms, washed, wiped dry, trimmed, and sliced
¼ lb. sharp cheddar cheese, grated (about 1 c. grated cheese)
1 c. sliced, pitted ripe black olives

1 T. barley or oat flour
½ t. salt
⅓ c. half and half
1 c. buttered crumbs from barley or oat breads

Spread mushroom slices on a cookie sheet and heat in a moderate oven until moisture begins to show in pan, 10–15 minutes. Remove mushrooms and place on paper towels, cover with more paper towels, and press out as much moisture as possible. Layer the mushrooms, cheese, and olives in an ovenproof casserole, making two layers of each. Combine flour, salt, and half and half. Pour over the mushroom mixture. Cover with crumbs. Bake at 350° about 40 minutes, or until brown and bubbly.

*Variations: *If you can use wheat*, you can substitute wheat flour for the barley or oat flour and wheat bread crumbs for the wheat-free crumbs.
For gluten-free, use brown rice flour and bread crumbs.

Sautéed Mushrooms

NO CORN, EGG, MILK, WHEAT,* OR GLUTEN*
Servings: 4

4 T. olive oil
1 lb. mushrooms, washed, wiped
    dry, trimmed, and thinly sliced
    (if small, leave whole)
2 cloves garlic, mashed

¼ c. chopped fresh parsley
¼ c. semidry Brown Rice
    Bread Crumbs (see page 13)
1 T. brown sesame seeds
1 T. lemon juice

Heat oil in a large frying pan. Toss mushrooms in oil over high heat until the moisture is evaporated and they are slightly colored. Mix garlic and parsley and add to mushrooms. Stir about 2 minutes. Combine crumbs and seeds. Stir into mushrooms until well blended and crumbs are slightly toasted. Sprinkle on the lemon juice.

*Variation: If you can use wheat and gluten, you can substitute wheat bread crumbs for the Brown Rice Bread Crumbs.

Mushrooms au Gratin

NO CORN,* EGG, OR WHEAT*
Servings: 4–5

1 lb. fresh mushrooms, washed,
    wiped dry, and trimmed
2 T. butter
⅓ c. yogurt
¼ t. salt

1 T. barley or oat flour
½ c. shredded sharp cheddar
    cheese
¼ c. chopped fresh parsley

Slice mushrooms through the stem, lengthwise, into ¼-inch slices. Heat butter in a large frying pan. Sauté mushrooms at moderate heat briefly. Cover pan for about 2 minutes, until juices exude. Blend yogurt, salt, and flour and stir in. Heat, stirring, until mixture is well blended and just comes to the boiling point. Pour into a shallow baking dish. Sprinkle with cheese and parsley. Bake at 400° until mushrooms are very hot and cheese is melted, about 4–6 minutes. This can be prepared ahead and refrigerated before baking. Remove from refrigerator 25–30 minutes before putting in oven. Allow for a longer cooking time.

Variations: *If you can use corn*, you can substitute 1½ t. cornstarch for the flour.

If you can use wheat, you can substitute unbleached wheat flour for the barley or oat flour.

For gluten-free, you can substitute brown rice flour for the barley or oat flour.

Vegetables à la Grecque

NO CORN, EGG, MILK, WHEAT, OR GLUTEN

This is an excellent make-ahead recipe. In fact, it *needs* to marinate to enhance the flavors. A day or two gives the best results, but it must have a minimum of 4–5 hours. Using a combination of several different vegetables produces an interesting party salad or first course or an enticing platter for a buffet; using just one or two vegetables produces excellent family fare. The vegetables are cooked in broth until tender yet crisp, and served cold.

3¼ c. water	2 cloves garlic, minced
⅔ c. dry white wine	1 T. chopped onion
6 T. lemon juice	5 peppercorns
⅓ c. olive oil	1 t. crumbled thyme
1¼ t. salt	1 t. tarragon
2 bay leaves	

Put water, wine, lemon juice, olive oil, salt, and bay leaves into a Dutch oven. Put remaining ingredients into a tea ball or cheesecloth bag. Add to broth mixture. Bring to a boil and simmer, covered, 10 minutes. Prepare your choice of the various vegetables listed below and cook separately as directed. As vegetables are done, remove them from the broth with a slotted spoon. When all vegetables are cooked, remove the tea ball. Cook broth until reduced to 1 cup. Cool slightly and spoon over vegetables. Cover, chill, and let marinate. At serving time, garnish with chopped fresh parsley.

Mushrooms: **Servings: 4–8**
Wash 1 pound white mushrooms and trim ends. Add to broth. Simmer 1 minute, or until just barely tender.

Crookneck or Zucchini Squash: Servings: 12–16
Trim ends and slice in half, lengthwise, 6–8 small squash. Add to broth, cover, and simmer about 5 minutes, or until tender yet crisp.

Carrots: Servings: 14–18
Trim ends, peel, and slice 6–8 small carrots on the diagonal about ¼ inch thick. Add to broth. Cover and simmer until tender yet crisp, about 7 minutes.

Eggplant: Servings: 10–12
Slice 1 medium-sized eggplant in half lengthwise. Slice halves lengthwise into ¾-inch-thick strips. Add to broth. Simmer until tender, about 5 minutes.

Celery: Servings: 12–16
Cut off tops and trim bottoms of 6 celery hearts. They should be 4–6 inches long. Cut lengthwise in half. Add to broth. Cover and simmer about 15 minutes, or until tender yet crisp. These are nice garnished with cherry tomatoes or strips of pimiento at serving time.

Other vegetables can also be used, cooked tender yet crisp in the broth.

Celeriac Salad

NO CORN, EGG, WHEAT, OR GLUTEN
Servings: 6

1 large or 2 small celeriac (celery root)
Broth (see page 7) or water
½ t. dry mustard
¾ t. salt
¼ c. tarragon or wine vinegar
2 t. caraway seeds (optional)

2 c. plain yogurt
1 t. sugar, or to taste
1 cucumber, thinly sliced
1 stalk celery, sliced
Lettuce
Radishes (optional)

Peel celeriac. Cut into bite-sized pieces and cook, covered, in 1 inch broth or salted boiling water until tender. Drain and cool. It should make 3 cups. Mix together mustard, salt, vinegar, seeds, yogurt, and sugar. Stir into celeriac along with cucumber and celery. Mound on lettuce. Garnish with radishes if you like.

Baked Squash with Apple

NO CORN, EGG, MILK,* WHEAT, OR GLUTEN
Servings: 2 (½ squash each)

1 acorn (Danish) squash
Safflower oil
Salt (to taste)

1 large apple, grated
Dash cinnamon
½ t. honey

Bake whole squash at 375° 30–40 minutes, or until almost soft. Remove from oven, cut in half, and scoop out seeds. Brush with oil. Sprinkle with salt to taste. Peel, core, and grate enough apple to fill the cavities. Mound into squash cavities. Sprinkle with cinnamon and spoon on a little honey. Bake at 375° 25–30 minutes, or until squash is tender.

*Variations: *If you can use milk*, you can substitute butter for the oil.

For an entrée, sauté ½ lb. pork sausage until no longer pink. Break up with a fork. Pour off grease. Spoon onto paper towels and pat to remove grease. Mix with grated apple. This is a complete meal with Carrot-Corn Bread (see page 58) and a tossed salad.

Eggplant "Cannelloni"

NO CORN, EGG,* WHEAT,* OR GLUTEN*
Servings: 6–8

1 large eggplant
Juice of 1–2 lemons
About ¼ c. olive or safflower
  oil
Brown rice flour or potato flour
1 c. grated mozzarella cheese
½ c. grated Parmesan or
  ricotta cheese

¼ c. chopped fresh parsley
3 oz. chopped cooked ham
  (approx.)
Salt, if needed
Grated Parmesan cheese
  (optional)

Peel eggplant. Cut lengthwise into thin slices. Dip into lemon juice, then oil. Coat slices with flour. Sauté in hot oil until soft and browned on both sides. Drain on paper towels. Combine cheeses, parsley, and ham. Taste to check for salt. Add if needed. Press mixture into a log and chill. Divide cheese mixture to equal number of eggplant slices and put one portion in center of each slice. Fold eggplant over filling to make a roll. Arrange seam-side-down in a baking dish. Pour Mushroom Sauce (see page 156) or Tomato Sauce (see below) over slices. Bake at 375° 20 minutes. Sprinkle with Parmesan cheese, if desired, and serve.

Variations: If you can use egg, mix egg into the filling mixture and blend to a smooth paste. Chill mixture.

If you can use wheat and gluten, coat eggplant slices in a mixture of wheat flour and raw wheat germ instead of the brown rice flour or potato flour.

If you can use gluten but not wheat, you can substitute oat flour for the brown rice flour or potato flour.

For a milk-free version, you can substitute a meat filling such as those for Chinese Dumplings or Potlickers (see pages 205–206, 207–208).

Tomato Sauce

Yield: 1–1½ cups

1 6–8-oz. can tomato sauce
½ c. beef or chicken broth
  (see page 7)
½–1 t. sweet basil

¼ t. oregano
⅛ t. thyme
⅛ t. sugar
⅛–¼ t. salt, if needed

Combine all ingredients in saucepan. Heat until well blended.

Sautéed Eggplant Slices

NO CORN, EGG, MILK, WHEAT,* OR GLUTEN*
Servings: 5–7 (2 slices each)

1 medium-sized eggplant
⅓ c. brown rice flour
¼ t. salt
1 T. toasted sesame seeds

Lemon juice
Safflower and sesame oil,
  combined

Peel and slice eggplant into ½-inch slices. Combine flour, salt, and seeds. Dip each eggplant slice in lemon juice and then into flour mixture, coating both sides. Cover bottom of pan generously with oil. Sauté in hot oil over medium heat until centers are tender and outside is crisp. Turn once. Add more oil when slices are turned so bottom of pan is again lightly covered. Drain on paper towels.

Variations: *If you can use wheat and gluten*, you can substitute whole wheat flour for the brown rice flour.

If you can use gluten but not wheat, you can substitute barley flour, potato flour, or oat flour, or a mixture of these.

Eggplant with Nuts

NO CORN,* EGG, WHEAT,* OR GLUTEN*
Servings: 5–7 (2 slices each)

1 medium to large eggplant
¼–½ c. olive or safflower
   oil
1 c. yogurt or sour cream
½ t. onion powder
1 T. potato flour or 1 T. brown
   rice flour

2 T. grated Parmesan cheese
1 T. sesame seeds
⅛ t. salt
Pine nuts or slivered almonds

Peel eggplant if desired. Cut crosswise into ½-inch slices. Brush both sides with oil and place in a shallow baking dish. Bake at 450° about 15 minutes, or until tender. Turn once. Combine remaining ingredients except nuts. Spread evenly on eggplant slices. Top with nuts. Broil about 6 inches from the heat until topping is slightly browned. Serve at once.

Variations: *If you can use corn*, you can substitute 2 t. cornstarch for the potato flour.

If you can use wheat or gluten, you can substitute unbleached wheat flour for the brown rice flour.

If you can use gluten but not wheat, you can substitute 1 T. barley flour for the brown rice flour.

Broiled Marinated Eggplant

NO CORN, EGG, MILK, WHEAT, OR GLUTEN
Servings: 4–5 (2 slices each)

1 small eggplant
½ c. olive or safflower oil
3 T. lemon juice
1 t. onion powder

½ t. garlic powder
½ t. salt
½ t. basil
½ t. oregano

Peel eggplant if desired and cut crosswise into ⅓-inch slices. Mix remaining ingredients in a bowl large enough to hold eggplant. Marinate for 30 minutes or more. Turn once. More oil can be added if needed to cover eggplant. Transfer with a slotted spoon to broiler pan rack. Brush with marinade. Broil about 5 inches from heat until slices begin to soften and slightly brown, 8–10 minutes. Turn and repeat until slices are very tender and slightly browned, 5–10 minutes.

Parmesan Baked Eggplant

NO CORN, EGG, WHEAT, OR GLUTEN
Servings: 5–7 (2 slices each)

1 medium-sized eggplant
6 T. sesame and safflower oil,
  mixed
¼ c. plus 1–2 T. grated
  Parmesan cheese, divided

¾ t. onion powder
½ t. salt
1 T. lemon juice

Peel eggplant. Cut crosswise into ½-inch slices. Combine oils, ¼ cup of the Parmesan cheese, and the onion powder, salt, and lemon juice. Dip eggplant into mixture, coating both sides. Place in a lightly greased ovenproof casserole. Bake at 400° 12–15 minutes, or until tender, turning once. Sprinkle the remaining 1–2 tablespoons Parmesan cheese on top. Place under broiler until cheese is lightly browned.

Eggplant Supreme

NO CORN, EGG, WHEAT, OR GLUTEN
Servings: 4–6

1 medium-sized eggplant
Salt
1 large onion, chopped
4 T. olive oil
½ t. salt
¼ t. basil
¼ t. thyme
½ c. dry white wine or broth
   (see page 7)

1 green pepper, seeded and
   chopped
½ c. tomato juice
½ c. grated Swiss or cheddar
   cheese
½ c. grated Parmesan cheese
½ c. pine nuts

Wash and peel the eggplant. Cut into ¾-inch cubes. Sprinkle with salt and let stand 45 minutes. Rinse and dry. In a large skillet, sauté the onion in the oil for 5 minutes. Add eggplant. Stir and cook until eggplant begins to brown. Stir in the ½ teaspoon salt, and the basil, thyme, wine, green pepper, and tomato juice. Cover and cook about 10 minutes, or until eggplant is translucent and moisture is absorbed. Turn down heat. Sprinkle cheeses and pine nuts over top. Cover and let sit one minute. Serve immediately.

Butternut Squash Casserole

NO CORN,* EGG,* WHEAT, OR GLUTEN
Servings: 12–14

An interesting flavor combination. Good as a hot dish or cold in place of a salad.

1 lb. butternut squash
2 T. lemon juice
1 t. grated lemon rind
⅓ c. chopped moist, dried apricots
1 c. white raisins
2 medium apples, pared, cored, and chopped

2 c. low-fat cottage cheese
¼ c. yogurt
1 t. cinnamon (approx.)
⅛ t. nutmeg
½ c. apple juice mixed with 1½ T. rice or potato flour
Chopped sunflower seeds or nuts

Peel and remove seeds and strings from squash. Grate by hand or in food processor (should be 4½–5 cups grated squash). Combine with lemon juice and rind. Combine apricots, raisins, and apple in a separate bowl. In a third bowl, combine remaining ingredients except seeds or nuts. Put two thirds of the squash mixture into a greased 9-inch ovenproof casserole. Spread evenly. Top with the fruit mixture, then the cottage cheese mixture. Add remaining squash. Spread evenly. Top with chopped sunflower seeds or nuts. Cover and bake at 475° 30 minutes. This gives the squash a crispy texture which is good as a salad. For a softer-textured squash, bake another 15–20 minutes, or until squash is tender.

*Variations: If you can use corn, you can substitute 2 t. cornstarch for the flour.

If you can use egg, you can substitute 1 lightly beaten egg for the apple juice mixture.

Parsnips with Pears

NO CORN, EGG, MILK,* WHEAT, OR GLUTEN
Servings: 4

Delicious!

3 medium parsnips
2 T. safflower oil
1 T. sesame oil
1 large D'Anjou pear

2 T. lemon juice
¼–½ t. ground ginger
¼ t. salt
½ t. honey

Wash and peel parsnips. Slice into ¼-inch slices. Combine oils in a saucepan. Stir in the parsnips. Add enough water to cover bottom of pan. Cover and steam until parsnips are nearly done and water is absorbed. Peel, core, and slice the pear. Sprinkle with the lemon juice. Add to parsnips. Combine ginger, salt, and honey. Stir into parsnips. Cover and simmer about 5 minutes, or until pears and parsnips are tender (*do not overcook*).

*Variation: *If you can use milk*, substitute 2–3 T. butter for the safflower oil.

Zucchini Fingers

NO CORN, EGG, MILK,* WHEAT,* OR GLUTEN*
Servings: 6

3 medium-sized zucchini
¼–⅓ c. brown rice flour
2–3 T. soybean milk (see page 16); tomato juice; or 1 t. lemon juice, 1 t. sesame oil and 2 T. water

Sunflower seed or sesame seed meal (see page 15)
3–4 T. olive or safflower oil

Cut lightly scraped zucchini lengthwise into eight strips. Roll strips in flour. Dip into milk. Roll in seed meal. Sauté in oil in a large frying pan.

Turn to brown on all sides. Drain on paper towels and keep warm in oven until all strips are cooked.

Variations: If you can use milk, substitute milk for the soybean milk.

If you can use wheat and gluten, you can substitute wheat flour for the brown rice flour and raw wheat germ or crushed dry cereal for the seed meal.

Zucchini-Spinach Casserole

NO CORN, EGG, MILK,* WHEAT, OR GLUTEN
Servings: 6

1 10-oz. package frozen chopped spinach, thawed and well drained

2 T. safflower oil, divided

¼ t. nutmeg

3 medium-sized zucchini

2 T. water

1 c. Seasoned Crumbs (see page 232) mixed with diced, crisp bacon

Press any excess moisture from spinach. Heat 1 tablespoon of the oil in a large frying pan. Add spinach. Sprinkle with nutmeg. Stir and cook until liquid evaporates. Remove to a bowl. Add 1 tablespoon more oil to the pan. Scrape and cut zucchini into ⅛-inch slices. Add to pan with the water. Cover and cook until zucchini is almost cooked, 3–4 minutes. Remove from heat. Spread half the zucchini in an 8-inch, greased oven-proof casserole. Spread on half the spinach mixture. Cover with half of the crumbs and bacon. Repeat layers, adding the rest of the crumbs. Cover casserole and bake at 350° 15 minutes. Remove cover and bake another 10 minutes, or until bubbly.

Variation: If you can use milk, you can use butter instead of oil and grated sharp cheese instead of the crumb and bacon mixture.

Baked Zucchini
with Seasoned Crumbs

NO CORN, EGG, MILK, OR WHEAT
Servings: 6–8

6–8 small zucchini
¼ c. Seasoned Crumbs (see below)

¼ c. olive oil

Cut squash in half, lengthwise. Trim ends. Arrange cut-side-up in a baking dish into which it fits closely in a single layer. Sprinkle with Seasoned Crumbs. Drizzle evenly with the olive oil. Bake, uncovered, at 350° about 40 minutes, or until zucchini is tender. Baste occasionally with more olive oil if squash looks dry. Serve hot or cold.

Variation: Use crumbs on broiled eggplant basted with olive oil; crookneck squash, halved and oiled; or green peppers, cut into quarters lengthwise with seeds and pith removed.

Seasoned Crumbs

NO CORN, EGG, MILK, OR WHEAT*
Yield: 1½ cups

Wheat-free bread (made of barley, oats, or light rye or a mixture of these)
½ c. minced fresh parsley
½ t. salt
1 clove garlic, minced

1 t. crumbled basil
¼ t. rosemary
¼ t. rubbed sage (bits of leaves, not powder)
5–6 T. olive oil

Whirl bread in a blender or food processor to make 1½ cups coarse crumbs. Combine crumbs with remaining ingredients. Blend thoroughly. Store excess in a tightly covered jar in refrigerator.

*If you can use wheat and gluten, French bread makes excellent crumbs.

Zucchini Casserole

NO CORN,* EGG, OR WHEAT*
Servings: 3–4

1⅓ c. coarsely grated zucchini
⅓ c. barley or oat bread
  crumbs
½ t. onion salt
⅓ t. mixed spices (see
  page 17)

1½ T. barley flour
2 T. butter, melted
¾ c. milk
Grated Parmesan cheese

Mix together the zucchini, crumbs, salt, and spices. Set aside. Stir flour into melted butter. Add milk slowly. Stir and cook until thickened. Stir zucchini into white sauce. Put into a lightly greased ovenproof casserole. Sprinkle with grated Parmesan cheese. Bake at 325° until bubbly.

*Variations: *If you can use corn*, you can substitute 1 t. cornstarch for the flour.

If you can use wheat and gluten, you can substitute unbleached flour for the barley flour, and wheat bread crumbs for the barley or oat bread crumbs.

For gluten-free, substitute brown rice flour for the barley flour.

Zucchini and Rice Casserole

NO CORN,* EGG, WHEAT,* OR GLUTEN*
Servings: 4–6

2 lb. zucchini
1 large onion, minced
2 cloves garlic, minced
¼ c. olive oil
2 T. brown rice flour
1 c. milk (or more)

1½ c. cooked brown rice
½ t. thyme
¾ c. plus 2 T. grated
  Parmesan cheese, divided
½ t. salt or to taste

Coarsely grate zucchini into a sieve set over a bowl. Press squash into sieve to extract juice. Retain the juice and the squash. Simmer onion and garlic in the oil about 5 minutes. Add the zucchini and toss about 2 minutes. Stir in flour. Cook another minute or two. Measure reserved juice and add enough milk to make 1½ cups. Blend it into the squash. Mix together rice, thyme, ¾ cup of the Parmesan cheese, and the salt. Mix into squash. Taste for seasoning. Pour mixture into a buttered baking dish. Sprinkle with the 2 tablespoons Parmesan. This can be prepared ahead and refrigerated until baking. Bring to room temperature before baking. Bake at 425° about 45 minutes, or until brown and bubbly and all liquid is absorbed.

Variations: If you can use corn, you can substitute 1 T. cornstarch for the brown rice flour.

If you can use wheat and gluten, you can substitute wheat flour for the brown rice flour or use 2 T. of potato flour.

If you can use gluten but not wheat, you can substitute barley flour for the brown rice flour.

Curried Squash Bake

NO CORN,* EGG, WHEAT,* OR GLUTEN*
Servings: 6–8

2 medium-sized zucchini
2 medium-sized crookneck squash
2 medium-sized summer squash (patty pan)
½ c. plain yogurt (or sour half and half)
2 t. Dijon mustard

½ t. curry powder
½ t. ground ginger
¼ c. finely chopped sunflower seeds
¼ c. grated Parmesan cheese
2 c. shredded jack cheese

Peel and cut squashes into ¼-inch slices. Steam about 5 minutes, or until barely tender. Combine yogurt, mustard, curry powder, and ginger. Place half the squash into a greased 2-quart ovenproof casserole. Top with half the yogurt mixture, seeds, Parmesan cheese, and jack cheese. Repeat layering. Cover and bake at 375° about 20 minutes, or until cheese is melted and mixture is bubbly.

Variations: If you can use corn, add 2 t. Worcestershire sauce to the yogurt mixture.

If you can use wheat and gluten, you can substitute toasted wheat germ for the seeds.

Yam Casserole

NO CORN, MILK,* WHEAT,* OR GLUTEN*
Servings: 4–6

1 lb. yams or sweet potatoes
   (about 3 medium)
2 eggs
2 T. honey
¼ c. safflower oil
½ c. orange juice
¼ t. salt

¼ t. cinnamon
¼ t. allspice
¼ t. nutmeg
Grated rinds of ½ lemon and
   ½ orange
2 T. finely chopped nuts or seeds

Wash, peel, and grind the potatoes in grinder or food processor with steel blade. Beat the eggs. Add honey, oil, juice, spices, and rinds. Stir in potatoes. Place in a well-greased ovenproof casserole. Bake at 325° uncovered, 45 minutes to 1 hour, or until the mixture is set and potatoes are cooked. Sprinkle top with chopped sunflower seeds or nuts.

Variations: *If you can use milk*, you can substitute milk for the orange juice.

If you can use wheat and gluten, you can substitute raw wheat germ for the chopped nuts or seeds.

Lima Bean Casserole

NO CORN, EGG, WHEAT,* OR GLUTEN*
Servings: 8–10

6 slices bacon
1 small onion, chopped
1 small green pepper, seeded and
   chopped
2 T. brown rice flour
1 t. dry basil

¾ c. chicken broth (see page
   7)
2 c. shredded Swiss, Monterey
   Jack, or cheddar cheese
2 10-oz. packages frozen baby
   lima beans, thawed

Fry bacon or cook it in microwave. Dice and set aside. Stir onion and green pepper into 2 tablespoons of the drippings. Stir in flour and basil.

Cook, stirring, until bubbly. Gradually stir in chicken broth. Cook, stirring, until thickened. Slowly add cheese. Stir until it melts. Steam lima beans 5–8 minutes, or until nearly cooked. Add beans and diced bacon to the cheese mixture. Spoon into a 2-quart ovenproof casserole. Bake at 350° about 20 minutes, or until bubbly and beans are tender.

Variations: *If you can use wheat and gluten*, you can substitute wheat flour for the brown rice flour.

If you can use gluten but not wheat, you can substitute barley or oat flour for the brown rice flour.

Baked Lima Beans

NO CORN,* EGG, MILK,* WHEAT, OR GLUTEN
Servings: 6–8

1 lb. large dry lima beans
2 qt. water
1 T. prepared mustard
¼ c. safflower oil
½ c. molasses

1 t. salt
1 t. ground ginger
¼ t. thyme
¼ t. dried parsley

Soak rinsed beans overnight in the water. Bring to a boil and simmer, covered, 30 minutes, or until tender. Drain, reserving 1½ cups of the liquid. Place beans in a 2½–3-quart ovenproof casserole or bean pot. Mix remaining ingredients including reserved liquid. Pour over beans. Bake at 350° 1½ hours, or until beans are cooked and liquid is absorbed.

Variations: *If you can use corn*, you can substitute ¼ c. dark corn syrup for ¼ c. of the molasses.

If you can use milk, you can substitute butter for the oil.

Lima Beans with Curry Sauce

NO CORN,* EGG, WHEAT,* OR GLUTEN*
Servings: 4–6

*1 10-oz. package frozen baby
    lima beans
2 slices bacon
1 small clove garlic, minced
½ medium-sized onion,
    minced
¼–½ t. curry powder (or to
    taste)*

*White Sauce with Mushrooms
    (see below)
1 T. dry white wine or milk
¼ c. sour half and half or
    sour cream
Homemade onion rings (enough
    to cover top of casserole)†*

Steam or boil the beans in a small amount of salted water. Drain well. Fry bacon until crisp. Remove from pan, drain, and dice. Sauté the garlic, onion, and curry powder in the drippings. When onion is soft, about 5 minutes, stir in the wine, White Sauce with Mushrooms, and half and half. Add beans and bacon. Put into greased 1-quart ovenproof casserole. Top with onion rings. Bake, uncovered, at 350° about 15 minutes, or until heated through.

    *Variation: *If you can use corn, wheat, and gluten, you can use ½ c. condensed cream of mushroom soup with the wine instead of making the White Sauce with Mushrooms.*

    †To make homemade onion rings, slice 1 large or 2 small onions, dip into potato flour or rice flour and fry in safflower or peanut oil. Or omit and substitute toasted sesame seeds.

White Sauce with Mushrooms

NO CORN, EGG, WHEAT, OR GLUTEN

*2 T. butter
1½ T. barley flour
¾ c. milk*

*½–¾ c. chopped, sautéed
    mushrooms (washed, dried,
    and trimmed)
Salt to taste*

Make a white sauce by melting butter, adding barley flour to make a roux. Add milk and heat, stirring until thickened. Stir in the mushrooms and add salt to taste.

Scalloped Turnips

NO CORN, EGG, WHEAT,* OR GLUTEN*
Servings: 6

Even if you do not usually like turnips, try this recipe. It is different and surprisingly good.

5–6 medium turnips
2 T. butter
1 T. brown rice flour
1½ c. half and half

½ c. grated Monterey Jack cheese
Grated Parmesan cheese

Peel and thinly slice the turnips. Steam until almost tender. Put in layers in a 1½-quart ovenproof casserole. Make a very thin cream sauce: Melt butter, stir in flour, slowly add the half and half. Cook until slightly thickened. Sprinkle the jack cheese over the turnips. Pour cream sauce over the cheese-covered turnips. Sprinkle with grated Parmesan cheese. Bake at 325° just until bubbly and browned, about 20 minutes. Turnips should be tender.

*Variations: If you can use wheat and gluten, you can substitute wheat flour for the brown rice flour.

If you can use gluten but not wheat, you can substitute barley flour for the brown rice flour.

Chayote Squash with Yogurt Sauce

NO CORN,* EGG, WHEAT,* OR GLUTEN*
Servings: 6

This is an interesting way to serve this mild-flavored squash.

3 chayote squash
1 c. unflavored yogurt
1 t. onion powder
1 t. sugar

2 t. brown rice flour
¼ t. salt
2 T. chopped fresh parsley

Peel and quarter squash. Cook in salted boiling water until nearly tender.
Transfer to a baking dish in a single layer. Combine remaining ingredients.
Spoon over squash. Bake at 350°, uncovered, for 15–20 minutes, or until
very hot.

*Variations: If you can use corn, you can substitute 1 t. cornstarch
for the flour.

If you can use wheat and gluten, you can substitute unbleached flour
for the brown rice flour.

If you can use gluten but not wheat, you can substitute barley flour for
the brown rice flour.

SOUPS

	NO CORN	NO EGG	NO MILK	NO WHEAT	NO GLUTEN
Indian-Style Split Pea Soup	X	X	X	X	X
Curried Split Pea Soup	X	X	X	X	X
Split Pea Soup with Pork	X	X	X	X	X
Hungarian Bean Soup	X	X	⊗	X	X
Navy Bean Soup	X	X	X	X	X
Black-Eyed Pea Soup	⊗	X	⊗	X	X
Italian Bean Soup	X	X	X	X	X
Kidney Bean Soup	X	X	X	X	X
Beef, Bean, and Barley Soup	X	X	X	X	X
Lentil-Vegetable Soup with Meatballs	X	X	X	X	X
Lentil Soup with Lemon	X	X	X	X	X
Creamy Lentil Soup	X	X		X	X
Lentil and Ham Soup	X	X	X	X	X
Baby Lima Bean Soup	X	X	X	X	X
Curried Peanut Butter Soup	⊗	X	X	X	X
Plain Peanut Butter Soup	X	X	X	X	X
Cranbeet Soup		X	X	X	X
Leberknodelsuppe (Liver Dumpling Soup)	X		X	⊗	⊗

⊗ means that the recipe includes instructions for adding that ingredient if allowed.

	NO CORN	NO EGG	NO MILK	NO WHEAT	NO GLUTEN
Cream of Lettuce Soup	X	X		⊗	⊗
Curried Eggplant Soup	X	X		X	X
Celeriac Soup	X	X	⊗	X	X
Cream of Parsnip Soup	X	X		X	X
Zucchini Soup	X	X	X	X	X
Chilled Zucchini Bisque	X	X	⊗	X	X
Blender Avocado Soup	X	X		X	X
Leek and Potato Soup	X	X		X	X
Cream of Potato Soup	X	X		X	X
Cucumber Soup	⊗	⊗	⊗	⊗	⊗
Fruit Soup	⊗	X	X	X	X

Indian-Style Split Pea Soup

NO CORN, EGG, MILK, WHEAT, OR GLUTEN

Servings: 5–6

1 cracked ham hock (about 1 lb.)
2 qt. water
1½ c. green or yellow split
  peas, picked over and rinsed
1 small onion, finely chopped
1 t. ground coriander
1 t. cumin

¼ t. turmeric
1 t. lemon juice
1 T. sugar
Salt
Chopped fresh parsley or chopped
  fresh coriander (optional)
Chopped salted peanuts (optional)

Place ham hock in a deep pan and cover with the 2 quarts water. Bring to a boil and simmer 10 minutes. Drain and save liquid. Set aside. Add peas, onion, and liquid to ham hock. Cover and simmer until peas are soft, about 1½ hours. Remove ham hock, discard bone and fat, cut meat into small pieces. Set aside. Remove peas with a slotted spoon. Put peas through a food mill or blend in a blender or food processor until smooth. Return peas to the pot. Add spices, lemon juice, and sugar and salt to taste. Add the ham bits. Simmer 10–15 minutes longer. Serve with chopped fresh coriander or parsley and chopped salted peanuts. (Use coriander sparingly as its flavor is very pronounced.)

Curried Split Pea Soup

NO CORN, EGG, MILK, WHEAT, OR GLUTEN
Servings: 4

*1 c. split peas, picked over and
    rinsed*
2 c. tomato juice
3 c. water
*A chunk of diced salt pork, a
    ham hock, or 4 slices diced
    uncooked bacon*
1 t. onion powder

½ t. garlic powder
1½ c. chopped celery
1½ c. chopped carrots
*½–1 t. curry powder (or to
    taste)*
½ t. salt (or to taste)
2 T. chopped fresh parsley

Combine peas, juice, water, pork, onion powder, and garlic powder in a
Dutch oven. Cook gently until peas are tender, about 1 hour. Add celery,
carrots, curry powder, and salt. Cover and simmer until vegetables are
tender. Add more liquid if needed. Just before serving, stir in parsley.

Split Pea Soup with Pork

NO CORN, EGG, MILK, WHEAT, OR GLUTEN
Servings: 6

*1 12-oz. package dried green or
    yellow split peas, picked over
    and rinsed*
2 qt. water
*1 lb. boneless pork or large ham
    hock*
*3 medium-sized carrots, cut into
    1-inch pieces*

*1 medium-sized onion, finely
    chopped*
½ t. whole marjoram
⅛ t. ground cloves or allspice
Salt

Place peas in a Dutch oven. Cover with remaining ingredients. Simmer
until peas are soft and pork is cooked, about 1½–2 hours. Remove
pork, discard bones and fat, cut meat into small pieces. Put soup through
blender, food processor, food mill, or strainer in batches. Return to pot.
Add pork bits and salt to taste. Reheat.

Hungarian Bean Soup

NO CORN, EGG, MILK,* WHEAT, OR GLUTEN
Servings: 8–10

2 c. dried pinto or cranberry
  beans
2 medium-sized carrots, peeled
1 parsnip, peeled
1 medium-sized onion, peeled and
  cut into chunks
2 large smoked ham hocks
2 lb. veal or beef bones
6 sprigs fresh parsley

½ t. garlic powder
1 t. salt
3 qt. water
1 T. safflower oil
1 T. brown rice flour
2 t. sweet Hungarian paprika or
  plain paprika
½ c. water

Pick over beans. Soak overnight in cold water. Discard water. In a large pot, combine carrots, parsnip, onion, ham hocks, bones, parsley, garlic powder, salt, and the 3 quarts water. Heat and simmer, covered, about 2 hours, or until ham is tender. Remove hocks and bones and set hocks aside. Strain soup, reserving carrots and parsnip. Return liquid to pot. Add beans and simmer, covered, until beans are tender, about 1 hour. Discard skin, bones, and fat from ham. Cut meat into small pieces. Slice carrots and parsnip. Add to soup along with meat. Adjust seasoning.

If possible, chill soup to congeal and remove fat, or run an ice cube over grease floating on top of soup to remove it. (Fat will adhere to the ice, but move quickly enough that the ice does not melt.) Heat soup again to simmering. In a small pan, heat the oil. Add flour and paprika. Cook until bubbly. Gradually add the ½ cup water, stirring constantly. Cook until thickened. Blend into soup and cook about 5 minutes longer.

*Variation: If you can use milk, you can substitute butter for the oil and serve with a dollop of sour cream.

Navy Bean Soup

NO CORN, EGG, MILK, WHEAT, OR GLUTEN
Servings: 4

1 c. navy beans
1 large ham hock

4 c. chicken stock or broth (see
page 7)
1 t. onion powder

Soak beans overnight. Pour off water, pick over beans, cover with fresh water, and bring to a boil. Pour off this water. When drained, combine beans with ham hock, chicken stock, and onion powder. Cook gently until beans are very soft and ham pulls away from bone, about 2 hours. Discard bones. Cut ham into small pieces. Return ham bits to soup. Mash some of the beans and stir in to thicken soup.

Black-Eyed Pea Soup

NO CORN,* EGG, MILK,* WHEAT, OR GLUTEN
Servings: 6

1 c. black-eyed peas
4 14-oz. cans or 7 c. regular-
strength beef broth
(see page 7)
1 medium-sized potato, peeled
and diced
1 stalk celery, finely chopped

1 large green apple, peeled and
sliced
1 large onion, chopped
1 t. curry powder
2 T. safflower oil
About 1¾ c. water or beef
broth

Pick over peas and soak overnight. Drain and discard water. Combine peas, broth, potato, and celery. Bring to boil and simmer, covered, until tender, 2–3 hours. Sauté the apple, onion, and curry in the oil until soft. Add to peas. Stir in water or broth to desired thickness. Whirl soup in blender or food processor until smooth. Reheat to serve.

*Variations: If you can use corn, add 2 t. Worcestershire sauce with the water or broth at the end.

If you can use milk, you can substitute butter for the oil and add 1¾ c. milk instead of broth or water at the end.

Italian Bean Soup

NO CORN, EGG, MILK, WHEAT, OR GLUTEN
Servings: 8–10

2 c. small red or cranberry beans
(see page 3)
8 c. water
¾ t. garlic powder
1 large onion, chopped, or 1 t.
onion powder
1½ c. thinly sliced carrots

1 c. finely chopped celery
½ c. tomato juice
2 large ham hocks, cut into
pieces
¼ c. tiny soup pasta, or ½
c. cooked brown rice
Chopped fresh parsley

Soak beans overnight. Pour off water. Pick over beans, cover with fresh water, and bring to a boil. Pour off this water. Now add 8 cups water and all the remaining ingredients except the pasta or rice and parsley to the beans. Bring mixture to a boil. Reduce heat and simmer, covered, until beans are soft, about 2½ hours. Lift out ham hocks, discarding skin, bones, and fat. Cut meat into bite-sized pieces. Set aside. Whirl soup in blender or food processor in batches if necessary. Return to pan with the ham bits. Add pasta or rice. Heat until pasta is cooked, about 5 minutes, or until rice is warmed. Serve sprinkled with chopped fresh parsley.

Pass grated Parmesan cheese if milk is allowed.

Kidney Bean Soup

NO CORN, EGG, MILK, WHEAT, OR GLUTEN
Servings: 6–8

1 c. kidney beans
8 c. water, divided
1 meaty beef bone
1 c. chopped carrots
1 c. chopped celery
1 clove garlic, minced

1 medium-sized onion, chopped,
or 1 T. onion powder
1 t. salt
2 c. tomato juice
½ c. dry sherry (optional)

Pick over beans and soak overnight. Drain. Add 3 cups fresh water. Bring to a boil. Boil gently 30 minutes. Drain off water. Add 5 cups fresh water and all remaining ingredients except sherry. Continue cooking until beans and vegetables are very tender, about 2 hours. Remove bone, scrape out any marrow, cut meat into small pieces, and return meat and marrow to soup. Add sherry if desired. The soup can be served as is or pureed in the blender or food processor with steel blade. If pureed soup is too thick, thin to desired consistency with water or tomato juice. Reheat, tasting for seasoning. Garnish with chopped parsley or a thin slice of lemon if desired.

Variation: Navy beans can also be used in this recipe.

Beef, Bean, and Barley Soup

NO CORN, EGG, MILK, WHEAT, OR GLUTEN
Servings: 6–8

¾ c. dried lima beans
2 lb. meaty beef soup bones
About 1 T. safflower oil
3 carrots, sliced
1 large onion, finely chopped
1 stalk celery, sliced
1 t. beef bouillon base (see page 7) or 1 c. homemade stock
1 t. dill weed
½ t. garlic powder
1 T. salt
2 T. chopped fresh parsley
¾ c. split peas, rinsed and picked over
½ lb. mushrooms, sliced, washed, trimmed, and diced
½ c. pearl barley

Pick over lima beans and soak overnight. Brush pan with oil and brown soup bones. (If skimpy, add about ½ pound beef chuck.) Sauté the carrots, onion, and celery in oil. Add bouillon, dill, garlic powder, salt, and parsley. Drain lima beans, retaining liquid. Add limas, peas, and bones (and meat) to pot. Add enough water to bean liquid to make 2 quarts (if stock is used, include it at this point). Cover and simmer about 2 hours, or until meat is tender and beans are cooked. Remove bones and meat. Cut meat into bite-sized pieces and set aside. Either leave the soup as is or put into blender or food processor with steel blade to make a thick puree. Add mushrooms and barley. Simmer until barley is tender, about 45 minutes. More water may be needed. Stir often. Add meat and adjust seasoning.

Note: Barley can be precooked in 1 cup boiling water to shorten the cooking time.

Lentil-Vegetable Soup with Meatballs

NO CORN, EGG, MILK, WHEAT, OR GLUTEN
Servings: 4–6

1 c. lentils, rinsed and picked over
2 c. water
1½ lb. lean ground beef or lamb
1 t. salt
½ t. ground cinnamon
1 t. cumin, divided
1 T. safflower oil
2 onions, finely chopped
2 cloves garlic, minced, or 1 t. garlic powder

2 medium-sized carrots, thinly sliced
1 medium-sized potato, peeled and cut into small cubes
2 stalks celery, sliced diagonally
Regular-strength beef broth (see page 7)
3 t. lemon juice, or to taste
Chopped fresh parsley

Cook lentils in the water until tender, about 35 minutes. Combine meat, salt, cinnamon, and ½ teaspoon of the cumin. Shape into about twenty-four balls. In a Dutch oven, brown in the oil. Remove meatballs from pan with slotted spoon. Discard all but 2 tablespoons of the drippings. Add onion and garlic to the pan. Cook, stirring, until onion is limp and golden. Add carrots, potato, and celery. Drain lentils, saving any liquid. Add enough beef broth to it to make 1 quart. Add beef broth to vegetables with the remaining ½ teaspoon cumin. Cover and simmer about 20 minutes, or until vegetables are tender. Add lentils and meatballs. Add more beef broth if needed. Simmer about 15 minutes. Stir in lemon juice. Adjust seasoning if necessary. Sprinkle with chopped parsley and serve.

Lentil Soup with Lemon

NO CORN, EGG, MILK, WHEAT, OR GLUTEN
Servings: 3–4

½ c. lentils, rinsed and picked
  over
3 c. water
1 slice uncooked bacon, diced
1 medium-sized onion, chopped,
  or ½ t. onion powder
1 T. chopped fresh parsley
1 clove garlic, minced, or ¼ t.
  garlic powder

1 large carrot, chopped
1 stalk celery, chopped
¾ t. salt
⅛ t. oregano
½ c. tomato juice
1 T. lemon juice
2 T. dry white wine
Lemon slices

Place lentils in a large pan with the water, bacon, onion, parsley, garlic, carrot, celery, salt, and oregano. Cover and simmer 1½ hours. Add tomato juice, lemon juice, and wine. Cook just until all ingredients are soft. Puree in blender or food processor with steel blade. Reheat if necessary. Adjust salt to taste. Serve topped with a slice of lemon. Recipe can be doubled or tripled.

Creamy Lentil Soup

NO CORN, EGG, WHEAT, OR GLUTEN
Servings: 6

1 c. lentils, rinsed and picked
  over
4 c. water
1 large potato, peeled and diced
1 small onion, finely chopped
2 T. butter or safflower oil

1 t. beef stock base (if allowed)
1 t. chicken-flavored stock base
  (if allowed)
½ c. milk or half and half
1 t. salt or to taste

Put lentils into a 3-quart kettle. Add the water. Bring to a boil. Add potato. Cover and simmer until soft, about 45 minutes. Sauté onion in butter or oil about 15 minutes. Add to lentils along with beef and chicken stock bases. Remove from heat and blend in food processor or blender until very smooth. Return to kettle. Add milk and salt to taste.

Lentil and Ham Soup

NO CORN, EGG, MILK, WHEAT OR GLUTEN
Servings: 6–8

3–4 lb. ham hocks, cut into
    sections
3 qt. water
2 bay leaves
1 t. Italian herbs or oregano
1 t. mixed pickling spices
1 medium-sized onion, finely
    chopped

1½ c. lentils, rinsed and
    picked over
1 c. peeled carrot chunks
3 small new potatoes, peeled and
    cut
12 pitted prunes, cut in half
Chopped fresh parsley

Cover ham hocks with water. Bring to a boil. Remove hocks and discard
water. Return hocks to pot. Add the 3 quarts water, herbs, spices, and
onion. Simmer about 2 hours. Remove ham, discarding fat and bones. Cut
meat into bite-sized pieces. Strain liquid to remove herbs and spices. Return
liquid to pan. Skim excess fat from broth. Reheat and add the lentils.
Cover and simmer 30 minutes. Add carrot, potatoes, and prunes. Cover
and simmer until beans and vegetables are tender, 25–30 minutes. Sprinkle
with parsley and serve.

Baby Lima Bean Soup

NO CORN, EGG, MILK, WHEAT, OR GLUTEN
Servings: 4

2 10-oz. packages frozen baby
    lima beans, thawed
1 qt. chicken broth, or 2½ 14-
    oz. cans regular-strength broth
    (see page 7)
1 medium-sized onion, sliced, or
    1 t. onion powder

1 large carrot, sliced
1 stalk celery, sliced
1 t. dill
½ t. salt or to taste
4 slices cooked bacon, crumbled
    (optional)

Combine all ingredients except dill, salt and bacon. Bring to a boil. Reduce
heat and simmer until beans are thoroughly cooked, about 15 minutes. Put

through a food mill, whirl in blender, or process in food processor with steel blade. Rewarm the puree. Add the dill and salt to taste. Add water if too thick. Sprinkle with crumbled bacon if desired.

Curried Peanut Butter Soup

NO CORN,* EGG, MILK, WHEAT, OR GLUTEN
Servings: 4

An interesting change and nourishing enough to be a luncheon entrée. Good with whole wheat or wheat-free toast, muffins, or sprout sandwiches and fruit.

3 T. peanut or safflower oil
⅔ c. chopped celery
⅔ c. chopped carrot
1 t. onion powder
½ t. curry powder
2 T. brown rice flour
3½ c. homemade chicken
stock or 2 14-oz. cans regular-
strength chicken broth (see
page 7)

⅔ c. chunky peanut butter
2 T. tomato sauce
1 t. soy sauce
Chopped peanuts (optional)

Heat oil. Add celery, carrots, onion powder, and curry powder. Cook, stirring, until vegetables are almost soft. Stir in flour. Gradually add chicken broth, peanut butter, tomato sauce, and soy sauce. Simmer, stirring, about 5 minutes. If too thick, thin to desired consistency with more broth or water. Pass chopped peanuts to be stirred in. (For those who can use milk, top soup with a dollop of plain yogurt before adding peanuts.)

Variation: *If you can use corn*, you can substitute catsup for the tomato sauce.

Plain Peanut Butter Soup

NO CORN, EGG, MILK, WHEAT, OR GLUTEN
Servings: 4

1 t. onion powder
¾ c. creamy peanut butter
3 c. chicken broth (see page 7)

Salt (to taste)
3–4 slices cooked bacon,
  crumbled

Mix onion powder into peanut butter in a large saucepan. Slowly add chicken broth. Stir until smooth. Simmer 10 minutes. Check seasoning and if salt is needed, add to taste. Sprinkle with crumbled bacon.

Cranbeet Soup

NO EGG, MILK, WHEAT, OR GLUTEN
Servings: 3–4

1 1-lb. can sliced or diced beets
½ c. whole cranberry sauce
1 c. homemade beef stock, or
  ½ 14-oz. can condensed
  beef broth (see page 7)
¾ t. onion powder
2 T. lemon juice

1 T. vinegar
1½ c. cranberry juice
¼ c. dry sherry (optional)
Salt (to taste)
1 c. diced peeled potatoes
  (optional)

Combine beets and cranberry sauce in blender or food processor with steel blade. *Do not completely puree*; leave some texture to the mixture. Transfer to a large saucepan. Add remaining ingredients. Heat. Taste for seasoning. Serve with a dollop of yogurt if allowed. This is also good served cold (without the potatoes) on a warm summer day.

Variation: *For a corn-free recipe*, use homemade cranberry sauce (see page 202).

Leberknodelsuppe
(Liver Dumpling Soup)

NO CORN, MILK, WHEAT,* OR GLUTEN*
Servings: 4–6

This is a favorite soup in Austria. A marvelous way to serve liver—it can be enjoyed even by those who do not usually like liver.

1 lb. beef liver, cut into bite-sized pieces
1 medium-sized onion, chopped
1 egg, well beaten
¾ t. salt
⅛ t. nutmeg
¼ c. finely chopped fresh parsley

1 t. grated lemon rind
⅓ c. fine wheat-free or gluten-free crumbs
Homemade or regular-strength beef broth (see page 7), allowing ¾–1 c. for each serving depending on size of bowl

Process liver and onion in a food grinder or food processor. Combine with all remaining ingredients except broth. Mold into golf-ball-sized dumplings with a tablespoon. Drop dumplings, a few at a time, into rapidly boiling, salted water. Reduce heat and boil gently 5–10 minutes, or until liver is cooked. Remove with slotted spoon and keep warm until all are cooked. Heat beef broth and pour over dumplings in soup bowls.

Variation: *If you can use wheat and gluten*, you can substitute wheat bread crumbs for the wheat-free, gluten-free crumbs. For gluten-free, use brown rice flour bread; for wheat-free, use barley, oat, or rye breads.

Cream of Lettuce Soup

NO CORN, EGG, WHEAT,* OR GLUTEN*
Servings: 4–6

2 T. butter or safflower oil
1 small onion, chopped
2 T. brown rice flour
2 t. beef stock base, or 2 bouillon
cubes (see page 7), in ¾ c.
boiling water, or ¾ cup
homemade stock

½ t. salt
2 c. half and half or rich milk
½ medium-sized head crisp
lettuce, shredded and cut
crosswise (about 4 c.)
Grated nutmeg or chopped fresh
parsley

Melt butter over medium-high heat. Sauté onion until soft. Stir in flour.
Dissolve beef stock base in boiling water. Add salt. Gradually stir into
onion mixture. Cook, stirring, until thickened and smooth. Add half and
half. Heat, stirring, to just below boiling point. Add lettuce to soup. Stir
until lettuce is heated. Serve immediately, sprinkled generously with nutmeg or chopped parsley.

*Variations: *If you can use wheat and gluten*, you can substitute wheat
flour for the brown rice flour.

If you can use gluten but not wheat, you can substitute barley flour for
the brown rice flour.

Curried Eggplant Soup

NO CORN, EGG, WHEAT, OR GLUTEN
Servings: 4

1 medium-sized eggplant
2 T. butter or safflower oil
2 t. onion powder
1 t. curry powder

4 c. chicken broth (see page 7)
⅔ c. half and half
Salt (to taste)
Chopped fresh parsley or chives

Trim and peel eggplant. Cut into ½-inch cubes. Heat oil in a saucepan.
Stir in onion powder and curry powder. Continue stirring 1–2 minutes.

Add eggplant and the 4 cups broth. Bring to a boil, reduce heat, and simmer until eggplant is very soft, 30–40 minutes. Puree in small batches in blender or food processor with steel blade. Strain to remove seeds. Return to pan. Add half and half and salt. Reheat for hot soup or chill, covered, several hours and serve in chilled bowls. Top with chopped parsley or chives.

Variation: *For milk-free Curried Eggplant Soup*, use safflower oil instead of butter and about ½ cup more broth instead of half and half, or enough to give the desired consistency.

Celeriac Soup

NO CORN, EGG, MILK,* WHEAT, OR GLUTEN
Servings: 6–8

3 T. safflower oil
2 c. chopped leeks
1 t. onion powder
3 T. raw short-grain brown rice
4 c. peeled and diced celeriac
  (celery root)

4 c. homemade chicken stock, or
  2 cans regular-strength
  chicken broth (see page 7)
2 c. more broth or water
½ t. salt or to taste
Chopped fresh parsley

Heat oil in a Dutch oven. Add leeks, onion powder, and rice. Mix, cover, and let cook, stirring several times until leeks are transparent, about 10 minutes. Add celeriac and the 4 cups broth. Heat to simmer and cook until vegetables and rice are very tender, 30–40 minutes. Whirl in food processor with steel blade or in blender in batches if necessary until very smooth. Return to pan. Add the 2 cups broth and salt to taste. Reheat. Serve sprinkled with chopped parsley.

Variation: *If you can use milk*, you can substitute 2 c. milk for the 2 c. broth or water.

Cream of Parsnip Soup

NO CORN, EGG, WHEAT, OR GLUTEN
Servings: 6–8

2 lb. parsnips
1 large onion, chopped
2 t. dry basil
2 14-oz. cans regular-strength
chicken broth or 3½ c.
homemade (see page 7)

2¼ c. milk
2 T. chopped fresh parsley
Salt
Garlic powder

Peel and cut parsnips into thin slices. In a large pot, combine them with onion, basil, and chicken broth. Cover, bring to a boil, and simmer until parsnips are tender, about 30 minutes. Whirl in blender or food processor with steel blade until mixture is smooth. Return to pan. Add milk, parsley, and salt to taste. Sprinkle with garlic powder. Reheat, stirring frequently, but do not boil.

Zucchini Soup

NO CORN, EGG, MILK, WHEAT, OR GLUTEN
Servings: 6–8

6 medium-sized zucchini
¼ lb. sliced bacon, separated
and cut in half
½ t. salt
½ t. garlic powder
½ t. mixed herbs (commercial
mix or own mix, see pages
17–18)

2 10-oz. cans regular-strength
beef broth plus 2 c. water, or
2 t. beef stock base plus 1 t.
beef bouillon plus 4 c. water
(see page 7) or 4 c. homemade
broth

Wash zucchini, remove ends, and cut into chunks. Put zucchini and bacon into a pot with the remaining ingredients. Cook 15–20 minutes, or until zucchini is soft. Remove bacon. Whirl soup in blender or food processor with steel blade, or put through a sieve. Reheat to serve.

Chilled Zucchini Bisque

NO CORN, EGG, MILK,* WHEAT, OR GLUTEN
Servings: 6–8

5 medium-sized zucchini (about
1¼ lb.)
4 T. safflower oil
1 medium-sized onion, finely
chopped, or 1 t. onion powder
2 14-oz. cans regular-strength
chicken broth (see page 7) or
3½ c. homemade

½ c. more broth
¼ t. nutmeg
Salt (to taste)

Wash zucchini, cut off ends, and thinly slice. Heat oil in a Dutch oven.
Sauté zucchini and onion until limp, about 5 minutes. Add the chicken
broth. Cover and simmer until vegetables are tender, about 10–15 minutes.
Whirl in blender or food processor or strain through a sieve until smooth.
Put into a bowl, add the ½ cup broth and nutmeg, and salt to taste.
Blend thoroughly, cover, and chill. Serve in chilled bowls or mugs.

*Variation: If you can use milk, use ½ c. half and half instead of
the ½ c. broth.

Blender Avocado Soup

NO CORN, EGG, WHEAT, OR GLUTEN
Servings: 3–4

1 large avocado, peeled, pitted,
and coarsely chopped
2 c. cold fat-free chicken broth
(see page 7)
1 c. commercial sour half and
half or plain low-fat yogurt

3 T. rum (optional)
1 T. lemon juice (decrease or
eliminate if yogurt is used)
½ t. curry powder
½ t. seasoned salt
3–4 thin lemon slices

Combine all ingredients except lemon slices. Whirl in blender or food
processor until very smooth. Serve chilled with a slice of lemon on top.

Leek and Potato Soup

NO CORN, EGG, WHEAT, OR GLUTEN
Servings: 4–6

*4 c. thinly sliced leeks, including
  some tender young tops*
1 medium onion, minced
3 T. butter or safflower oil
2 c. diced or shredded potato
*2 14-oz. cans regular-strength
  beef broth (see page 7) or
  3½ c. homemade beef stock*

2 c. half and half or milk
Salt (optional)
*Chopped parsley or chopped
  chives*

Sauté leeks and onion in the butter or oil. Add potatoes and broth. Cover and simmer, stirring occasionally, about 15–20 minutes, or until vegetables are soft. Whirl in blender or food processor until mixture is very smooth. Return to pan. Stir in half and half. Add salt if needed. Reheat. Serve sprinkled with chopped parsley or chives.

Variations: *To make Vichyssoise*: Chill. Stir in a dollop of sour cream before serving

To make Senegalese Soup: Add 1 c. chopped celery and a touch of curry powder to the leeks and potatoes. Serve chilled.

Cream of Potato Soup

NO CORN, EGG, WHEAT, OR GLUTEN
Servings: 3–4

2 c. diced potato
*2 c. chicken stock or broth (see
  page 7)*
2 strips bacon, diced
¼ large onion, finely chopped

2 c. rich milk (approx.)
Salt
Dash of nutmeg or mace
Grated Parmesan cheese

Combine potatoes and broth. Boil until potatoes are soft, about 15 minutes. Whirl in blender or food processor until very smooth. Fry bacon until crisp. Remove from pan and drain. Sauté the onion in the drippings. Drain any excess drippings. Add onion and bacon to potatoes. Stir in milk to desired thickness. Add salt to taste. Serve with a dash of nutmeg or mace. Pass grated Parmesan cheese.

Cucumber Soup

NO CORN,* EGG,* MILK,* WHEAT,* OR GLUTEN*
Servings: 4

1 c. chopped onion
4 T. safflower oil
2 T. brown rice flour or potato flour
2 14-oz. cans regular-strength chicken broth (see page 7) or 3½ c. homemade stock

2 c. peeled, seeded, and diced cucumber
2 T. dill weed
Salt (to taste)
Thin cucumber slices

Sauté the onion in the oil until soft. Sprinkle on flour. Stir in flour and cook over moderate heat 2–3 minutes. Add broth and cucumber. Bring to a boil. Lower heat, and cook, covered, until cucumber is tender, about 15 minutes. Whirl in blender or food processor until very smooth. Return to pan. Reheat but do not boil. Add the dill weed and salt to taste. Serve either hot or cold with a slice of cucumber floating on top.

*Variations: If you can use corn, you can substitute 1 T. cornstarch for the flour.

If you can use egg, lightly beat 2 egg yolks and stir into soup before reheating.

If you can use milk, stir ½ c. half and half into soup before reheating (if adding egg yolks, stir cream into beaten yolks, then stir mixture into soup) and substitute 6 T. butter for the oil if desired.

If you can use wheat and gluten, you can substitute wheat flour for the brown rice flour.

Fruit Soup

NO CORN,* EGG, MILK, WHEAT, OR GLUTEN
Servings: 8–10

This is a very versatile dish that can be used as a first course, in place of salad, or as a dessert with chopped nuts sprinkled on top and a dollop of yogurt or sour cream if allowed. A great variety of fruits can be combined for many variations.

1 c. chopped moist dried peaches
1 c. chopped moist dried apricots
½ c. chopped moist dried pears
½ c. seedless raisins
½ medium-sized lemon, thinly sliced
1 stick cinnamon, about 3 inches, or 1 t. ground cinnamon

6 c. combined fruit juices† (reserve 2 T.)
1 c. chopped crisp apple or pineapple chunks
2 T. arrowroot or 4 T. potato flour
⅛ t. salt
½ c. mild honey (or to taste)
⅓ c. rum or brandy (optional)

Combine the dried fruit, raisins, lemon, cinnamon, and liquid. Bring to a boil. Reduce heat and simmer 10 minutes. Remove from heat. Add apple or pineapple chunks. Combine arrowroot, salt, and the 1 T. reserved juice. Stir into fruit mixture. Add the honey and rum or brandy if desired. Simmer mixture, stirring, until thickened and fruit is tender, about 15 minutes. Adjust liquid if too thick by adding more juice. Serve hot or cold. (Do not reheat if arrowroot is used as arrowroot-thickened food will not stay thick if reheated.)

Variations: *If you can use corn*, you can substitute cornstarch for the arrowroot.

Other fruits such as prunes, dried figs, mandarin orange sections, dried apples, canned plums, diced papayas, mango or grapes can be added or substituted as desired.

---

†Use a combination of 3 cups water and 3 cups of any combination of the following you wish: orange juice, pineapple juice, grape juice, apple juice, or cranberry juices.

MISCELLANEOUS

	NO CORN	NO EGG	NO MILK	NO WHEAT	NO GLUTEN
Tofu Salad Dressing	X	X	X	X	X
Tofu Pimiento Cheese	⊗	X	X	X	X
Tofu Whipped Cream	X	X	X	X	X
Tofu Spread or Dip	⊗	X	X	X	X
Yogurt Orange Salad Dressing	X	X		X	X
Yogurt Roquefort or Blue Cheese Dressing	⊗	X		X	X
Honey-Fruit French Dressing	X	X	X	X	X
Thousand Island Dressing		X		X	X
Salmon Ball Hors d'Oeuvres	X	X		X	X
Mustard Sauce	X	X	⊗	⊗	
Dill Sauce	X	X	⊗	⊗	⊗
Creole Tomato Sauce	X	X	X	X	X
Easy Tomato Sauce	⊗	X	X	X	X

⊗ means that the recipe includes instructions for adding that ingredient if allowed.

Tofu Salad Dressing

NO CORN, EGG, MILK, WHEAT, OR GLUTEN
Yield: 1½ cups

6 oz. soft tofu, prepared as
  directed on page 125
2 cloves garlic, minced
4 T. lemon juice
1 T. safflower oil

2 t. ground coriander
½ c. finely chopped fresh
  parsley
1 T. soy sauce

Process tofu in a blender or food processor with steel blade until smooth and creamy. Blend in remaining ingredients. Store in a covered jar in refrigerator.

Tofu Pimiento Cheese

NO CORN,* EGG, MILK, WHEAT, OR GLUTEN
Yield: 1¼–1½ cups

1 t. plain gelatin
2 T. cold water
2 T. lemon juice
2½ T. safflower oil
8 oz. soft tofu, prepared as
  directed on page 125

2 oz. pimiento, drained
  (½ can)
½ t. salt
1 small clove garlic, chopped
¼ c. chopped cashews

Soften gelatin in cold water. Let sit 5 minutes. Heat, stirring, until gelatin is dissolved. Stir in lemon juice and oil. Set aside. Process tofu in a blender or food processor with steel blade until smooth and creamy. Add pimiento, salt, and garlic. Add gelatin mixture. Whirl until smooth and thoroughly blended. Stir in cashews. Turn out into a bowl or mold and chill until firm. Serve with raw vegetables or crackers.

*Variation: If you can use corn, add ½ t. Worcestershire sauce with the pimiento.

Tofu Whipped Cream

NO CORN, EGG, MILK, WHEAT, OR GLUTEN
Yield: ½ cup

4 oz. soft tofu, prepared as
directed on page 125

1 T. honey
1 t. vanilla (or to taste)

Process tofu in a blender or food processor with steel blade until smooth and creamy. Add honey and vanilla and blend thoroughly.

Tofu Spread or Dip

NO CORN,* EGG, MILK, WHEAT, OR GLUTEN
Yield: 2 cups

½ t. plain gelatin in ⅔ T.
lemon juice
8 oz. soft tofu, prepared as
directed on page 125
3 T. olive oil or sesame or
safflower oil

½ t. salt
½ c. chopped olives
¼ t. onion powder
⅛ t. garlic powder

Warm gelatin in lemon juice. Combine ingredients in blender or food processor and blend thoroughly. Store in refrigerator.

*Variations: If you can use corn, add ¼ t. Worcestershire sauce.

Add 1 4-oz. can drained, finely diced pimiento instead of the olives. This can be stirred into the tofu mixture or whirled into mixture in blender or food processor until smooth.

To make tofu more like cheese in flavor, add nutmeg, paprika, and celery salt in equal amounts and pepper if desired.

Yogurt Orange Salad Dressing

NO CORN, EGG, WHEAT, OR GLUTEN

This is best for fruit salads.

1¼ c. low-fat yogurt
2 T. frozen orange juice
    concentrate, thawed

1–2 T. honey, or to taste

Combine in blender or food processor until well blended. Store, tightly covered, in the refrigerator.

Variation: Add 1½ fresh mint leaves, or 1 scant T. dried leaves, and 1–2 T. lemon juice. Combine with yogurt as above.

Yogurt Roquefort
or Blue Cheese Dressing

NO CORN,* EGG, WHEAT, OR GLUTEN

1 c. low fat yogurt

¼ c. (approximately)
    Roquefort or blue cheese

Combine in blender or food processor until well blended. Store in refrigerator.

Variation: *If you can use corn*, add ¼ t. Worcestershire sauce.

Honey-Fruit French Dressing

NO CORN, EGG, MILK, WHEAT, OR GLUTEN

½ c. safflower oil
½ t. paprika
4 t. honey
¼ t. salt

2 T. grapefruit juice
2 T. orange juice concentrate
1½ T. lemon juice

Combine all ingredients in blender or food processor. Blend until thoroughly mixed. Store in refrigerator. Shake before using.

Thousand Island Dressing

NO EGG, WHEAT, OR GLUTEN

2 c. low-fat cottage cheese
½ c. buttermilk
3 T. vinegar
¼ c. catsup
¼ t. prepared mustard

¼ c. pickle relish
1 t. finely chopped green onion
2 t. chopped green olives
   (optional)

Combine cheese, buttermilk, vinegar, catsup, and mustard in blender or food processor. Remove to bowl and add relish, onion, and olives. Store tightly covered in refrigerator.

Variation: For corn-free, use ¼ c. tomato sauce (see page 268), 1 T. chopped capers, ¼ t. dill weed, and ¼ t. onion powder instead of catsup, mustard, and pickle relish. Green olives are optional.

Salmon Ball Hors d'Oeuvres

NO CORN, EGG, WHEAT, OR GLUTEN
Yield: 10–12 balls

1 7¾-oz. can salmon, drained
4 oz. cream cheese
½ T. lemon juice
1 t. corn-free white horseradish*

⅛ t. paprika
1 t. onion powder
½ c. sunflower seeds
1½ t. chopped fresh parsley

Combine salmon, cream cheese, lemon juice, horseradish, paprika, and onion powder in blender or food processor with steel blade. Blend until smooth and creamy. Chill several hours, until firm enough to handle. With two spoons, make ten to twelve small balls. Whirl sunflower seeds in blender. Combine ground seeds with parsley. Roll balls in seeds. Place on waxed paper. Cover and chill as long as overnight. Serve with squares of toasted rye or whole wheat bread, if allowed, or Brown Rice Crackers (see page 61). Or, make one large ball and serve with raw vegetables.

*If horseradish has unidentified vegetable oil, omit for corn-free; substitute ½ t. chervil or tarragon, and ¼ t. each sweet basil and oregano.

Mustard Sauce

NO CORN, EGG, MILK,* OR WHEAT*

3 T. safflower oil
2 T. barley flour
1 c. chicken stock, homemade
(see page 7), or canned if
allowed

1 T. lemon juice
½ t. dry mustard mixed with 1
t. water to form a paste
Salt to taste

Heat oil, stir in flour, and slowly stir in broth and lemon juice. Cook, stirring, until thickened. Add mustard and taste for seasoning. Add salt if needed. Serve warm.

*Variations: If you can use milk, you can substitute butter for the safflower oil or use a mixture of both.

If you can use wheat, you can substitute unbleached wheat flour for the barley flour.

For gluten-free, use brown rice flour instead of the barley flour.

For Caper Sauce, add 1–2 T. capers, drained, to the Mustard Sauce.

Dill Sauce

NO CORN, EGG, MILK,* WHEAT,* OR GLUTEN*
Yield: 3–3½ cups

5 T. safflower oil
6 T. brown rice flour or potato
  flour
1 t. onion powder
¼ t. celery salt
3 c. heated chicken broth,
  homemade (see page 7), or
  commercial if allowed

½ t. dried or 2 t. fresh
  chopped dill, or to taste
2–3 T. dry sherry (optional)
Salt to taste

Heat oil. Stir in flour and cook, stirring, 1–2 minutes. Add onion powder and celery salt. Slowly add broth, stirring constantly. Beat with a wire whip until thickened to consistency of a soft custard. Add the dill and sherry, and salt if desired.

Variations: *If you can use milk*, you can substitute 6 T. butter for the safflower oil.

If you can use wheat and gluten, you can substitute wheat flour for the brown rice or potato flour.

If you can use gluten but not wheat, you can substitute barley flour for the brown rice flour.

Creole Tomato Sauce

NO CORN, EGG, MILK, WHEAT, OR GLUTEN
Yield: 1½–2 cups

This sauce is good on fish or over noodles, meat loaf, Lentil Loaf, pastas, or frozen in small containers to be used as needed in place of catsup.

2 c. canned okra
1 large onion, chopped
2 cloves garlic, chopped
1 medium-sized green pepper,
* seeded and chopped*

3 T. safflower oil
1 8-oz. can plain or hot tomato
* sauce*

Sauté okra, onion, garlic, and green pepper in the oil until onion is soft. Blend. Add tomato sauce, mix well, and heat.

Variation: For a thicker sauce for pizza, stir 1 T. of potato flour or 2 T. of barley flour (or 2 T. of wheat flour if allowed) into the sautéed vegetables.

Easy Tomato Sauce

NO CORN,* EGG, MILK, WHEAT, OR GLUTEN
Yield: 1–1½ cups

1 16-oz. can stewed tomatoes†
½ small lemon, thinly sliced
1 small bay leaf

¼ t. honey
¼ t. basil

Combine all ingredients. Heat to boiling. Let simmer 5 minutes. Remove from heat and let steep 5–10 minutes. Blend in food processor with steel blade or in blender. Strain to remove tomato seeds.

   *Variation: *If you can have corn*, add 1 t. Worcestershire sauce.

†Check ingredients for corn syrup and omit Worcestershire.

APPENDIX

USDA Table of Food Contents

The following chart is taken from *The Composition of Foods*, U.S.D.A. HANDBOOK #8. It will quickly give you comparative values to aid in planning better meals. The figures are for 100-gram (approximately 3½-ounce) portions, an average serving for most foods. However, for something like bran this is the equivalent of about 2 cups and for liquids about ½ scant cup.

Key: (0) = none or amounts too small to measure
      − = No reliable information available.

FRUIT	Calories	Protein (gr)	Fat (gr)	Carbohydrate (gr)	Calcium (mg)	Phosphorus (mg)	Iron (mg)	Sodium (mg)	Potassium (mg)	Vitamin A (I.U.)	B1—Thiamin (mg)	B2—Riboflavin (mg)	Niacin (mg)	Vitamin C (mg)
Apples, raw	58	0.2	0.6	14.5	7	10	0.3	1	110	90	0.03	0.02	0.1	4
Apricots, raw	51	1.0	0.2	12.8	17	23	0.5	1	281	2700	0.03	0.04	0.6	10
Avocado, California	171	2.2	17.0	6.0	10	42	0.6	4	604	290	0.11	0.20	1.6	14
Bananas	85	1.1	0.2	22.2	8	26	0.7	1	370	190	0.05	0.06	0.7	10
Cantaloupe	30	0.7	0.1	7.5	14	16	0.4	12	251	3400	0.04	0.03	0.6	33
Cherries, sweet	70	1.3	0.3	17.4	22	19	0.4	2	191	110	0.05	0.06	0.4	10
Cherries, sour	58	1.2	0.3	14.3	22	19	0.4	2	191	1000	0.05	0.06	0.4	10
Dates	274	2.2	0.5	72.9	59	63	3.0	1	648	50	0.09	0.10	2.2	0
Grapefruit, raw pulp	41	0.5	0.1	10.6	16	16	0.4	1	135	80*	0.04	0.02	0.2	38
Grapes, raw	69	1.3	1.0	15.7	16	12	0.4	3	158	100	0.05	0.03	0.3	4
Lemons, raw	27	1.1	0.3	82.0	26	16	0.6	2	138	20	0.04	0.02	0.1	53
Oranges, raw	49	1.0	0.2	12.2	41	20	0.4	1	200	200	0.10	0.04	0.4	50
Peaches, raw	38	0.6	0.1	9.7	9	19	0.5	1	202	1330	0.02	0.05	1.0	7
Pears, raw	61	0.7	0.4	15.3	8	11	0.3	2	130	20	0.02	0.04	0.1	4
Pineapple, juice-pack	58	0.4	0.1	15.1	16	8	0.4	1	147	60	0.10	0.03	0.3	10
Prune-type plums, raw	75	0.8	0.2	19.7	12	18	0.5	1	170	300	0.03	0.03	0.5	4
Prunes, uncooked	344	3.3	0.5	91.3	90	107	4.4	11	940	2170	0.12	0.22	2.1	4
Raisins, natural uncooked	289	2.5	0.2	77.4	62	101	3.5	27	763	20	0.11	0.08	0.5	1
Strawberries, raw	37	0.7	0.5	8.4	21	21	1.0	1	164	60	0.03	0.07	0.6	59

*Most white-fleshed varieties have about 109 International Units per 100 grams, although some have as low as 10 IUs; red-fleshed have about 440 IU

GRAINS

Barley	349	8.2	1.0	78.8	16.0	189	2.0	3	160	0	0.12	0.05	3.10	0
Bulgur wheat, hard red	354	11.2	1.5	75.7	29.0	338	3.7	—	229	0	0.28	0.14	4.50	(0)
Corn, sweet raw	96	3.5	1.0	22.1	0.3	111	0.7	trace	280	400	0.15	0.12	1.70	12
Corn flour	368	7.8	2.6	76.8	6.0	164	1.8	1	—	340	0.20	0.06	1.40	(0)
Farina, dry, enriched	371	11.4	0.9	77.0	25.0	107	2.9	2	83	0	0.44	0.26	3.50	0
Oatmeal, dry	390	14.2	7.4	68.2	53.0	405	4.5	2	352	0	0.60	0.14	1.00	0
Rice, brown, raw	360	7.5	1.9	77.4	32.0	221	1.6	9	214	0	0.34	0.05	4.70	0
Rice bran	276	13.3	15.8	50.8	76.0	1386	19.4	trace	1495	(0)	2.26	0.25	29.80	(0)
Rice polish	265	12.1	12.8	57.7	69.0	1106	16.1	trace	714	(0)	1.84	0.18	28.20	(0)
Rye flour, medium	350	11.4	1.7	74.8	27.0	262	2.6	1	203	0	0.30	0.12	2.50	0
Wheat germ	363	26.6	10.9	46.7	72.0	1118	9.4	3	827	0	2.01	0.68	4.20	0
Whole wheat flour, hard	333	13.3	2.0	71.0	41.0	372	3.3	3	370	0	0.55	0.12	4.30	0
Whole wheat flour, soft	364	9.7	1.0	76.9	20.0	97	1.1	2	95	0	0.08	0.05	1.20	0
Wheat bran, crude	213	16.0	4.6	61.9	119.0	1276	14.9	9	1121	0	0.72	0.35	0.21	0

FISH

Cod, raw	78	17.6	0.3	0	10	194	0.4	70	382	0	0.06	0.07	2.2	2
Flounder, baked	202	30.0	8.2	0	23	344	1.4	237	587	—	0.07	0.08	2.5	2
Haddock, raw	79	18.3	0.1	0	23	197	0.7	61	304	—	0.04	0.07	3.0	—
Halibut, raw	100	20.9	1.2	0	13	211	0.7	54	449	440	0.07	0.07	8.3	—
Herring, raw Atlantic	176	17.3	11.3	0	—	256	1.1	—	—	110	0.02	0.15	3.6	—
Herring, raw Pacific	98	17.5	2.6	0	—	225	1.3	74	420	100	0.02	0.16	3.5	3
Mackerel, raw Pacific	159	21.9	7.3	0	8	274	2.1	—	—	120	—	—	—	—
Perch, raw	118	19.3	0	0	—	192	—	—	—	—	—	—	—	—

	Calories	Protein (gr)	Fat (gr)	Carbohydrate (gr)	Calcium (mg)	Phosphorus (mg)	Iron (mg)	Sodium (mg)	Potassium (mg)	Vitamin A (I.U.)	B1—Thiamin (mg)	B2—Riboflavin (mg)	Niacin (mg)	Vitamin C (mg)
FISH (cont.)														
Salmon, raw Atlantic	217	22.5	13.4	0	79	186	0.9	—	—	—	—	0.08	7.2	9
Salmon, canned silver	153	20.8	7.1	0	244	288	0.9	351	339	80	0.03	0.18	7.4	—
Salmon, broiled/baked	182	27.0	7.4	0	—	414	1.2	116	443	160	0.16	0.06	9.8	—
Snapper, red/gray, raw	93	19.8	0.9	0	16	214	0.8	67	323	—	0.17	0.02	—	—
Scallops, steamed	112	23.2	1.4	—	115	338	3.0	265	476	—	—	—	—	—
Flatfish (sole) sand dabs raw flounder	79	16.7	0.8	0	12	195	0.8	78	342	—	0.05	0.05	1.7	—
Tuna, canned in oil drained solids	197	28.8	8.2	0	8	234	1.9	—	—	80	0.05	0.12	11.9	—
Tuna, canned in water solids & liquids	127	28.0	0.8	0	16	190	1.6	41	279	—	—	0.10	13.3	—
LEGUMES														
Chick peas (garbanzos)	360	20.5	4.8	61.0	150	331	6.9	26	797	50	0.31	0.15	2.0	—
Kidney beans, dry raw	343	22.5	1.5	61.9	110	406	6.9	10	984	20	0.51	0.20	2.3	—
Lentils, cooked	106	7.8	trace	19.3	25	119	2.1	—	249	20	0.07	0.06	0.6	0
Lentils, raw	340	24.7	1.1	60.1	79	377	6.8	30	790	60	0.37	0.22	2.0	—
Lima beans, cooked unsalted	138	8.2	0.6	25.6	29	154	3.1	2	612	—	0.13	0.06	0.7	—
Navy beans, raw	340	22.3	1.6	61.3	144	425	7.8	19	1196	0	0.65	0.22	2.4	—
Navy beans, cooked	118	7.8	0.6	21.2	50	148	2.7	7	416	0	0.14	0.07	0.7	0
Peas, black-eyed, dry raw	343	22.8	1.5	61.7	74	426	5.8	35	1024	30	1.05	0.21	2.2	—
Peas, black-eyed, cooked	76	5.1	0.3	13.8	17	95	1.3	8	229	10	0.16	0.04	0.4	—

LEGUMES (cont.)

Peas, split, raw	348	24.2	1.0	62.7	33	268	5.1	40	895	120	0.74	0.29	3.0	—
Peas, split, cooked	115	8.0	0.3	20.8	11	89	1.7	13	296	40	0.15	0.09	0.9	—
Soybeans, raw	403	34.1	17.7	33.5	226	554	8.4	5	1677	80	1.10	0.31	2.2	0
Soybeans, cooked	130	11.0	5.7	10.8	73	179	2.7	2	540	30	0.21	0.09	0.6	0

MEAT

Beef, choice muscle, raw	301	17.4	25.1	0	10	161	2.6	—	—	50	0.07	0.15	4.2	—
Veal, medium fat, raw	190	19.1	12.0	0	11	193	2.9	90	320	—	0.14	0.25	6.4	—
Lamb, choice raw, 23% fat	263	16.5	21.3	0	10	147	1.2	75	295	—	0.15	0.20	4.8	—
Chicken, light, cooked	166	31.6	3.4	0	11	265	1.3	64	411	60	0.04	0.10	11.6	—
Chicken, dark, cooked	176	28.0	6.3	0	13	229	1.7	86	321	150	0.07	0.23	5.6	—
Turkey, flesh, cooked	190	31.5	6.1	0	8	251	1.8	130	367	—	0.05	0.18	7.7	—

ORGAN MEAT

Liver, beef, raw	140	19.9	3.8	5.3	8	352	6.5	136	281	43,900	0.25	3.26	13.6	31
Liver, calf, raw	140	19.2	4.7	4.1	8	333	8.8	73	281	22,500	0.20	2.72	11.4	36
Liver, chicken, raw	129	19.7	3.7	2.9	12	236	7.9	70	172	12,100	0.19	2.49	10.8	17

MILK PRODUCTS

Cow's milk, 3.7% fat	66	3.5	3.7	4.9	117	92	trace	50	140	150	0.03	0.17	0.1	1
Cow's milk, skim	36	3.6	0.1	5.1	121	95	trace	52	145	trace	0.04	0.18	0.1	1
Cow's milk, half & half	134	3.2	11.7	4.6	108	85	trace	46	129	480	0.03	0.16	0.1	1

CHEESES

Cheddar cheese	398	25.0	32.2	2.1	750	478	1.0	700	82	1310	0.03	0.46	0.1	0
Cottage cheese, uncreamed	86	17.0	0.3	2.7	90	175	0.4	290	72	10	0.03	0.28	0.1	0

	Calories	Protein (gr)	Fat (gr)	Carbohydrate (gr)	Calcium (mg)	Phosphorus (mg)	Iron (mg)	Sodium (mg)	Potassium (mg)	Vitamin A (I.U.)	B1—Thiamin (mg)	B2—Riboflavin (mg)	Niacin (mg)	Vitamin C (mg)
CHEESES (cont.)														
Cream cheese	374	8.0	37.7	2.1	62	95	0.2	250	74	1540	0.02	0.24	0.1	0
Parmesan	345	21.2	28.0	2.2	590	393	0.6	—	—	1140	0.08	0.50	0.2	0
Swiss, domestic	393	36.0	26.0	2.9	1140	781	0.4	734	149	1060	0.02	0.73	0.2	0
Yogurt, low fat	50	3.4	1.7	5.2	120	94	trace	51	143	70	0.04	0.18	0.1	1
NUTS														
Almonds, dried	598	18.6	54.2	19.5	234	504	4.7	4	773	0	0.24	0.92	3.5	trace
Brazil nuts	654	14.3	66.9	10.9	186	693	3.4	1	715	trace	0.96	0.12	1.6	—
Cashews	561	17.2	45.7	29.3	38	373	3.8	15	464	100	0.43	0.25	1.8	—
Filberts	634	12.6	62.4	16.7	209	337	3.4	2	704	—	0.46	—	0.9	trace
Peanuts, roasted w/skins	582	26.2	48.7	20.6	72	407	2.2	5	701	—	0.32	0.13	17.1	0
Walnuts, English	651	14.8	64.0	15.8	99	380	3.1	2	450	30	0.33	0.13	0.9	2
VEGETABLES														
Beans, lima fordhook, boiled	99	6.0	0.1	19.1	20	90	1.7	101	426	230	0.07	0.05	1.0	17
Beans, baby lima, boiled	118	7.4	0.2	22.3	35	126	2.6	129	394	220	0.09	0.05	1.2	12
Beans, snap, boiled	25	1.6	0.2	5.4	50	37	0.6	4	151	540	0.07	0.09	0.5	12
Bean sprouts, mung, raw	35	3.8	0.2	6.6	19	64	1.3	5	223	20	0.13	0.13	0.8	19
Beets, boiled	32	1.1	0.1	7.2	14	23	0.5	43	208	20	0.03	0.04	0.3	6
Cabbage, raw	24	1.3	0.2	5.4	49	29	0.4	20	233	130	0.05	0.05	0.3	47
Carrots, raw	42	1.1	0.2	9.7	37	36	0.7	47	341	11,000	0.06	0.05	0.6	8
Celeriac (celery root)	40	1.8	0.3	8.5	43	115	0.6	100	300	—	0.05	0.06	0.7	8

VEGETABLES (cont.)

Celery, raw	14	0.8	0.1	3.1	31	22	0.2	88	239	230	0.02	0.03	0.3	6
Chayote, raw	28	0.6	0.1	7.1	13	26	0.5	5	102	20	0.03	0.03	0.4	19
Corn on cob, sweet, boiled	96	3.3	1.0	21.0	3	89	0.6	trace	196	400	0.12	0.10	1.4	9
Cucumber, peeled raw	14	0.6	0.1	3.2	17	18	0.3	6	160	trace	0.03	0.04	0.2	11
Eggplant, boiled	19	1.0	0.2	4.1	11	21	0.6	1	150	10	0.05	0.04	0.5	3
Jerusalem artichoke, raw	7.75	2.3	0.1	16.7	14	78	3.4	—	—	20	0.20	0.06	1.3	4
Kale, raw	53	6.0	0.8	9.0	249	93	2.7	75	378	10,000	0.16	0.26	2.1	186
Lettuce	13	0.9	0.1	2.9	20	22	0.5	9	175	330	0.06	0.06	0.3	6
Mushrooms, raw	28	2.7	0.3	4.4	6	116	0.8	15	414	trace	0.01	0.46	4.2	3
Parsley	44	3.6	0.6	8.5	203	63	6.2	45	727	8500	0.12	0.26	1.2	172
Parsnips, cooked	66	1.5	0.5	14.9	45	62	0.6	8	379	30	0.07	0.08	0.1	10
Peas, frozen cooked	68	5.1	0.3	11.8	19	86	1.9	115	135	600	0.27	0.09	1.7	13
Peas, fresh cooked	71	5.4	0.4	12.1	23	99	1.8	1	196	540	0.28	0.11	2.3	20
Potatoes, raw	76	2.1	0.1	17.1	7	53	0.6	3	407	trace	0.10	0.04	1.5	20
Pumpkin, canned	33	1.0	0.3	7.9	25	26	0.4	2	240	6400	0.03	0.05	0.6	5
Spinach, raw	26	3.2	0.3	4.3	93	51	3.1	71	470	8100	0.01	0.20	0.6	51
Spinach, frozen, cooked	23	3.0	0.3	3.7	113	44	2.1	52	333	7900	0.07	0.15	0.4	19
Squash, summer, all varieties cooked	14	0.9	0.1	3.1	25	25	0.4	1	141	390	0.05	0.08	0.8	10
Squash, winter, all varieties baked	63	1.8	0.4	15.4	28	48	0.8	1	461	4200	0.05	0.13	0.7	13
Sweet potatoes, raw	114	1.7	0.4	26.3	32	47	0.7	10	243	8800	0.10	0.06	0.6	21
Tomatoes, raw	22	1.1	0.2	4.7	13	27	0.5	3	244	900	0.06	0.04	0.7	23
Turnips, raw	30	1.0	0.2	6.6	39	30	0.5	49	268	trace	0.04	0.07	0.6	36
Yams, raw	101	2.1	0.2	23.2	20	69	0.6	—	600	trace	0.10	0.04	0.5	9

MISCELLANEOUS

	Calories	Protein (g)	Fat (g)	Carbohydrate (g)	Calcium (mg)	Phosphorus (mg)	Iron (mg)	Sodium (mg)	Potassium (mg)	Vitamin A (I.U.)	B1—Thiamin (mg)	B2—Riboflavin (mg)	Niacin (mg)	Vitamin C (mg)
Eggs, raw & hard-cooked*	163	12.9	11.5	0.9	54	205	2.3	122	129	1180	0.11	0.30	0.1	0
Gelatin, dry unflavored	335	85.6	0.1	0	5	6	.5	—	—	0	—	—	—	1
Honey, strained or extract	304	0.3	0	82.3	5	—	.5	5	51	—	trace	0.04	0.3	—
Molasses, light	252	—	—	65.0	165	45	4.3	15	917	—	0.07	0.06	0.2	—
Molasses, blackstrap	213	—	—	55.0	684	84	16.1	96	2927	0	0.11	0.19	20.0	0
Rice, bran	276	13.3	15.8	50.8	76	138	19.4	trace	1495	0	2.26	0.25	29.8	0
Sesame seeds, dry whole	563	18.6	49.1	21.6	1160	616	10.5	60	725	30	0.98	0.29	5.4	0
Sunflower seeds	560	24.0	47.3	19.9	120	837	7.1	30	920	50	1.96	0.23	5.4	0
Tofu	72	7.8	4.2	2.4	128	126	1.9	7	42	0	0.06	0.03	0.1	0
Soybean milk	33	3.4	1.5	2.2	21	48	0.8	—	—	40	0.08	0.03	0.2	0

*2 large eggs average 120 grams

Index of Recipes with Allergy-Causing Ingredient Excluded

NO EGG

NO MILK

NO WHEAT

General Index

Titles of Related Interest from PLUME

☐ **THE ALLERGY ENCYCLOPEDIA edited by The Asthma & Allergy Foundation of America and Craig T. Norback.** The one book no asthma or allergy sufferer should be without! Prepared by doctors—the only complete medical guide to causes, symptoms, treatments, cures, diet, clinics, camps and organizations for the allergy/asthma sufferer. (256291—$8.95)

☐ **THE WORLD ALMANAC® WHOLE HEALTH GUIDE by David Hendin.** Based on over six years of extensive research, this valuable guide offers information on such topics as finding and checking out a doctor, patient's rights, saving money on prescriptions, mental health problems and how to find help, child abuse, the elderly, sources for acquiring even more information, and much more. (251451—$4.95)

☐ **THE BARBARA KRAUS SODIUM GUIDE TO BRAND NAME AND BASIC FOODS.** Expanded edition. A dictionary listing of nearly 6,000 brand names and basic foods with their sodium counts. The perfect reference for people concerned with keeping their sodium intake under control. (254248—$6.95)

☐ **CALORIES AND CARBOHYDRATES by Barbara Kraus.** Fifth revised edition. This most accurate and dependable caloric and carbohydrate guide gives counts of many brand-name and fast-food products as well as of basic foods. Recommended by doctors for weight control. (253985—$6.95)

☐ **THE TAPPAN CREATIVE COOKBOOK FOR MICROWAVE OVENS AND RANGES by Sylvia Schur.** From breakfast for one to dinner for twenty —prepare over 400 delectable dishes designed for microwave ovens or standard stoves. (253128—$6.95)

All prices higher in Canada.

To order, use the convenient coupon on the next page.

Titles of Related Interest from PLUME

To order, use the convenient coupon on the next page.

Guides to Good Eating from PLUME